From the reviews of *Hotel Tiberias*:

'One half of Hope's story describes the romantic derring-do soldiering of Hackett, whose steps are traced in a modern-day journey to "Palestine", the other tracks the more elusive figure of Grossmann, from a family of Templars who settled in Palestine . . . Hope writes so honestly about his lost German family that we share his urgent desire to acquit them of charges of Nazi sympathies . . . it is heartening to see [Grossmann] rescued from wartime slanders by a grandson who never knew him but will not let him fade'   *Sunday Times*

'Hope indicates a new direction in the British travel book: a post-colonial search for roots and for explanations in their families' involvement in the recent history of the British imperial endeavour'   *TLS*

'Hope is a seasoned travel writer and his descriptive writing is vivid and convincing . . . [*Hotel Tiberias*] achieves real pathos. All families have their hidden as well as public histories. *Hotel Tiberias* gives us a poignant glimpse into a particularly dramatic example'   *Independent on Sunday*

'The politics of the Middle East are sketched with verve ...
Hope's meditation on his grandfather's suicide and the region's
history is written with conviction and clarity'

Scotland on Sunday

'Hope takes us down all sorts of intriguing avenues and gives
us a vivid and unusual perspective on an endlessly fascinating
chapter of the twentieth century'   Edward Stourton, *Tablet*

'Moving, intelligent, highly readable and occasionally extremely
funny, this is a fine book indeed'   *Geographical Magazine*

By the same author

Outcasts of the Islands

HOTEL TIBERIAS

A Tale of Two Grandfathers

SEBASTIAN HOPE

HARPER PERENNIAL
London, New York, Toronto and Sydney

Harper Perennial
An imprint of HarperCollins*Publishers*
77–85 Fulham Palace Road
Hammersmith
London W6 8JB

www.harperperennial.co.uk

This edition published by Harper Perennial 2005

1

First published by HarperCollins*Publishers* 2004

A catalogue record for this book is available from the British Library

ISBN-13 978-0-00-713021-4
ISBN-10 0-00-713021-X

Set in Bembo by Rowland Phototypesetting Ltd, Bury St Edmunds, Suffolk
Maps by John Gilkes
Printed and bound in Great Britain by Clays Ltd, St Ives plc

Nescire autem quid ante quam natus sis acciderit, id est semper esse puerum. Quid enim est aetas hominis, nisi ea memoria rerum veterum cum superiorum aetate contexitur?

> To be ignorant of what occurred before
> you were born is to remain a child forever.
> For what is the worth of human life unless
> it is woven into that of our ancestors by
> the records of history?
> CICERO, *Orator*, XXXIV, 120

In memory of
Dore Vorster
1906–2003

and
despite Barnaby

CONTENTS

ILLUSTRATIONS

1. Captain J. W. Hackett c. 1937. (Private Collection)
2. TOP: The German colony of Haifa. (J. Schumacher, 1877)
   MIDDLE: Postcard of the Jerusalem Hotel in Jaffa in 1917.
   (Courtesy of Yoel Amir)
   BOTTOM LEFT: Members of the largely German Jaffa Sports
   Club c. 1892.
   BOTTOM RIGHT: Templer cemetery, Haifa. (Sebastian Hope)
3. TOP: Tiberias: the lake shore, photographed by Richard
   Grossmann before 1900. (Courtesy of University of
   Dundee Archive Services)
   MIDDLE LEFT: The beginnings of the Hotel Tiberias, 1894.
   (Tiberias Municipal Archive)
   MIDDLE RIGHT: Hotel Tiberias and citadel from the minaret
   of the mosque, 1913. (Courtesy of Yoel Amir)
   BOTTOM: Tiberias: view over the town and mosque of
   Daher al-Amr from the roof of the Hotel Tiberias,
   c. 1910. (Courtesy of Yoel Amir)
4. TOP LEFT: Frieda and Richard Grossmann's wedding day,
   1904. (Private Collection)
   TOP RIGHT: The widowed Frieda and her three children:
   Dore, Rix and Fritz, c. 1920. (Private Collection)
   MIDDLE: Margaret, Fritz and Rix skiing on Mount
   Hermon, 1938. (Private Collection)

BOTTOM: Hotel Tiberias, c. 1934. (Private Collection)

5. TOP: The Lido, c. 1937. (Private Collection)

MIDDLE: Staff of the Scottish Hospital watch the landing of a flying boat on Lake Tiberias, c. 1932 (Courtesy of University of Dundee Archive Services)

BOTTOM: The Feingold party, 1938. (Tiberias Municipal Archive)

6. The last picture of Fritz Grossmann at the Lido with his two daughters, Brigitte and Liesl, June 1938. (Private Collection)

7. TOP: Rix reading *Esquire* magazine in Tunis, 1943. (Private Collection)

BOTTOM: Frieda's brother Alfred Ruff, his wife Anna and their daughter Elfride in Tatura internment camp, Victoria, Australia, 1945. (Australian War Memorial)

8. TOP: Frieda on the hotel terrace revisiting Tiberias in 1969. (Private Collection)

BOTTOM: The former Hotel Tiberias, today's Meyouhas Youth Hostel. (Sebastian Hope)

ACKNOWLEDGEMENTS

In the past I have mostly written about people I did not know before I started writing about them. Often I wrote about getting to know them. I wrote about them in as intrusive a way as they would permit, or as I saw fit. Mostly I knew there was little chance of a come-back from my subjects, who lived in faraway places, but on the few occasions I have met people after I have written about them their reaction has been gratifyingly positive.

On this occasion my subjects are in part people whom I have always known, or rather who have always known me: my own family. Reactions have been more mixed, yet this book could not have been written without their help, especially that of my mother, Bridget Hope. Many of the contemporary documents that proved crucial to Shan Hackett's story would not have come into my hands had she not realised their interest to me. My brother Alexander and his partner Clare Smith came to my rescue at a time when I had nowhere to write and let me use a room in their home as an office. My father, Timothy Hope, has played his part as military adviser. My aunt and grandmother have made a considerable contribution to this final version; they have been generous with their comments and diligent in their corrections. I deeply regret that the process has been such a painful one for them. I refer those wanting a more complete biography of General

Sir John Hackett to Roy Fullick's book: *Shan Hackett: The Pursuit of Exactitude* (Leo Cooper, 2003).

My German relatives too have been extremely helpful and supportive, especially Rix Grossmann and Dore Vorster. Many of the illustrations, and anecdotes, came from their collections, and Dore's daughter and son-in-law, Ursel and Ortwin Leder, provided the copy of the hotel's luggage label on which the cover of this book is based. I have dedicated this book to Dore's memory.

While I was travelling in the Middle East there were many people who helped me along my way and some without whose assistance and interest this book would be much the poorer. In Amman, Major Tawfiq Mousa Ahmed shared his memories of the Trans-Jordan Frontier Force. In Israel I owe a great deal to Elisheva Ballhorn, ex-archivist of Tiberias municipality, and her successor, Jehudit Cohen, was also helpful. The late Professor Alex Carmel was an inspirational figure for many both in and outside Israel and I feel honoured to have met this pioneering academic. Yoel Amir, a collector of historical postal documents, has been very generous in sending me images from his collection, some of which are reproduced here. For many years Irène Lewitt kept Frieda Grossmann's diary safe and delivered it up when asked. Not only did that selfless act enable me to gain invaluable insight into my great-grandmother's daily life, but also to send copies of their mother's diary to her two surviving children.

In England I have received much assistance from Martin Higgins who has shared his extensive knowledge of and con-tacts with the Templers. He has put me in touch with relatives I never knew I had, like Felix Haar, and other Templers in Australia whom I thank for their help: Alfred Klink, Horst Blaich and Dieter Ruff. I would also like to thank David Byrne, Nitza Spiro, Jill Lomer of the Thomas Cook Archive,

Rupert Chapman and Felicity Cobbing of the Palestine Exploration Fund, the staff of the University of Dundee Archive, and Dermot Doran of the British Airways Archives and Museum Collection.

My editors Richard Johnson and Lucinda McNeile have been patient, supportive and brutal in just the right measure, and this is a much better book for their efforts. My agent David Miller has given me unstinting encouragement since I first told him the outline of this story in 1998 and in large part it is due to him that I have been able to pursue my research. They have had a lot to put up with, but they have not had to live with me while I have been writing this book. My wife Lisa deserves more than thanks, and maybe an abject apology would be a good place to start, before putting her through it all over again.

The passage on pp. 39–40 from *Cairo in the War 1939–1945* (Copyright © Artemis Cooper, 1989) is reproduced by permission of Felicity Bryan and the author. That on pp. 196–7 from *Tiberias* by Helga Dudman (1988) is reproduced courtesy of Carta, Jerusalem.

FAMILY TREE

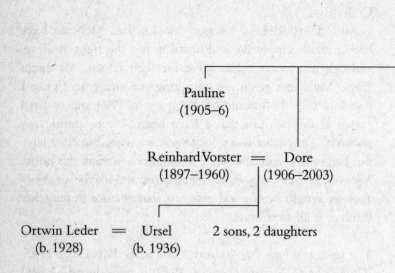

Pauline
(1905–6)

Reinhard Vorster = Dore
(1897–1960) (1906–2003)

Ortwin Leder = Ursel   2 sons, 2 daughters
(b. 1928)   (b. 1936)

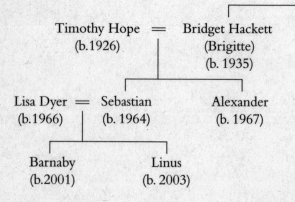

Timothy Hope = Bridget Hackett
(b.1926)   (Brigitte)
              (b. 1935)

Lisa Dyer = Sebastian   Alexander
(b.1966)   (b. 1964)   (b. 1967)

Barnaby   Linus
(b.2001)   (b. 2003)

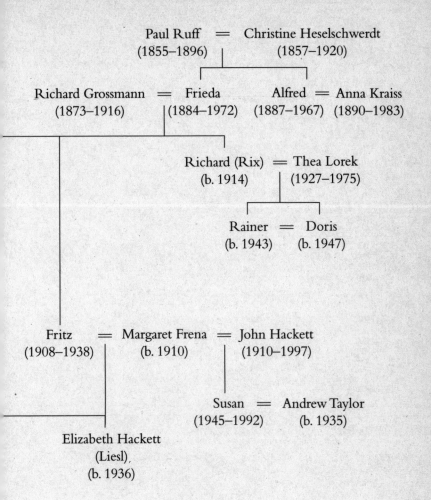

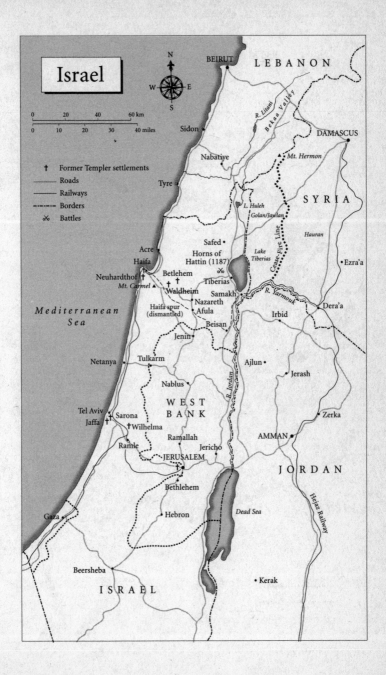

Israel

N
W · E
S

| 0 | 20 | 40 | 60 km |
| 0 | 10 | 20 | 30 | 40 miles |

† Former Templer settlements
— Roads
— Railways
- - - Borders
⚔ Battles

LEBANON
BEIRUT
Sidon
Nabatiye
R. Litani
Bekaa Valley
DAMASCUS
Mt. Hermon
Tyre
L. Huleh
Golan/Jawlan
SYRIA
Hauran
Safed
Acre
Haifa
Neuhardthof
Mt. Carmel
Betlehem
Waldheim
Horns of
Hattin (1187)
Tiberias
Lake
Tiberias
Cease-Fire Line
Ezra'a
Samakh
R. Yarmouk
Haifa spur
(dismantled)
Nazareth
Afula
Beisan
Dera'a
Irbid
Jenin
Ajlun
Netanya
Tulkarm
Mediterranean
Sea
Nablus
R. Jordan
Jerash
WEST
BANK
Zerka
Tel Aviv
Sarona
Jaffa
Wilhelma
Ramle
Ramallah
Jericho
AMMAN
JERUSALEM
JORDAN
Bethlehem
Hebron
Dead Sea
Hejaz Railway
Gaza
Beersheba
Kerak
ISRAEL

The Middle East in 1939

Cherkessk

Grozny

U. S. S. R.

GEORGIA · Tbilisi

Caspian
Sea

AZERBAIJAN

ARMENIA · Baku

Yerevan

Manzikert
(1071)

L. Van
· Van

Tabriz

Diyarbakir

· Urfa

·TEHRAN

R. Euphrates

Mosul ·

SYRIA

R. Tigris

· Kirkuk

Tikrit ·

I R A N

BAGHDAD

Kerbala ·

N

W·E

S

I R A Q

SAUDI
ARABIA

Basra ·

KUWAIT

Persian
Gulf

0	200	400	600 km
0	100	200	300	400 miles

PROLOGUE

I was sixteen when I found out. We were going on holiday to Scotland with another family. The car was already loaded at 6.30 a.m. with everything from frozen food to an inflatable dinghy. My mother, my brother and I were standing in the kitchen, ready to leave the moment my father said, let's go, so as not to start the twelve-hour drive on a bad note – we would have to keep our nerve for his overtaking manoeuvres on the A9. Mum said almost as an aside that we were not to be surprised if we heard the other paterfamilias refer to Grandpa as her step-father – why? – because he is. 'Grandpa adopted Lizzie and me when he married Granny. Our real father was her first husband, and he died when we were very small.' And then my father said, let's go.

My world did not fall apart. I did not feel betrayed or deceived because we had not been told sooner. I did not feel as though my own sense of identity had been weakened. As the August countryside passing by in car window-sized frames gave way to the purple hills of the Highlands, I wondered if my relationship with my grandfather would change now he was my step-grandfather. I saw no reason why it should. He was the only one I had ever known – I could not remember my father's father. We were the only grandchildren he had. Even though we were not related by blood he could never be anything other than our Grandpa. The real surprise was

1

that our mother was not entirely the person I thought she was. I had passed through that stage of early adolescence when you think your parents don't know anything about you, and I was beginning to realize how little I knew about them. Family gatherings thereafter became opportunities to observe the newly revealed relationships at work.

John Winthrop Hackett, my step-grandfather, was a great man. He was a career soldier who had reached the rank of major at the outbreak of the Second World War. He had what they call a 'good war' and was a brigadier by the end. He had shown great bravery, receiving wounds and decorations in equal measure. As a leader he had inspired enduring devotion in his subordinates, not least because of his maverick attitude towards his own superiors. He rose to the rank of full general and commanded the British Army of the Rhine during the deep mid-winter of the Cold War. He had been commander-in-chief of the British forces in Northern Ireland in the late 1960s and still featured in those IRA assassination wish-lists that were discovered scribbled on Rizla papers and the backs of envelopes bearing the new decimal stamps. He was dubbed a Knight Grand Cross of the Order of Bath. He had even been tipped for the top army job, but a frank letter to *The Times* on the ability of NATO to withstand a non-nuclear offensive, in which he asserted that Russian tanks would be in Paris in forty-eight hours, so infuriated his political masters that he was denied, it is said, this final promotion.

He was also a scholar. He had read Greats at New College, Oxford, having the precocity to complete that degree in two years and sit the finals for one in History the following summer. It was said that he did not know which to be, a soldier or a don, and that he became a soldier in a prolonged bout of donnish absent-mindedness. Even after becoming a soldier he gained a B. Litt. for his thesis on Saladin's campaign against the Principality of Antioch in 1188. After he retired from the army he became Principal of King's College, London. It was his last public appointment. Granny and Grandpa lived in a narrow house on Campden Hill that had a security grille in front of the garden doors and a twisting wooden banister, perfect for sliding down, that I scratched from top to bottom with the buckle of my belt.

In 1975 Grandpa retired and he and Granny moved to a mill house in the Cotswolds that they had bought some years previously. It was an event that had an impact on my family too: we had to vacate the mill. We had lived there for five years, and it was the longest that we had stayed anywhere. My father was also a career soldier, a major at the time of his secondment to the Wessex Yeomanry in Cirencester, which was to be his last posting. I was six when we moved in. I had already had four different homes, three of which I could remember, army married quarters in Canada, Dorchester and Sevenoaks. While I remembered them all with affection, Coberley Mill was the best place a boy who loved woods and streams could possibly find himself. Leaving a house so old and so alive, the creaking boards below which water trickled through the old mill race, leaving the sylvan hollow in the Churn Valley was a wrench; moving into a house on the corner of a B road in the middle of a village near the M4, surrounded by flat land, was both a shock and a disappointment. Long stretches at boarding school augmented my alienation from our new 'home'.

Visiting Granny and Grandpa was also to revisit childhood memories. At first my brother and I would leave the lunch-table early and scramble onto the oak that had fallen across the stream where we used to have our tree house, or put on gumboots and rebuild a dam with nuggets of clay. Crayfish live in the banks, trout in the pools. Later on we would sit with the adults listening to their serious talk upstairs in the drawing room, whose windows framed the big ash tree at the top of the cowslipped bank where the tyre-swing used to hang. The room itself had changed, the yarra boards covered with pale carpet, the windows double-glazed. The image of how it once had been faded quickly, but every now and again I would look out over the millpond and see myself on an oil-drum raft paddling upstream, a wartime mission deep in the jungles of Burma.

These birthdays and anniversaries, Boxing Days and Easters were always difficult occasions for my father. He may have married the general's daughter, but he was a different type of soldier. In 1944, at the age of seventeen, he had left school without sitting his Highers, grown a moustache, lied about his age and joined up. The war ended before he could be posted – 'the atom bomb saved my life,' he says – but his career did not lack active service: Palestine; Korea; Malaya. He met my mother during his regiment's tour of duty in West Germany. Five days after I was born in 1964 he left for fourteen months, fighting insurgents in the Radfan. He was a regimental soldier by nature and did not attend Staff College, partly because of his strong anti-intellectual bias. Grandpa, battlefield commander, sought out the weakest point and attacked. Any discussion on any topic between the two men invariably ended in Grandpa correcting my father's use of English, and my father taking umbrage. He would always lose more than the argument, his composure and his temper being frequent casualties of the engagement.

'Shan' Hackett was not an easy man with whom to have lunch. We never knew what his mood would be when we arrived. We never knew what part of his memoirs, his correspondence or his military punditry he would be rehearsing that day, or how he would try to suck us into the quicksand of a discussion. Sometimes he would start right in with the barbs, like the time he asked my father, who had recently gone to work for an insurance company, 'How's trade?' as he walked through the door. Sometimes, when the approach work was slower, it was possible to avert the clash. It did no good to change the subject, as Shan needed no opening to bring up the topic again and reiterate his position, but one could harry at the margins and draw fire. We developed a variety of survival tactics. My grandmother and my brother would keep their heads below the parapet. My mother and my aunt Elizabeth sought distraction in the preparation and supply of food, although Lizzie was fond of joining the fray and could always retreat outside for a cigarette. She never married.

My strategy was to engage, but without the irritability that made my father vulnerable. I tried not to let his corrections and interruptions either anger or deflect me. I was not always successful; one discussion we had when I was nineteen, a particularly weighty debate that centred on dukes in bathing suits, ended when I called him a mental masturbator. 'Dear boy,' he said, 'I do so enjoy our talks. They remind me of my time at university.' I too had come to enjoy our rigorous exchanges.

The only person who did not have a strategy was Susan, the only child Margaret and Shan had together, primarily because she did not seem to need one. She was Daddy's Little Girl, as the youngest daughter often is, though there was never any suggestion that this favouritism stemmed from her being his only natural child. She had her own name for him, 'Fred', and as a Christmas present from her an ordinary-looking tie with the letter 'F' repeated in a mock heraldic design was a comedic *tour de force*. Susan's husband, Andrew Taylor, a lean, urbane man, had been an officer in the Gurkhas. His career thereafter took them to Australia and Hong Kong. They separated and divorced in the 1980s, Susan moving back to London. She died of pneumonia on Christmas Day 1992.

Though married to his favourite – or maybe because of that – Andrew was no more exempt from the general's displeasure than was my father. Matters came to a head one Guy Fawkes Night, my grandfather's birthday, when the two sons-in-law felt so insulted that they made a pact never to come to one of these 'parties' again. When the next occasion swung round my father declined the invitation, telling the general they would both have a more enjoyable day if he did not attend, and I was thrust into the front line.

It goes without saying, or rather it does all too frequently in English families, that I loved, love all these people. I was also immensely proud of Grandpa. I found exciting his talk of letters to *The Times*, of correspondence with eminent people and comrades in arms, of speaking engagements and radio interviews and the writing of forewords – I relished these dispatches from a life of the mind and of letters that was absent in my own home. He published a war memoir in 1977 called *I Was a Stranger* and though I was too young to appreciate the quality of the writing, the story it told was straight out of the war comics that passed around my school. Five years later he published a bestseller, a future-history entitled *Third World War*. It was translated into many languages, but its crowning achievement was to have been clearly visible on Ronald Reagan's desk in a *Time* picture of the Oval Office.

I Was a Stranger told the story of Brigadier Shan Hackett's experience of the Battle of Arnhem, the airborne attempt to capture bridges across the Rhine in September 1944. He was in command of the 4th Para Brigade, a force he had raised eighteen months previously. The brigade had participated in the invasions of Sicily and the Italian mainland. It made a vital contribution to the success of the Taranto landing, taking the harbour and establishing a beach-head, but Operation Market Garden, as the plan for capturing the Rhine crossings was codenamed, was far more ambitious. It failed. The 4th Para showed great bravery and sustained heavy losses before they surrendered. Hackett had been wounded twice. The bullet in the thigh seemed the more serious, but when he reached the military hospital in Arnhem it was discovered that a piece of shrapnel had entered his abdomen and shredded his large intestine – 'two sections and twelve perforations, you know'. Grandpa still had the vest he was wearing at the time. The German doctors gave up on him, but a South African surgeon called Lipmann Kessel, who had also been captured, operated and stitched the serviceable pieces of his gut together with such skill that his life was saved.

Hackett was the most senior officer to have been captured, but as the allied forces had parachuted in without badges of rank and regiment, the Germans did not realize they had a brigadier in their custody. On the third day after his operation two Dutch resistance workers walked into the hospital disguised as orderlies, dressed the brigadier as one, and walked him out past the guards. He was taken to the house of a Dutch family where he was hidden for nearly five months while he recuperated. His strength regained, he set out for the Allied lines with another Dutch resistance worker. They crossed Holland by bicycle to rendezvous with Canadian commandos on the banks of the Meuse.

The title of the book shows what was most important to Hackett: the courage and self-sacrifice of the de Nooij family. One of the few books he had to read during his convalescence was a copy of the New Testament in the Greek of its earliest editions. The title is a quotation from Matthew, chapter 25, verses 35–6: 'I was an hungred, and ye gave me meat: I was thirsty, and ye gave me drink: I was a stranger, and ye took me in:/ Naked, and ye clothed me: I was sick and ye visited me: I was in prison and ye came unto me.'

It was not long after the memoir was published that the film *A Bridge Too Far* was released. Grandpa escaped portrayal, and for him it was the one good thing about the film. For me, it reinforced my perception of the Second World War, that the Allies were right, but that the Germans had the best kit.

One does not have to come from an army family to be aware of weapons and war from the age of about three. Boys everywhere play with guns, have toy soldiers, fight imaginary battles. When we lived in Dorchester, our war games took place in a copse behind the house and were given an added reality by the fact it had once been the site of an army post. The barbed wire still stood in places and the ground bore signs of trenches. You could easily find shell cases in the undergrowth and I once came upon some live rounds, but the best thing I found was a helmet, a proper Tommy steel helmet half covered by dead leaves. It was added to the army paraphernalia around the house, from caps and clothes in the dressing-up box, to things stored in ammo boxes in the garage and ashtrays made from the base of a tank round.

I graduated from Dinky toys to making plastic models of war planes and gunboats, though as my father had served in armoured cars and tanks these were my favourite kits. A Japanese firm, Tamiya, made the best models and their range had a preponderance of German hardware. I do not know exactly how it came about, but I became almost obsessive about the German Panzer Mark IV tank. It is a particularly male condition, the urge to collect and complete series of things, to bring order to the world. It is a compulsion, and I had fixed on the Panzer Mark IV in my quest for perfection. Apart from the standard turreted configuration, with either short or long barrel, the tank's elegant chassis provided a most versatile armoured platform on which to mount other types of artillery – vast mortars, anti-aircraft guns, field pieces. In all there were fifteen variations on the Panzer Mark IV theme. I rattled through the ones covered in the Tamiya range, and then began to hybridize the kits. It was a phase that passed on encountering puberty and punk rock.

I never played with the models – I might have broken them. I never imagined them rolling in regiments across Northern Europe killing people. Somehow it escaped me that Grandpa had actually faced German tanks in battle. My only experience of real tanks placed them as things to be clambered over at the Bovington Tank Museum. My pleasure was in the assembly of the models, an incremental achievement of painting and gluing that brought the set closer to completion. Curiously, for a music genre that advocated anarchy in the UK, punk records also provided a collecting opportunity in the form of limited edition sleeves and vinyl colours. Grandpa's comment on punk, that it was 'repetitive thump and whine', led both to my assertion that all music was by its very nature repetitive and to a tedious, though unharassed, luncheon for everyone else.

Our perennial discussion though centred on language. As a student of literature and modern languages I shared his keen interest in its use, and having studied both Latin and Greek I could appreciate some of his bugbears – 'logo' and 'nomad' should be pronounced with a short first vowel to accord with their Greek derivation, the 'e' of 'economy' should always be long by the same token, and 'the *hoi polloi*' was a tautology that betrayed both pretension and ignorance. He was a hard master, but he led by example. He continued to read works in both Latin and Greek throughout his life. When my Greek

'O' level came close he tutored me in one of the set texts, Book VI of the *Odyssey* which opens with the hero and his hyacinthine locks being washed ashore on Nausicaa's island. As well as speaking French, German and Italian, Grandpa had learned Arabic as a young man, and continued to receive instruction in its weak verbs into his seventies.

By the time the exam results came, I knew he was not my blood relative and I wondered if, in retrospect, there had been any clues to that fact. The only ones I could pinpoint were in talk of his own family. He was extremely proud of his Norman-Irish ancestry, of the thirteenth-century church in Tipperary where his family coat of arms was escutcheoned on the wall. His father had emigrated to Western Australia and had left it late in life to have children; the fourth of five, his only son, being born in 1910 when he was sixty-seven. Sir John Winthrop Hackett senior died when Shan was six. He had amassed a sizeable fortune through his mineral holdings and ownership of the *West Australian* newspaper, a fortune his will stipulated would go to the University of Western Australia should his young widow remarry. She did; money thereafter was in shorter supply. Nonetheless, Shan was due to take up a place at Winchester College in England at the age of thirteen, but a severe case of glandular fever caused him to miss the intake. Instead he went to the Geelong Grammar School, near Melbourne. Maybe it was his father dying when he was still so young, or maybe it was as a result of his frequent visits to Ireland while he was at Oxford, but reconnecting with his family's history seemed to be his chief motivation for joining the army. In fact he often denied that he had ever joined the army. What he had done was quite different; he had joined his great-grandfather's regiment. And there it was, always 'my great-grandfather', never 'your great-great-great-grandfather', never 'our family coat of arms'. Appropriately, when asked to suggest supporters for his banner in the Bath Chapel at Westminster Abbey, it was Susan's deflating wit that supplied the owl and the pussycat.

I knew all this about Grandpa, and more, but I knew next to nothing about my real grandfather and my mother had not offered much detail when she introduced me to him. The time came to ask. One of the reasons her real father was not spoken about, she said, was because he had committed suicide, and she had not been told of it until the eve of her wedding in 1961. At that point I had no conception of the matrix of guilt and blame and shame that holds the survivors. My view of the act was still formed by the notions of Romantic literature and rock and roll.

He was a German called Fritz. Fritz Grossmann, or rather Großmann. He was a hotelier in Palestine, co-owner and manager of the Hotel Tiberias in the town of the same name. My mother was three when he died and she could remember very little about him. She remembered how he shuffled his feet in the slippers he wore around the house, him going to sleep in the afternoons with a newspaper over his face. She remembered one time standing in the enclosed circular bed at the foot of a fruit tree, crying because there were ants crawling over her bare feet, and her father saying, 'Well, just come out of there then.' As for the reasons for his suicide, it was said he had a depressive nature. His debts were also mentioned, but no one really knew why he did it. He had borrowed heavily to build a Lido at the hotel's private beach on the Sea of Galilee, but the unsettled situation in Palestine and the events in Europe that led to war caused the tourist trade to fall away. When war came, his Austrian-born widow Margaret, her two daughters, her sister and her mother-in-law were interned by the British authorities together with all 'enemy aliens' in Palestine. Shan Hackett had already been courting her for some time, and continued to call on her in the internment camp. They were married in Jerusalem in 1942. Margaret followed Shan to Egypt, while the two girls stayed with their grandmother – Granny G – and went to school in Jerusalem. In 1944 they all left for England, but Granny G stayed behind in the land of her birth.

The hotel had been administered by the Custodian for Enemy Property for the duration of the war, and an Arab manager installed. I believe Granny G intended to return to her home and business when it was over, but the hotel was eventually confiscated by the new Israeli government. She lost everything. The compensation, which did not arrive until the 1960s, was of a token nature. She lived in Beirut for a number of years before moving to Germany where she died.

Most of us have grown up hearing anecdotes not just about ourselves, but also about our parents and grandparents, stories that build into a received family history, forming our sense of where we come from and who we are. Happy or sad, they make up an oral tradition to which the family continuously adds. While the telling of my family narrative was still turning up new digressions and sub-plots, the salient points I thought of as settled. It was astonishing to discover a whole section of the main story line, and such a dramatic one, had remained untold for so long, astonishing to realize I had German relatives of whom I had never even heard. My sense of self may not have been weakened, but it had certainly been broadened.

Army children often have a problem answering the question, 'Where do you come from?' It can even affect one's national status; my brother has a Canadian passport. I had never thought of myself as anything other than English, even though I knew my grandmother was Austrian, and despite having visited our relatives in Graz I did not think of my mother as anything other than English either. It seemed absurd that her application for a driver's licence in the mid-1970s should be questioned because she had been born in Haifa.

There was all the difference in the world between being quarter Austrian and being half German. The former I regarded as a recessive element in my make-up, diluted by a generation and distant enough to be left out of account; the latter could not be so easily ignored. When I opted to study German as an 'A' level it was because I got on with its grammatical certainties. Now I knew my mother had been a little German girl called Brigitte Grossmann once upon a time, I wondered (for as long as it took to dismiss the idea) if I might have inherited an aptitude. Did she still, if ever, think of herself as German? We never spoke the language together, although she had taught me to count to ten in German when I was four years old, a time when I still spoke English with a Canadian accent. I had lost the accent quickly on returning to England, just as she seemed to have lost the command of her first language.

As I could not ignore the fact that I was half German, I had to consider whether it ought to make a difference to my behaviour. I was not about to start cheering for Germany in a World Cup qualifier, but shouldn't I stop the name-calling 1918, 1945, 1966 John Bull jingoism? After all, wasn't it possible that members of my own family had played for the opposition in all three contests? Unlikely in 1966, but still possible in theory. Shouldn't I own up to the Germanic part of my ancestry, take on the responsibilities of being German, the guilt? The people I told seemed to assume I would, and would break the flow of a tirade against, say, what Germans do with their beach towels in Mallorca to make placatory reference to my ancestry – 'no offence', assuming their remarks could offend. I did not know enough about my newly revealed family to feel that bothered.

The subject of Fritz Grossmann came up only twice more in the next thirteen years. Occasionally a story was told about the girls' childhood in Palestine, usually as a digression from some other topic – a news item about rabies inoculation reminds my mother of the time she was bitten by a dog in Tiberias and of the long needle required to pierce the solar plexus; a picture of flat bread being fished out of a *tandoor* in Peshawar transports Lizzie to the Old City of Jerusalem. Although younger, Liz seemed to feel much more of a connection with the German side of the family than my mother did as a result of her closeness to Granny G. At one time she had been a regular visitor to our relatives there. It was after one of her visits that a folder of photocopied documents and pictures appeared in our kitchen. Among them was the first photograph I had seen of my real grandfather.

It showed a man of medium build smartly dressed in a light summer suit and wire-rimmed glasses. The jacket is buttoned over a striped tie. The trousers have turn-ups. He has dark wavy hair and a sun-tanned face which is inclined down and slightly away from the camera so it cannot be clearly seen. In each brown hand he holds that of a small girl in a short cotton dress, white socks and sandals. Nearest the camera stands my mother, wearing the serious expression of an eldest child reminiscent of my own at the same age. Furthest away is Lizzie, peering round her father's legs at the lens. She is almost two and looks to have the potential for mischief. They stand on a gravel path edged with black and white stones. There is a bit of a lawn and a flowerbed; a rose climbs up the wall of a white-washed brick building in the background. A palm frond intrudes from the left. The picture was taken at the Lido on the Sea of Galilee, my mother said.

The only other time my real grandfather was mentioned, and then not even by name, was at a dinner in a restaurant in London. It was winter, almost a year after Susan's death, and I had been flat-sitting her apartment while it was on the market. Granny and Grandpa and Lizzie had come up for the night, something to do with the Order of the Bath as I recall, and certainly the conversation came round to one of Grandpa's favourite subjects – his ancestry and coat of arms. I do not remember exactly how it came up, or who suggested I take a more active interest in compiling the Hackett history. It was an idea that had to be nipped in the bud and, reckoning they knew that I knew already, rather than offend with a direct refusal I said I would be more interested to find out about my real grandfather. Lizzie let out an exclamation of horror. I may have been breaking a family taboo, but it was too late to take back the words, and what with the wine and the wide open opportunity, I wanted to say more. I said that Grandpa was the only grandfather I had known and that I loved him as much as a grandson could, but the fact remained he was not my blood relation. As a consequence there was 25 per cent of my genetic inheritance about which I knew nothing and was curious, and which I could no longer deny. My interest was noted and it was said that we would talk about the matter at a more appropriate time.

The time more appropriate never did come. Grandpa's reminiscences began to stretch further back, leaving behind the smouldering issues of the Cold War and Northern Ireland and revisiting his years in the Eastern Mediterranean. One day he would be reiterating the argument he had advanced at the time, that Rhodes rather than Sicily should have been the site of the Allied counterattack in 1943; on another he would be reliving a cavalry charge against Arab irregulars, sabres drawn, while serving with the Trans-Jordan Frontier Force, and as an aside, 'that was when I first met your grandmother'. Frequently he told stories that we had heard before, often using the exact same form of words as he had on the previous telling. He was rehearsing his memoirs. He was given a dictaphone one birthday, but he did not start to use it until shortly, too shortly, before his death.

Coberley Mill began to show signs of it's aging occupants. Tubular handles in a hospital-white plasticized finish appeared in doorways and bathrooms. A stair-lift was installed. The rituals of gathering remained broadly the same, although the bottle of champagne before lunch became New Zealand sparkling. Nonetheless, Grandpa would still produce his silver swizzle stick and defizz it somewhat. The trout in the pool below the millpond sluice grew fatter on the bread we threw them. Ducklings disappeared one by one. Dippers flitted past the drawing-room window. If Grandpa was now less inclined to argue, he was more prone to insult, and Lizzie bore the brunt of this.

The isolation that made up so much of the charm of the house came to be a liability for eighty-year-olds. The narrow lane leading down the hill from the main road arrived steeply at a bridge over a stream; snow made it impassable. If that were to coincide with a power-cut or a problem with the boiler or a burst pipe . . . The loneliness of the spot must have made it seem vulnerable to burglary. One day, when my grandparents were away, a gang of thieves reversed a pick-up through the heavy oak front door. To silence the burglar alarm they tore the bell off the wall and threw it into the millpond. What they could not have realized was that, ever since the IRA threats against Grandpa's life, the alarm had been hard-wired to Special Branch in Cheltenham. A rapid reaction unit had the place surrounded in thirty minutes.

In the new year of 1997 Grandpa went for a walk up the lane and was discovered sometime later lying on the verge. His balance had not been good for a number of years, but it was not clear whether he had fallen and then suffered a stroke or the other way round. He was admitted to hospital, and then to a rehabilitation centre where his recovery progressed to the point where he was able to go home. Soon after, though, he developed jaundice and returned to hospital for more tests. These revealed he had cancer of the liver.

The old soldier faded away over that spring and summer, as the Halle-Bopp comet waned. The warrior became meek, and I would push him in his wheelchair to feed the fish, or to inspect the lambs in the meadow where I had played kiss-chase as a boy with the girls from the farm in the village. He stayed at home until the end. The final phase of his illness came at the beginning of September. The last time I saw him he was yellow and swollen. His hands were puffed up and dimpled at the knuckles. His eyes were closed. His carer had said that he might be able to hear so I should talk to him, but I could not find anything to say. I sat watching his chest rise and fall as he took gulping dry breaths, between which there were interminable intervals, so long I had to wonder if he would ever breathe in again. I bent over him to tell him I loved him, to kiss him goodbye. His moustache tickled my cheek.

Grandpa often said he could start the day only if when he turned to *The Times* obituary page his was not there. What the comment said about him depended on which camp you were in, those who thought him an egotistical martinet, and those who found in his amused take on public life irreverence and self-deprecation. The former resented being told that 'egotistical' should be pronounced with a short 'e'; for them his querulousness was merely a way of showing off that he was cleverer than you. The latter were inclined to see a certain intellectual mischievousness in his pedantry. Besides being the subject of jest, the ritual of turning to the obituary page first was for him a *memento mori*, an acknowledgement that the day would arrive when his own appeared there.

When it came, the obituaries were indeed encomious. Condensed into fifteen hundred words his public career glittered with decorations and honours. His qualities as a scholar, soldier and leader were dwelt upon. His sense of humour and approachability were mentioned in the same breath as his pedantry, or rather, to quote his entry in *Who's Who*, an interest in 'the pursuit of exactitude, called by some pedantry'. It was a fitting send-off for one of the breed obituarists know collectively as 'the Moustaches', the heroes of the Second World War. At his memorial service in St Martin-in-the-Fields Church there were five field marshals, three air marshals, and thirty-six assorted generals among the eight hundred people who attended.

Shan and Margaret were married for fifty-five years. She was his *Schatz*, his treasure. The pain she suffered during his last illness was terrible to behold; her sadness after his death was deep indeed, and into it intruded the sublunary necessity of ordering his affairs. Before his death King's College, London, had been offered and accepted the gift of his papers. He had left an ample record of himself which was still being archived four years later, and as the papers were sorted through and boxed up, occasionally a gem would emerge. One item that caught my eye was a large Manila envelope containing the photographs and negatives he had taken while touring the Crusader Castles of Northern Syria for his thesis on Saladin. As I had an enlarger at home I offered to print them for Granny.

My father had taught me to print black and white photographs using pictures he had taken during the Korean War – helicopters and tanks in the snow, cherry-blossom time in Japan. His father, a Fellow of the Royal Photographic Society, had taught him. I had become interested in old printing processes – carbon and cyanotype and gum bichromate – and in the world such old photographs portrayed, so to come across a hoard of negatives from the 1930s was exciting. That they showed an obscure corner of the world made these even more intriguing. Grandpa had occasionally spoken about this journey down the Orontes Valley on a mule, and having had similar experiences in Asia I was eager to work on the pictures.

They are not good photographs. Though Grandpa listed painting among his hobbies, had even attended art school, he did not have an eye for taking pictures and he was further disadvantaged by the camera he was using, 'a poor camera, borrowed from a brother officer' whose bellows leaked light. The flat noonday sun deprives the scrubby hills and tumbled masonry of all contrast and bleaches the sky to a dull white. Where the ruins are substantial and well preserved, the photographs fail to capture the spirit of the place. Admittedly they were not taken for a wholly pictorial purpose, but even as illustrations they are disappointing.

Nevertheless, however good or bad they are, these were 1/60th of a second slices of May 1935 in Northern Syria. They were part of the source material for a story that had become a family legend, proof that it really had happened. I wondered what else had survived from that time, and what I could find out about my real grandfather. If such discoveries could be made about a family legend, why not a family mystery? The telling and re-telling of the events recorded in a family's oral history seldom follow the same path twice. The self-contained episodes are re-combined according to theme. Their chronology becomes obscured and the larger story fragmented. Yet I felt certain that if I could track down more concrete evidence to which to anchor the anecdotes, I would be able to reassemble these pieces into a narrative that would not only tell what had happened sixty years previously in Palestine, but also how the protagonists came to be there in the first place. Maybe I would even find out why my real grandfather had committed suicide. At the least I might find his grave.

PART ONE

'The East is a career,' wrote Benjamin Disraeli in his novel *Tancred, or The New Crusade* published in 1847, but just what sort of career lay ahead for John Winthrop Hackett was far from certain. His regiment, the 8th King's Royal Irish Hussars, the regiment in which his great-grandfather had served in the eighteenth century, arrived in Port Said on 29 December 1933 aboard the *Nevasa*. 'I was glad', he wrote, 'to be in the East again.' He was so glad, he embarked upon an all-night bender with a group of other young officers. They started at the casino and dined at the Eastern Exchange Hotel, before being led by 'a persuasive person in a blue dressing gown' to an unsavoury part of the town where a floor-show was staged for them in an equally unsavoury establishment. For some who served in the 'sensuous and despotic' Orient their career was a headlong one towards dissoluteness.

The first time Shan Hackett passed through Egypt he had been a serious Australian teenager en route to a place at New College, Oxford. He returned with a taste for champagne, two degrees and a thirst to learn about the world; as an officer in the British (rather than the Australian) Army he would have the chance to see some of it. There may also have been a financial motive. His widowed mother had remarried and the bulk of his father's fortune had gone to various public institutions as a result. In life his father had been a philanthropist, but in death he was more than beneficent; his endowment to the University of Western Australia remains, in real terms, the largest single bequest to an academic establishment in Australian history. They named a wallaby after him. Shan said later that he was glad he had not inherited a fortune as it would have made him bone idle, yet the modest means left to his mother were severely depleted by the Great Depression. He may have come from 'the uppermost crust' of Australian society, but he was frequently short of money while he was at Oxford, not least because he ran with a rich crowd, and in 1931 he pledged to join the army on graduating, thereby supplementing his irregular allowance with a subaltern's pay.

He was an unlikely-looking soldier, short of stature, only five foot six, and slight, but he had a competitive toughness, resulting perhaps from his antipodean upbringing, which earned him a half-blue at lacrosse, and a physical recklessness that directed him to the biggest jumps while out hunting. He had grown up with horses, and a part of the allure of joining the 8th King's Royal Irish Hussars stemmed from the fact it was still a mounted regiment. As strong was the desire to make his name outside Australia, where, because of his father's standing, he would never have been sure that his achievements were entirely his own. He was only too aware of the burden he had inherited with his father's name. He was both proud of his family history and eager to escape its colonial confines. In joining his great-grandfather's regiment he was at once honouring his ancestry by reconnecting with his Irish forbears and striking out for himself.

All these circumstances led the second lieutenant unsteadily to Port Said's waterfront at dawn on the morning of 30 December. His companion, a captain in the East Surrey's, was even shakier than Hackett, on whom it fell to hail a passing dinghy and negotiate a passage back to the *Nevasa*. The fisherman and his wife rowed them across the still harbour. It was so calm and quiet that the sound of a dog barking reached them from miles away, quiet that is until the captain started singing at the top of his voice, the raucous song bouncing between the hulls of the dimly lit ships lying at anchor. They paid double the agreed fare. The fisherman presented them with a crab which they gave to the sentry, who signed them in as having returned at midnight.

No amount of coffee could restore Shan for the arduous day ahead and his mood was as flat as the desert through which the train ran towards their barracks at Abbassiyya, just outside Cairo. The sand stung his eyes. The station was crowded with men from the 14th Hussars who were to leave that night and his sore head could have done without the band that led them into the troops' quarters. There was no let-up that night either as he had friends in the departing regiment and so did not get to bed until midnight. He had slept for only eleven hours in the preceding four days; the following night being New Year's Eve, his aggregate was not set to rise by much. There was a party at Shepheard's Hotel. On New Year's Day there were arrangements to be made for the start of training the following morning, after which Shan paid a visit to the stables to see his pair of polo ponies. So ended his first three days as an officer of the Cairo Cavalry Brigade.

By the time the British took control of Egypt in 1882 the country had been ruled by foreigners for more than two thousand years, ever since Alexander the Great was confirmed as Pharaoh by the priests of Memphis in 332 BCE. Greek was supplanted by Roman rule in 30 BCE, whose centre shifted eastward to Constantinople during the fourth century CE. The Byzantines were defeated in their turn not only by a new Arabian power, but also by a new religion. The armies of Islam established a camp before the walls of the Byzantine fortress, Babylon-in-Egypt, in 641, from which the city of Cairo grew. As a province in the empires of Islam, Egypt was ruled in succession by the Umayyad dynasty of Damascus, the North African Fatimids, the Abbasid Caliphs of Baghdad, the Kurdish Ayyubids, Mameluke sultans, whose origins lay in the Caucasus and Kipchak Steppe, and finally, from 1517, by the Ottoman Turks. Even when the country did regain a degree of autonomy at the beginning of the nineteenth century it was under the leadership of an Albanian officer in the Ottoman Army, Mohammed Ali, who could not speak Arabic. His successors, first as khedives and then as kings, remained in power until 1952.

The rise of Mohammed Ali reversed the isolationism of the Ottoman era and once again the Red Sea route to India and the East lay open. The British established a coaling station at Aden in 1839, and together with the French invested heavily in Egypt. Factories were established and irrigation work in the Nile Delta brought a million new acres under cultivation, planted with cash crops like cotton and sugar cane. With modernization came westernization among the non-Egyptian ruling elite, and an ever-increasing national debt. In the 1850s the British built a railway from the Red Sea to Alexandria to carry their Indian trade, and in 1859 the French began work on the Suez Canal. It opened ten years later, during the reign of Khedive Ismail, Mohammed Ali's profligate grandson, a reign which saw the undertaking of vast public projects. Egypt's cultivated area increased by 15 per cent as a result of the digging of more than 8000 miles of new irrigation canals; her railway network was extended by some 900 miles, and, in imitation of Haussmann's remodelling of Paris, Ismail built a new European-style quarter next to the old walled city of Cairo. The khedive declared, 'My country no longer belongs to Africa; it is part of Europe,' but to achieve this end he had borrowed £25 million at punitive rates of interest. In 1875 Ismail was forced to sell Egypt's 44 per cent stake in the Suez Canal – the British government, then under Prime Minister Benjamin Disraeli, bought the shares for £4 million – but it was not enough to save the country from bankruptcy the following year. To protect their interests, the British and the French took control of Egypt's finances and for a while the schedule of repayments was maintained, until European dominance and the increased level of taxation became insupportable. Ismail's policies only inflamed the situation, and he was exiled in 1879. His son Tewfiq failed to control the upsurge of nationalist sentiment; the country stood on the brink of anarchy. A strong Anglo-French fleet was sent to Alexandria, though the French contingent withdrew in protest at the hard line adopted by the British towards the nationalist leader, Colonel Arabi. The decisive engagement came at Tel el-Kebir in September 1882 where Arabi's forces were defeated with the loss of ten thousand men. British casualties totalled fifty-seven dead and twenty-two missing. The British occupied Cairo.

William Gladstone, who had succeeded Disraeli as prime minister, was faced with a dilemma. His sentiments were naturally anti-imperialist. He had once said that it was as unnecessary for Britain to make a colonial possession of Egypt as it was for a man with property both in the north of England and the south to want to own all the inns along the way; all that the landowner required of those inns was that they should be 'well-kept, always accessible, and [furnish] him, when he came, with mutton-chops and post-horses'. Moreover, French and Ottoman opposition to the establishment of a British colony might have triggered a European war. Yet after the battle of Tel el-Kebir, the British were in possession of Egypt, more by force of circumstance than design, and despite frequent protestations that their departure was imminent their rule lasted seventy-four years.

While the undignified imperialist scramble for the acquisition of African colonies at the end of the nineteenth century was in full swing, Egypt remained stable under the guidance of the British 'agent and consul-general', Sir Evelyn ('Over') Baring, later Lord Cromer. A former viceroy of India, he was the power behind the khedive's throne and appointed British advisers to every cabinet minister's office. He had stereotypically Victorian ideas concerning 'subject races', of which the Egyptians were one, and 'governing races' of which the British were the exemplar. He did not think it worthwhile to educate the Egyptian peasants, the fellahin, beyond the most basic level and looked to the old Turco-Circassian landlords and military classes to provide civil servants. He set about the eradication of corruption and curtailed all public works except irrigation. Within ten years, Egypt had returned to solvency, but Cromer never achieved his stated ambition: to relieve the British exchequer of the cost of maintaining a military presence in the country. The country was relieved of him in 1907, but his ideas about the native Egyptians' unfitness to rule lingered on.

The nature of the British occupation changed dramatically with the entry of the Ottoman Empire into the Great War on the side of Austria-Hungary and Germany. Egypt was still nominally an Ottoman territory, but it could not become a British one without alienating France. The compromise was to declare it a Protectorate, and then fill it with troops. Britain's main concern was to safeguard the Suez Canal, but once the only Turkish attack on the waterway had been repulsed, Egypt was used as the launch-pad for the Syrian campaign and the Gallipoli landing, and to supply the Arab uprising in the Hejaz. The defeat and disintegration of the Ottoman Empire brought Britain new responsibilities in the Middle East – a League of

Nations mandate for the government of part of Syria, and the position of Protector to the Gulf Emirates and the newly created kingdoms of Trans-Jordan and Iraq. Cairo became Britain's regional headquarters and the permanent garrison was enlarged accordingly.

    🔥   🔥   🔥

At 8.15 on the morning of 2 January 1934, Hackett's squadron, sixty-nine men and horses, formed up on the parade ground and moved off into the desert. As a schoolboy in Australia Shan had been inspired by reading Robert Graves's book *Lawrence and the Arabs* and, when it appeared in the Geelong Grammar School library a year later, T. E. Lawrence's abridgement of *Seven Pillars of Wisdom* entitled *Revolt in the Desert* (1927). The latter was the first book he ever started to reread immediately on finishing it. Now he found himself part of a small mounted force riding out into a desert morning. He drank in the scenery. They crossed a sandy plain strewn with iron-stone pebbles where the Egyptian infantry was parading to the accompaniment of a band. 'On the right hand were hills, the near ones bright red with little yellow ochre foothills, the farther ones blue. They were savagely torn and great rents in them were filled with rich blue and plum coloured shadows.' The squadron advanced to the top of one of these foothills, Signal Hill, and took their bearings. To the north lay Heliopolis, a garden suburb the British had constructed before the Great War. It was built in a quixotic style, a fantastic blend of European and Asian architecture that threw up such follies as a private residence modelled on a Hindu temple. In the morning light it looked like stage scenery. Beyond Heliopolis was the RAF aerodrome, which consisted of a few hangars beside an area of desert that had been levelled and cleared of stones. To the left of that stood the Abbassiyya barracks, and to the west Cairo, al-Qahira, 'the City of Mars', crowded onto the banks of the Nile. This plain, these foothills, served as the regiment's training ground for the next three months.

After two weeks of little more than exercising the horses, the training began in earnest. Officers wore swords and their mounts were caparisoned with the brass-bound, plumed regimental saddlery. The squadron's first task was to ride on a compass bearing for 6000 yards, to be calculated according to regulation paces. Next they walked, trotted and cantered on the 'pace track', a distance of 440 yards marked out with white cairns, timing each pass, then onto the 'wheeling track', turning in a figure of eight. It was during these manoeuvres that Shan noticed his plume had worked loose. While they continued to trot and wheel and reform their columns, he tried to loosen its straps so that he could stow it away, but almost unbridled his horse in the process. The result was the straps trailed on the ground and the plume dangled. Hackett bemoaned his 'congenital unsmartness' that was always inviting 'extra and unseen disaster'.

It was not his first gaffe. There was the occasion where he had worn a Tyrolean hat he had been given for Christmas – he was banned from ever wearing it again – and another time he had appeared at a funeral wearing the wrong kind of uniform trousers – he was sent off to change. Twice he had been late for the morning parade, and once the squadron had moved off without him, taking his empty mount with them. Twice he had forgotten his duties when ward officer and had failed to set the watch, but the sergeant-majors expected as much from junior officers and nothing was said. The continuing field drill provided opportunity for plenty more mistakes – dismounted attacks, night manoeuvres, extending and closing in squadron column, artillery formation, line of troop column, patrolling by troops. It was even said that he had got lost on one occasion, a heinous crime, and he continued to have trouble with his plume.

While Hackett was critical of himself, he was not un-questioning of the army. He remembered a 'most heretical' conversation with his squadron commander, who asserted 'there was no such thing as foreign service in the British Army, only home service abroad,' and suggested Hackett might apply for a colonial job at the end of his commission. Hackett commented, displaying the analytical thinking he brought to bear on the world, and especially on military matters: 'I suppose any corporate body when it travels preserves the immunity of its constituents from outside influence to some degree. A regiment seems to do so very largely.' He also cited the corporate attitude as contributing to his own incompetence:

> I do not know in my own mind whether this assumption of complete ignorance is a good thing or a bad. Two years in the Oxford University OTC taught me a good deal about section work and section leading, my two attachments with the Bays taught me something about stable management and ... manoeuvres ... But here and perhaps wisely absolute ignorance is assumed. The only trouble is I have always been as competent (or as anything else!) as people expect and here consequently I have been grossly incompetent. I started on the wrong leg. But there have been fewer raspberries the last day or two. . . .

The day's training ended at lunchtime – 'half a day's wages, we always said, for half a day's work,' Hackett observed. Occasionally there was a lecture in the afternoon, but for the most part the officers were free to do what they wanted. Shan spent many of his afternoons with his polo ponies. By way of preparation for their tour of duty overseas the officers had clubbed together to purchase a string of 120 unmade ponies, bought from breeders in Australia and shipped to Egypt ahead of their arrival.

Polo was then in its international heyday and greatly encouraged in the cavalry regiments of the British Army, where it served, as it had since its origins in Persia, as a training game for mounted combat. It had been introduced by Muslim invaders into India, where the first British clubs were started by tea-planters in Assam in 1859 and by colonial administrators in Calcutta in 1860. Officers of the 10th Hússars saw a game there in 1866 and immediately formed a club of their own. They played a series of exhibition matches against the 9th Lancers in Richmond Park in 1870, and from England the game was exported to the United States and Argentina, where it became a national sport. By the 1930s big games in Buenos Aires attracted as many as sixty thousand spectators. For British cavalry regiments India was still the place to play, although the game was to be found in even the smallest colonial outpost, and the 8th King's Royal Irish Hussars were due to spend five years in the subcontinent after their two-year tour in Egypt. Their aim was to arrive on the broad maidans of India after two years of warm-up matches with a team ready to take on the dragoons and lancers and hussars already there. Not only does the purchase show what the officers of the 8th Hussars thought they would be doing with their time, but also a great confidence in the continuation of the imperial peace; at the beginning of 1934, although the seeds of war had already been sown, there was no reason to suppose it would not last.

Shan's ponies were both grey Arab stallions 'with pretty heads and plenty of quality'. They had both played a good deal, unlike Hackett who had never played before. They were cared for by his syce, Dahab, who called both horses 'him bony'; Shan called them Joey and Kishmul and many other things besides. He spent hours in the 'polo pit' – a wooden horse set up so that a player could practise hitting the ball, rather than his pony, with the long flexible mallet. He spent afternoons knocking about on his own, though his ponies had other ideas: 'Joey had sudden fits of taking charge which lasted just long enough to make me miss a shot each time, and Kishmul, wanting to go on a bit, crabbed away from the ball.' He practised so much his hands blistered, but all these exercises could not prepare him for the hurly-burly of the game. In his first match he was 'carried away twice and quite failed to hit the ball except by accident. I didn't know where to go except when it was too late to go there and got generally cursed.' Next time out, 'four incompetent chukkas' at the Gezira Club, he started by 'striking the ball the wrong way and then rarely, after that, striking it at all. Seem to be continually in the wrong place or fouling people. . . .' He did improve with practice and, though he never won a place in the regiment's first team, which toured internationally, he played the game with the same energy he brought to everything he did.

After two weeks of 'withering sobriety', Hackett was ready for a party, 'a blind' as he had come to say. It started innocently enough. On an earlier trip into Cairo, while shopping for a picture frame, he had found a copy of *Vanity Fair*, but only the first volume. He had sat reading in a cafe, feeling '"out of school" and more myself than I had in a long time'. Now he wanted to get the second volume and after buying it repaired to the Shepheard's Hotel bar where he had arranged to meet a fellow officer. They proceeded to drink seven champagne cocktails. 'After the fourth I began to feel very well and after the seventh refused to go home.'

Shepheard's Hotel was usually where such evenings began.

It was an institution amongst Cairo hotels, the first to be built there in the European style. Egypt's opening to European trade and influences under Mohammed Ali attracted a growing number of visitors and in 1841 Shepheard's opened its doors to them. If Mark Twain is to be believed the hotel was 'the worst on earth except the one I stopped at once in a small town in the United States' – if believed, because he then reproduces an extract from his journal about the place, the Benton House, that shows off all his comic flair, and Twain was not known to let the truth get in the way of a good story. His observation that 'all the donkeys in Christendom and most of the boys in Egypt, I think, are at its door' is more credible. Whatever its state when Twain visited in 1868, during the 1870s it became the hotel to which the British firm Thomas Cook and Son sent their tourists. In the same year that the hotel had opened, Thomas Cook had organized an excursion by a chartered train from Leicester to Loughborough to attend a temperance meeting, and so gave rise to the modern travel industry. The hotel prospered greatly through this association, expanded, modernized and refurbished in 'Eighteenth Dynasty Edwardian'. By the 1920s, when trips to Egypt became all the rage in the wake of the discovery of Tutankhamun's tomb, it was simply the grandest hotel in Cairo, a landmark in its own right and a base from which to visit other parts of the Middle East.

In the late afternoon the hotel's shady terrace was the place to meet. The terrace was raised up to head-height above the level of Ibrahim Pasha Street, and partly covered by a balcony supported on cast iron pillars. Waiters in tarbushes and long white tunics moved between the wicker chairs and tables. A pianist played an upright in a self-absorbed manner. If the weather was too hot, or too cold, mixed company could gather below the dome of coloured glass in the Moorish Hall; the Long Bar was an all-male preserve. In the evening the hotel's dress code was strictly enforced and male diners had to wear dinner jackets. On nights when the Pharaonic ballroom was opened up, white tie was required. Yet for all its formality the parties held there could become very raucous, and then more often than not the pair of bare-breasted caryatids that flanked the grand staircase would fall victim to some puerile outrage.

For the young officers of a cavalry regiment, the social season gathered pace in February and March as the polo season reached its climax. The whirl of cocktail parties and balls also coincided with the preparations for brigade manoeuvres. The lack of sleep began to take its toll on Shan and as the heat began to mount the regimental exercises became torturous. He recalled 'days spent in a blind sweating fury of galloping drill', how he 'sat on a burning hilltop and watched unfortunate men crawling over sharp rocks'. He continued to do his job 'almost right, but wrong enough to get cursed for it'. Shan's youth and energy carried him through, and he even found time to play polo, maintain a considerable correspondence, read Thackeray's *Vanity Fair* and D.H. Lawrence's *The Plumed Serpent* (written only eight years before), and begin learning Arabic.

Hackett chose a comfortable spot from which to reflect on his first three months in the Cairo Cavalry Brigade – a deckchair aboard the SS *Aquitania* as she crossed the Mediterranean. It was the beginning of April. He was going off on leave, to Italy for a holiday before returning to England, and the limbo of transit afforded him the opportunity to recall such moments as the morning after the 12th Lancers' Ball, riding out at six 'full of champagne and exalted to the verge of immortality'.

It is a commonplace to say that Egypt is the Nile. The truth thus obscured by cliché might be better expressed as: Egypt depends on the management of the Nile. Flood control and irrigation enabled the kingdoms of the Pharaohs to rise and remain the keys to the country's prosperity. But dependence on the Nile has also limited Egypt's development upstream of the delta, to the river valley, the narrow fertile strip closed in by rocky hills and desert: 99 per cent of the population lives on 5 per cent of the land. Travel but a short distance east or west from the life-giving watercourse and an uncompromising wilderness starts abruptly at the point where the irrigation pipes end. From outer space the thin green ribbon is merely the boundary between the Libyan Desert, part of the Sahara, and the 'Eastern Desert', the Sahara al-Sharqiya that borders the Red Sea. From the air, approaching Cairo airport from the south and looking east, there is very little on the ground to suggest proximity to a city of seventeen million people. A drab empty plain stretched out under a blanket of yellowish cloud, the plains on which the 8th Hussars had trained. The RAF aerodrome has grown into the busiest airport in Africa.

The taxi driver wiped the dust off the back seat. Turning the key in the ignition activated a robotic voice somewhere behind the dashboard: '*bism illah ar-rahman ar-rahim*', 'in the name of Allah, the Merciful, the Compassionate', an appeal for protection before entering the Cairo traffic that was not unwarranted. The driver raced to catch up with the nearest traffic jam only to decide it was not moving slowly enough, so he raced off to find a worse one. Just as the traffic looked as though it might be moving again, he decided he had been better off before and did another U-turn from the nearside lane in order to rejoin the first queue. It was a game of inches, who could get just far enough ahead to cut into another lane, who could get closest to his neighbour. A large medallion hung from the rear-view mirror, the name of Allah on one side and Muhammad on the other, angular gold letters on a black ground. It fretted against a string of blood-stone beads. The driver was not worried about the delay, even though he was not on the meter. He saw it as an opportunity to talk up his Lovely-Jubbly Pyramid Tour. After all, everyone who came to Cairo visited the Pyramids, so why not straightaway? 'First the Biramid – the Great Biramid, the Sfiks, rider camel, lovely-jubbly – then to the hotel, no?' His eyes inquired in the mirror. It was the only time he used it, even after the blockage was behind him and the taxi was speeding past blocks of flats, under grimy flyovers blackened by diesel fumes from the buses and lorries that were as slalom gates to any Cairene car driver. On curves, the beads and the medallion hanging plumb measured the increment of the vehicle's list. It seemed to be a matter of honour among young male pedestrians to step off the curb without looking. There was no question of waiting for a gap in the traffic – as if there were one. They followed the theory that every road was crossable at the precise moment that they wanted to cross it and set out to test that belief at every opportunity. Their bravado was sometimes breathtaking, their timing immaculate, finding fleeting spaces between the cars. Some crossed with the insouciance of a sleepwalker in a silent movie, others, like matadors, stood side-on between lanes, sighting along the left shoulder at the charging black and white taxis, swaying out of the way of wing mirrors that would gore them through. The high-rise apartment blocks gave way to the once-elegant avenues of Khedive Ismail's European quarter, the Cairo that Hackett knew. Turning into a side street off what was once Fuad I Avenue, clogged with cars parked two deep at the curb, the taxi pulled up outside the Windsor Hotel. 'Biramid tomorrow?'

The chief appeal of the Windsor Hotel is claimed to be its old-fashioned atmosphere. It is said to have preserved the charm of the British era, but anyone who took the hotel to be representative of that time would be convinced that the past was a scruffy place. It has more in common with a dilapidated south-coast boarding house than the grandeur and *luxe* of Shepheard's, the Meena House or the Continental. Rather than being old-fashioned it is merely old; the dark wood panelling and scuffed reception desk, the antique cage lift that is started and stopped by well-judged use of the resistor lever, the door-lock so worn it had to be picked with its own key, the lumpy bedstead, the plumbing. The dining-room smelled of over-boiled vegetables. The sheets piled on the landing were grey. Even the metal detector, a detached portal standing a little inside the front door as a sop to those guests who remembered the bombing of a tour-bus outside the Egyptian Museum and the massacre of fifty-eight tourists at Luxor in 1997, even this was old. Only the room rates showed signs of renovation. After the British withdrew to their bases on the Suez Canal in 1946, the building continued to be used as a club for non-commissioned officers. The bar on the first floor has retained the homely gentility of a pub lounge, a brass foot-rail and high-stools, settles upholstered in velveteen, stools fashioned from beer barrels, old travel posters on the walls. An Egyptian TV crew was using it as the location for a scene of a period drama and was blocking all access to its exceptionally cold beer.

In the postwar years negotiations between the British and Egyptian governments dragged on and failed to produce mutually acceptable terms for Egypt's independence. The situation for the occupiers changed during the course of one day in January 1952. Egyptian frustration had led to increasingly frequent guerrilla attacks against the British positions in the Canal

Zone. Local policemen were involved in the sabotage. The
British responded to one particular incident by surrounding
the police station in Ismailia and demanding the surrender of
those inside. The minister of the interior ordered them to
resist; fifty policemen and five British soldiers died when the
building was stormed. Protests in Cairo the following day
turned into riots by late morning. The mob set fire to many
buildings in the European quarter, targeting especially British-
owned and frequented property and establishments, though
French, Italian, Greek, Armenian and Jewish businesses were
also torched. The day came to be known as Black Saturday
as a result of the clouds of smoke and ash that filled the air.
The arsonists appeared to be well-organized in small groups,
each of which had a list of targets and a supply of combustible
materials. Plans for such an action must have long been in
place. The day's events were encouraged by government min-
isters and condoned by the police. The Turf Club, as a bastion
of the British class and colonial systems, was high on the
rioters' list. Hackett described it as being 'like one of the less
exclusive bits of St James's complete with stags' heads'. It
had been a club 'to which no Egyptians were allowed in
membership, though sometimes, greatly daring, some member
might take one of the more distinguished Egyptians there with
him. This wasn't popular. . . .' Neither was the club with the
Cairenes and the mob showed particular savagery towards its
members. Artemis Cooper in her book *Cairo in the War*
describes what happened.

> Just after 1.30 the Turf Club was attacked. For the past few
> weeks, the Club had been protected by a police guard of some
> forty men, but this had mysteriously dwindled to four by the
> time the gang arrived. [T]hey broke down the front door, and
> immediately started smashing furniture and making piles of it

on the ground floor, which were set alight with bundles of hessian . . .

Of the forty-odd members who were in the Club at the time, most were on the ground floor and managed to get out by the back door. But several were prevented from escaping by the crowds outside, and were pushed back into the flames. Two Englishmen who were trapped on an upper storey jumped out of the windows. The first broke his back on the roof of a small shed beneath, and must have died soon after; but the second let himself down into a small courtyard on knotted sheets. He was kicked and beaten to death with iron bars. The bodies of the two men were then brought together, and a great pile of material was put on top of them to make a bonfire . . . While the Turf Club was under attack, a lorry full of police drove by. They did not stop, and the crowd cheered. Inside the building, a number of other Britons were savagely mutilated before being tossed onto bonfires.

Shepheard's Hotel went up in flames shortly afterwards, though with less loss of life. The offices of Thomas Cook and BOAC, Barclay's Bank and W. H. Smith's followed. Other groups organized by the Muslim Brotherhood attacked targets they considered immoral, such as bars, nightclubs and cinemas. Though much of Cairo's 'West End' was on fire by nightfall, both the large synagogue on Sharia Adly Pasha and the Opera House were spared.

'The Opera House didn't burn down till years later,' said Mr Doss, owner of the Windsor. 'The wardrobe master had been stealing for years, and suddenly there was going to be an audit. Of course they would discover he had not bought all the costumes he said he had, so he set fire to the wardrobe to cover his tracks.' Verdi had written *Aida* for the grand opening of the Opera House in 1871; a hundred years later as a result of this petty larceny the building burned to the ground. 'They tried to burn this place down in 1952, but it survived because it is mostly brick and had very thick iron gates. Then it was empty. The NCOs did not come back.' The British did consider moving on the capital – the destruction of foreign property during the Alexandria riots of 1882 had provided them with the excuse for occupying the country in the first place – but the world had changed and Britain could no longer ignore its opinion. When the revolution came six months later on 23 July 1952 it met only token resistance. Public approval of the events of Black Saturday had made its success inevitable, and that day's frenzied destruction had purged it of the need for violence. A group of military commanders known as the Free Officers forced King Farouk to abdicate and he went into exile in Italy. He was succeeded briefly by his infant son, the great-great-great-great-grandson of the Albanian Mohammed Ali, but less than a year later Egypt became a republic with General Muhammad Neguib at its head. It was the first time an Egyptian had ruled the country since Alexander the Great.

In 1979, three years after General Sir John Hackett retired from his post at King's College, he gave an interview to a researcher from the Imperial War Museum for its sound archive. A second recording was made twelve years later and together the two sessions last four and a half hours. They reveal as much about Hackett's public persona as the events recounted. They cover his time in the Middle East and his experiences during the Second World War. On both occasions he speaks with such fluency and precision, displaying his great range of knowledge and power of memory. The 81-year-old general of the last two reels is a little more forgetful and in the last fifteen minutes he repeats a story he finished telling the first time but ten minutes earlier. Yet even this repetition reveals just how polished his performance is; in retelling the story he uses the same form of words and the same intonation as he did on the first occasion.

There is a clunk as the tape recorder is turned on, and then the interviewer's voice some way from the microphone states, 'Sir John Hackett, reel one. When did you first go to the Middle East, Sir John?' From the first syllable of Hackett's reply – a mere 'er' – you can see his three-piece tweed suit, his regimental tie, thin grey hair slicked flat over capacious pate, pale blue eyes, arched nostrils, the clipped moustache. He says: 'Er, other than a brief visit to Egypt for twenty-four hours off a P&O ship . . .' and continues without a pause for the next eleven minutes, until the interviewer finally interjects into Hackett's flow on a trivial point and produces nothing but a digression. He keeps quiet after that, saying during the following twenty minutes only 'Just milk, please' to Lady Hackett's enquiry as to how he took his tea. Shortly after there is the sound of a door-latch lifting as somebody leaves the room, the rattle before the thumb-plate is depressed and the wrought-iron latch rises with a clack. It is instantly recognisable as the door furniture of the drawing room at Coberley Mill. As a spoon chinks against a saucer the pattern on the china becomes visible.

Hackett's is a voice from a different era, the accent betraying no hint of his Australian upbringing, the pronunciation received, patrician and retaining elements of pre-war vowel sounds – not so affected that he says 'haice' for 'house', or 'awff' for 'off', but there is a hint of that diction, which it seems has survived into the twenty-first century solely among members of the Royal Family, when he says 'lawst' for 'lost'.

He is a man who has become accustomed to people listening to what he has to say, and a military manner creeps in occasionally; at one point he corrects himself with a bluff 'no, as you were . . .' He paints a picture of life in the Cairo Cavalry Brigade with fondness, 'a very healthy, agreeable, highly social life . . . with a lot of leave . . . a life that has disappeared. Nobody worked in the afternoon, you weren't expected to . . . Every officer was expected as a matter of course to have his visiting cards and [you] had to go through a ritual of calling on the designated people when first you arrived.' The formality of British society abroad is encapsulated in this custom, the obligatory calls on the High Commissioner and the commanders of the British Troops in Egypt and the Egyptian Army. 'Your card had on it "Mr J. W. Hackett, Cavalry Club". You would no doubt be asked to attend garden parties later.'

'Of course we had a good deal of fun . . .' and to illustrate this the general recounts a tale of Cairo high-jinx that occurred one Saturday night in Shepheard's Hotel:

the souffragi who was at the cloakroom counter . . . was an old Egyptian whom I knew quite well. He was sick, he'd had injections that day and was very, very unwell but didn't like to disclose this because he thought it might even jeopardize his job so I took over from him, put on his clothes and his tarbush . . . he was a fair coloured Egyptian and I was pretty sunburnt as we all were. His clothing fitted me and all that evening I spent taking the coats of people I knew and then putting them on again without being recognized by one of them, except a businessman there who looked round in surprise when in an excess of professional zeal I not only helped him into his coat, but put my hand up inside his great coat to settle his tailcoat down underneath it by a tug at the tails, which of course is the right thing to do, but which the souffragi had never done and he was so surprised at this extra special treatment, I suppose I was a little flown with wine for I had a bottle of champagne under the desk and was refreshing myself from time to time, he was so surprised that he looked round and was the only person that evening who recognized me. *But he didn't say anything to you?* He said, 'Hello it's you is it?' and I said, 'Yes, but please don't tell anybody.' Later the souffragi had recovered and came back and took over from me, and I put on my tailcoat again and went and rejoined the party from which I had absented myself, and nobody asked any questions. Anyway it was an agreeable and not an unfunny life. . . .

Hackett's interest in academic study had not ended when he left Oxford. 'I used to spend my long leave partly in Bodley,' he tells the interviewer, 'and partly in the Reading Room of the British Museum at work on a campaign of Saladin.' He does not specify a year, but, by the time the next long leave came around in April 1935 and Hackett embarked on a journey to Syria, he was already well acquainted with the mediaeval accounts of Salah al-Din's life and the Third Crusade. It could perhaps be inferred that Shan's rediscovery of his scholarly ambitions was in part a reaction to the social riot of February and March 1934. In January he had 'contrived to read a few pages of Halphen's *L'Essor de l'Europe* most days', but that had gone by the board as the polo season neared its climax. At any rate, he returned from leave with renewed academic vigour. In the quiet months of July, August and September, when the other half of the regiment's officers were on leave and the rest languished at their summer camp in Alexandria, Hackett applied himself to learning Arabic more seriously. He began to study for the army's preliminary interpretership examination and his plans to visit Syria the following spring added incentive.

Also during his visit to Oxford, the focus of his study seems to have shifted away from the Third Crusade itself and settled on the events of two years earlier. The change is telling. The Christian expedition of 1190 came to be led by an Anglo-Norman king, Richard Coeur de Lion. It was the first crusade to have a large contingent from England, funded by the first poll tax, the Saladin Tithe. T.E. Lawrence, Hackett's hero as a schoolboy, could trace his ancestry to an Anglo-Norman knight who had served in Richard's army, and he had taken an obsessive journey through the Levant in 1909 visiting as many Crusader castles as he could for his BA thesis. His final tally was thirty-six, having walked nearly nine hundred miles in three months. Hackett too had knightly Norman forebears and his initial interest in the Third Crusade must have involved an element of atavism. When, however, he came to submit the subject for his B. Litt. thesis, after a year as an officer in command of a light cavalry unit, his interest fell not on the stalemate that confined Richard's reconquest of the Holy Land to a coastal strip, but on Salah al-Din's brilliant campaign against the Crusader states in 1187 and 1188 whose success had prompted the Third Crusade in the first place.

In July 1187, Salah al-Din had won a battle over the Crusader Kingdom of Jerusalem at the Horns of Hattin so decisive that by December all its former territory was under his control, with the exception of the port of Tyre. When the next campaigning season came round in May of 1188 he was preparing an attack against the two remaining Crusader states, the County of Tripoli and the Principality of Antioch. His efforts were concentrated on the latter, since, realising his success against Jerusalem would bring a renewed Christian invasion, he was attempting to block the route across Asia Minor taken by all the previous crusading armies. It was this swift campaign in particular that formed the subject of Shan's thesis. For Hackett the study became a lesson in military planning, in how to keep a large force in the field and use it to best effect against static positions, as well as an historical analysis of contemporary sources. He hoped it would make him a better soldier.

To travel from Cairo to Damascus by train, changing at Haifa onto the Samakh spur of the Hejaz Railway, was an easier proposition in 1934 than it is today. Unfortunately, Hackett's first impressions of the Holy Land, unlike those of many before him, of crossing the Jordan and climbing up the Yarmuk Valley to Dera'a, are not recorded; no diary of the journey has been found. From Damascus a road continued north to Homs where it met the road to the coast, an ancient trade route that runs through the gap between the Lebanon and al-Nusayriyah ranges. The riches of Asia reached the Mediterranean along this route and made wealthy the ports of Trablus and Tartus (Tripoli and Tortosa of the Crusaders). It was the route that Salah al-Din took in July 1188, in the shadow of the strongest Crusader castle in the Levant, Krac des Chevaliers. Its own impregnability could not stop Salah al-Din picking off its outlying defences and passing on to lay siege to Tortosa. Dated photograph captions put Hackett in Tortosa late in April 1935.

As is to be expected in a scholarly thesis, there is little in the way of personal material in the paper, but there is much that is characteristic of its author. Hackett's notes suggest his first recourse was to the *Mediterranean Pilot* and its geographical detail, as though reconnoitring the coast for an invasion of his own. From this work he gleaned such essential facts as the depth of the Orontes at its mouth and the mean annual rainfall of Jaffa. Yet one piece of information did make it into the final analysis. The *Pilot* identifies a spring that rises offshore in the bay below Markab castle, causing an area of disturbed water. Hackett uses this feature, mentioned in the chronicles, to locate the closest point to the shore accessible to the Sicilian fleet from Tripoli and demonstrate that the road between the sea and the castle's outposts, along which Salah al-Din had to pass, was indeed within their bowshot; ibn al-Athir records the rapid construction of breastworks from which to return fire. Elsewhere, a military eye is cast over ibn al-Athir's account of the fall of Saône castle at the end of July 1188, an account which conflicts with that of the other Arab chronicler, Baha al-Din. Hackett resolves the uncertainty by establishing the only place where a direct assault on the walls could have been successful and so fixes the position of Salah al-Din's key battery: 'For the actual emplacement, I selected a slight levelling out of the forward slope of the ravine, a little below the highest point, and experiments conducted with the aid of three small Arab boys convinced me that it was well within mangonel range.' One assumes the boys were armed with slings or the like.

The same acuity is brought to bear on the castles of Bakas-Shogr, Bourzey, Darbsak and Baghras and their fall to Salah al-Din, but Hackett shows his tactical appreciation of the campaign nowhere more than in his analysis of the Kurdish commander's supply problems. His examiners were prompted to remark that he had 'to some extent rediscovered Saladin's lines of communication . . . Mr Hackett's work, though short, is a remarkably good example of the critical discussion of literary evidence in the light of field work.' It was not until 1937 that he received their verdict.

In his IWM recordings Hackett offers some insight into why it was so delayed and so brief. 'I wrote this up in my spare time,' he claims, 'without missing, I may say, a single party or a single chukka of polo. It was rewarded by the Regius Professor's observation on it . . . that "this is a model . . . of what such a work should be." ' Hackett remembers the exact words used by the examiners forty-two years previously. It is a fact he does not need to embellish, but there is a hint of broidery in his recollection of 'spending a lot of time on a mule up and down the Orontes Valley living with Arabs'. It was in truth no more than a week and maybe as few as two days actually on a mule, yet the experience obviously made an impression on the 24-year-old that lasted longer. During more than a year in Egypt he had never been in contact with local people so intimately and for so long. One can easily imagine him caught up in the romance of the journey. He could not have kept himself from thinking, as he rode through the Syrian wilderness, that he had glimpsed what Lawrence had experienced in Arabia. Spring stood on the threshold of summer as they rode beside the marshes of the valley floor from Bourzey to Apamea. His companions and other people met along the way can be seen occasionally in his photographs, a young man with a hawk on his wrist, another wearing a bandoleer of rounds for his old rifle. At night he would have sat with them around the fire wrestling with the local form of Arabic and hunks of mutton. As for Lawrence, by then T.E. Shaw, he died in a motorcycle accident two weeks after Hackett reached Apamea.

Parties and polo were not the only things that kept Shan from writing his thesis. No sooner had the regiment returned to Cairo in October 1935 from their summer camp than the Italians invaded Abyssinia. Britain and Italy stood on the brink of war.

On a steep-sided spur overlooking the road to Antioch stand the remains of Baghras castle, which once guarded the southern approach to the Beylen Pass. In its shadow, an old man in a bobble hat was leading his pony loaded with field tools up the rough path behind the village, through the almond orchards and olive groves towards the scrubby hills beyond. The sound of hooves on stone, the clanking of metal on metal passed, an echo of ancient sieges, and quiet returned, the breeze making the poppies sway, rustling through the stunted trees growing out of the castle wall, a lark celebrating the bright air. Lizards basked on the fallen stones in the uppermost court, overgrown with bramble and dog rose, the castle's only remaining defenders.

It is everything a ruined castle should be, a perfect place for the village boys to play. They scramble up the slope below the walls and edge along their base, slipping through a breach into the long lower gallery where horses and livestock were once stabled. A rock fall at the far end provides a ramp to the next level, a dim vaulted chamber whose furthest window frames a bank of poppies drifting down from the upper court. There, between the Knight's Hall and the Templar Chapel, the fiercest fighting takes place, the victors mounting the ruined ramparts and frightening themselves at the sheer drop into the ravine below.

The Beylen Pass is the natural route for any southbound army to take across the Amanus Mountains. Alexander the Great marched through in pursuit of the Persian King Darius; Roman legions followed some two hundred and fifty years later. They called the pass 'Pilae Syriae', the Pillars of Syria, and it was probably they who built the first fortification at Baghras. The Byzantines strengthened the position as the armies of Islam moved northwards in the seventh century; it came to stand on the border of the two empires. When the Crusaders took Antioch in 1098 they built up its defences and much of what remains today dates from the twelfth century, despite subsequent sieges and occupations. While its design is Norman, Hackett concluded from the use of small roughly shaped sets its construction was probably executed by Armenian masons. Its defence, and that of Darbsak, the stronghold on the pass's northern flank, was entrusted to the Knights Templar. Through the summer of 1188 the garrison watched the line of low hills to the south-east for signs of Salah al-Din's approach.

Standing in the Templar Chapel under a barrel vault that has stood for nine hundred years it is easy to think that not much has changed since Hackett visited on 1 May 1935, but his photographs show that the process of dilapidation has continued in the meantime. They show a sturdy aqueduct that is no longer to be seen bridging the defensive ditch cut through the spur; the stones have been carted off and reused elsewhere. The finer pieces of dressed masonry from the windows and the doorways have also disappeared. Geographical features have proved even less permanent. In the background of one shot of the aqueduct there is a glint of water from the shallow Amouk Lake; it no longer exists, drained and brought under the plough. The castle is even in a different country now; in 1935 Syria's northern border reached the Mediterranean at Payas, bringing both Alexandretta and Antioch, now Iskenderun and Antakya, within the French mandate. At the outbreak of the Second World War this region, known as the Hatay, was ceded to Turkey partly in the hope of securing her neutrality.

Both Baghras and Darbsak had surrendered quickly to Salah al-Din; Antioch was left without a single defence and seemingly at his mercy, but the expected siege never even began. With his skirmishers raiding up to the very walls of the city, dissension spread amongst his men and their commanders.

They had been campaigning from May to late September. Ramadan was coming and they wanted to go home. They had land to plough. A truce was concluded that was to run until the end of the following April when, if no help had arrived, Antioch was to be surrendered to the Sultan. May 1189 came, but no Muslim army with it, rather news that Frederick Barbarossa, the 70-year-old Holy Roman Emperor, had just set out from Regensburg with a largely German army, more numerous than any Crusading force before it. As Salah al-Din foresaw, they took the land route, slowly, to Constantinople and Konya, where they defeated a Seljuk army the following May. The road to Antioch through the Christian Kingdom of Cilician Armenia was open to the Crusaders, but in June the German Emperor drowned while crossing a river and his army lost heart. Some stragglers reached Tyre by sea from Tarsus, but most went home. The real threat from Europe, the sea-borne armies of Philip II of France and Richard Coeur de Lion of England, did not arrive until the following spring. Antioch remained in Christian hands for another eighty years.

Ahmad Bey scanned Hackett's photographs of Antioch street scenes with the magnifying glass he normally used to read the newspaper, looking for people he knew; he was old enough to have appeared in them himself. Passing by the camera along the market street are Arab boys in galabiyas riding donkeys, men wearing Western jackets over the long robe, a youth from the hills in riding pantaloons, soft-soled buskins and collarless coat with embroidered sleeves. Three men in Western suits stand talking by a telegraph pole, the one in the homburg set at a jaunty angle looks straight into the lens. Only the Turkish greengrocer is bare-headed, wearing a waistcoat over his white shirt, standing with his arms crossed in front of his displays of fruit and vegetables; everyone else is wearing a skull-cap or a tarbush or a peaked cap. There is only one woman to be seen, swathed in a white veil. Taken together the pictures look like the raw material for an illustration from a Tintin adventure. Ahmad Bey maintained the sartorial conventions of yesteryear as well as his gentlemanly Ottoman title, wearing a jacket and tie even in retirement, smoking cigarettes through a yellowed bone holder. He called for a round of tea.

Most days Ahmad Bey is to be found here, once a barber's shop, now a sort of social club for his passing friends. It stands in the acute angle between two converging roads, a rhomboid room commanding the confluence, glazed on three sides, both observation platform and hall of public audience. Ahmad's family were Turks who had been granted land in the Hatay at the time of the Ottoman conquest in 1516 and he still had large holdings. His tenants could bring their problems to him here. Turkish rule, administered by an army of bureaucrats, the janissaries, made up of Christian converts from the empire's European lands, replaced that of the Mamelukes of Egypt, soldier-slaves from the Caucasus, but for the local peasantry the certainties of the seasons, taxes and death abided.

Ahmad Bey's tenantry was largely Arab. 'But if you ask them if they want to be part of Syria again, they will say no, like me. They can see it is better in Turkey. They can see there is no freedom there. In Turkey there is democracy, in Syria a dictator. Yes, the economy could be better, but Syria's is worse. Here there is modern education and a free press. Even the Christians,' he gestured down the road towards the Orthodox church, 'even they want to be in Turkey. The people who say the Hatay should go back to Syria are all in Syria. What about joining Europe? The people who say yes are also wrong. Look,' he pointed to a calendar on the wall distributed by a political party, 'that is what we Turks should join, the countries of the other Turks.' On a map of the

Middle East and Central Asia the countries of the Turks and the regions of other countries where Turks were in the majority formed a single green block, with Northern Cyprus stuck out in the Mediterranean: the lands of the Azeris, the Kazaks, Uzbeks, Turkmen, Kyrgyz, Uighurs as well as Turkey.

The idea of a pan-Turkic federation is not a new one. It first found political expression in the 1880s among the Turks of the Crimea and lower Volga and its doctrine of the 'unity of language, thought and action' of all Turkic peoples was taken up in Istanbul as the Empire's fortunes waned. The formation of nation-states in Europe along the lines of ethnicity and language – Italy and Germany – at the expense of declining empires, provided a paradigm not only for the Ottomans' Slavic and Arab subject nations, but also for the Turks themselves. The collapse of the Soviet empire revived the dream, but the opportunity was largely spurned. 'Too busy looking west to turn east,' said Ahmad Bey. Below the map were printed a pair of quotations from the twin heroes of nationalism, Ataturk and Alp Arslan, who defeated the Byzantines at the battle of Manzikert in 1071, opening Asia Minor to Turkish conquest. 'Ah, and here is someone who can translate them better than I,' he claimed. At the door were two modestly dressed Western women, one older, slight, the other in her early twenties and robust in a corn-fed North American way. The younger one clutched a book to her chest that looked like a vinyl-covered day-to-a-page diary and turned out to be a New Testament, ragged with bookmarks. Their arrival demanded another round of tea.

Christine, the older woman, had been working as a missionary in Turkey for the last decade, and Sandi had been sent to join her for a few months by their church in Canada. As Christine and Ahmad Bey talked in Turkish, Sandi seemed to drift off into a world of her own, smiling inwardly and making repeated searches in her text. She found something that made her raise a fist and let out a mini-whoop of the kind usually heard at sporting events. Christine and Ahmad stopped to look at her. 'Oh, I'm sorry. I just found the great text I thought of when Yusuf was explaining the Holy Trinity to his wife on the back of that envelope.' They had just come from a home visit with one of Christine's few converts. She smiled indulgently at Sandi's outburst.

'Here are two texts,' said Ahmad pointing to the calendar, 'for you, Christine, to translate.'

'Well, everyone knows that saying of Mustafa Kamal – "happy he who can call himself a Turk" – you see it spelled out in whitewashed stones on the hillsides behind barracks. This second one, "*Size öyle bir vatan aldim ki ebediyen sizin olacaktir*", is something about how good the country is and how Alp Arslan is giving it to the Turks forever – like a Promised Land, eh, Ahmad Bey?'

'No such thing. If you have the land, it's yours; if you don't have it no one can promise it to you.' Christine had an amused expression when she spoke, more playful than beatific, and it seemed she and Ahmad frequently enjoyed such discussions. 'Oh, we talk about history and religion and the history of religion,' said Ahmad. 'In the Middle East they are the same thing. What else is there to talk about and where better to do it? You know that both St Peter and St Paul preached in Antioch and it was here that the followers of Jesus the Nazarene were first called Christians.'

'And St Simeon, the guy on the pillar,' Sandi chimed in. 'That's why I wanted to come here. The pastor at the church organised a fund-raiser last summer where we recreated living on a pillar. It was a lot of fun. We built a pillar about twenty feet high and we took it in turns. We stayed up there for thirty days.' Christine had taken her to the ruins of the monastery that grew up around the hermit's pillar, high on a hill above the Orontes River. The stump of the pillar still stands; Sandi had had her picture taken sitting on the top. 'And he was up there thirty years. Praises.'

◬ ◬ ◬

The end of the nineteenth century saw the colonial powers involved in an unseemly scramble for territory in Africa. Europe's two newest countries, Italy and Germany, saw their chance to join the club; their problem was to find an opening. The Portuguese ruled Angola and Mozambique. The Belgians had the Congo. The French and the British converted their trading interests in West and Sub-Saharan Africa into colonial rule. The Spanish held the Western Sahara and enclaves in Morocco, eventually French, as were Algeria and Tunisia. The Ottomans, nominally, ruled Libya. After the British took control of Egypt in 1882, the French threat to the headwaters of the Nile made it necessary to extend their power into the Sudan. The Germans made room for themselves in Cameroon and South-West Africa, agreeing their sphere of influence in East Africa by treaty with the British. The only place for the Italians to gain a foothold was in the Horn of Africa.

The Italian presence there began in 1869, less than a decade after Italy had reunited, freeing itself from the rump of Habsburg and Bourbon rule. Following the example of the British and the French in Seylac and Djibouti, the Italians established a coaling station at Aseb on the Danakil coast. Their ambitions did not end there. In 1885 they took another port, Massawa, on the Eritrean coast to the north, and in the space of four years extended their rule to such a degree that the Emperor of Abyssinia, Menilek II, was forced to cede the whole province to them. Their attention was then turned towards the

Somali coast where they acquired two small protectorates in the north and succeeded to the interests of the British East Africa Company in the south. A direct attack against Abyssinia in 1896 was defeated, but Italy's colonial intentions were stated for all to see, inscribed at the gateway to the Mediterranean on its consular building in Port Said: 'Rome – once again at the heart of an Empire.'

In 1911 the Italians invaded Libya and during the resulting war with the Ottomans they took ten of the twelve Greek islands that make up the Dodecanese. In 1915 Italy joined the Allied camp and though largely unsuccessful against the Austrians, gained territory in the Tyrol and at the head of the Adriatic. Italian ambitions towards the Dalmatian coast and Albania were disappointed. Though it retained control of the Ottoman islands taken in 1912, Italy did not receive the possessions it had been promised on the Turkish mainland, and furthermore the Treaty of Saint-Germain proscribed Italian expansion in Africa.

The First World War was called the Great War until the Second World War started. It was supposed to be the last colonial war. Its closing territorial arrangements were to be ordered on Woodrow Wilson's 'principle of nationality'. Italy, which had regained its own nationality within living memory, felt cheated of the empire that was its birthright. Within a year of gaining office in 1922, Mussolini, at the head of a party whose symbol was the fasces of Imperial Rome, instructed his governors in Libya and Somalia to consolidate Italy's power and this they did with enough vigour to prompt the last uncolonized state in Africa, Abyssinia, to join the League of Nations.

As a force for world peace, the League of Nations was even more ineffectual than its successor. When it acted – such as in its support of a Jewish Homeland in Palestine – and when it failed to act – such as against Hitler's remilitarization of the

Rhineland in 1936 – the consequences were alike: new conflicts. Abyssinia appealed to the League in vain as Italian forces encroached inland from the Somali coast, until the Italians provoked a skirmish at the Oasis of Welwel that provided the excuse for Italy's invasion. The colonial powers of Europe expressed their horror. The League of Nations imposed sanctions on Italy that had no bite since they did not include oil; Mussolini conceded that if they had he would have had to withdraw in a week. (At that time nobody knew that the Italians in Libya were sitting on one of the largest oilfields in the world.) In May 1936 Emperor Haile Selassie went into exile and the world worried about other things once more. The era of the appeasement of Fascism had begun.

The British protested strongly against the Italian trespass into their Nilotic sphere of influence, but took no direct action against their erstwhile allies. Britain did not have the military resources in Egypt and the Sudan to counter the Italian invasion. Moreover, to have attacked the Italians in Abyssinia would have not only threatened stability on the European mainland, but also prompted an attack against Egypt by Italy's forces in Libya. Such an invasion would not have lacked local support. Since 1911 an increasing number of Italians of all types had settled in Alexandria and Cairo; the waterfront in Alexandria had come to resemble 'a broken-down version of Naples', according to Lawrence Durrell. King Fuad had been educated in Italy and numbered many Italians among his household. Realising the vulnerability of their own position, the British in Egypt could only take measures to discourage Italian ideas of further expansion, and these had a profound effect on the future of the 8th Hussars. Hackett recalls:

> we were hastily mechanized and put into locally adapted Ford
> V8 pick-ups mounted with a Vickers Vertier machine gun

and, rather ill-trained and inexperienced as mechanized troops, we went out into the desert. The war didn't break out, and we went as far as Mersa Matruh, up to the Wah and down to the Oasis of Siwa some of us, and then back to Cairo. This raised a problem about the regiment's [imminent transfer to] India, since the Indian government only wanted cavalry on horses. The remainder of our foreign tour was therefore cancelled and the regiment stayed in Cairo, so that by the outbreak of war [it] had been stationed there for some six years. Now this had one very important effect upon the officers in the 8th Hussars, in that, in the expectation of a seven-year tour in India and with high ambitions in the polo world, we, the officers of the regiment, had mobilized all the funds we possibly could, regimental and private, to finance the purchase of a string of unmade polo ponies . . . We found ourselves with a string of very, very high class polo ponies on our hands, far better than could commonly be found in Cairo, where we won all the tournaments there were to win – and there were quite a few of these . . . We were loaded with these things and couldn't get rid of them; there was no market for them in Egypt. So we sent a team to California with some of them to play them and sell them there. We sent a team to Austria to play and sell them in Hungary. We sent a team back to Hurlingham . . . to sell them in London. And when war broke out we still had a very considerable number of ponies.

△ △ △

Madame Wafa'a asked: 'Why are you British so keen on sports?' It was an unlikely question from the Cultural Secretary of the Gezira Sporting Club, which relied on the continuing keenness on sport of the Egyptian upper classes, and indeed she was an unlikely-looking employee. Her wimple-like head-gear and all-covering robe proclaimed the orthodoxy of her Islamic observance, while at the swimming pool women, both married and not, stripped down to bikinis. Her humorous, almost flirtatious manner may have been at odds with her dress, but it was difficult to imagine where her own keenness on sport might lie. 'Your British officers were crazy for sport, even during the war, even when the Germans were so close to Alexandria they were still playing polo here. Crazy!' She had a point. Why were British officers so obsessed with sport? She had touched on a deep vein of socioeconomic ore that ran through the substrata of the British Empire: the quasi-feudal British class structure.

The French in their imperial dealings viewed their overseas territories as an integral part of France, which is why the European Union has constituencies in the Pacific and the Caribbean. The British thought of their colonies as possessions separate from the Mother Country. Their peoples were to be kept at arm's length, and British soldiers and civil servants were regarded with suspicion if they fraternized too much with the locals. To maintain their otherness the British re-created their own exclusive society wherever they went. Their priorities in this endeavour are discernible in Cairo. Very shortly after British forces arrived, their officers established the Gezira Sporting Club on land granted to the army by Tewfik, Mohammed Ali's great-grandson, long before work began on All Saints Anglican Cathedral. Before the democratizing of warfare in the two world wars, British officers were drawn almost exclusively from the ranks of the aristocracy and landed gentry. Second, third, fourth sons would become politicians, clergymen, soldiers and colonial administrators, creating a remarkably uniform social ethos within the Empire, based on the values instilled at public school. If success in such an institution was judged by one's peers on sporting rather than academic criteria, so demonstrating too much professional zeal in one's work in later life was in as bad taste as talking about money. The Empire was administered by gifted amateurs with a notion of fair play. What really mattered were the team games that had won the battle of Waterloo, allegedly, such country pursuits as the British landowner enjoyed, transposed in Egypt to shooting doves and quail and hunting jackals, and above all polo and racing.

What colonized countries adopted from the British sporting heritage can be seen both in terms of political attitudes towards the colonizers and of class. Cricket is a useful indicator. In Ireland resistance to English rule extended to boycotting 'barrack games' like cricket, while in Southern Africa, Australasia and initially in the Caribbean it was the preserve of the white settlers. Where British rule lasted longest – in India – the game became a part of the indigenous culture, chiming with the way time passes on the subcontinent; where they came latest – Malaya – the game is hardly known. The fellow feeling that existed between the British officer class and the Indian warrior caste led to the mirroring of the British Army in India by the Indian Army and the creation of a truly Anglo-Indian game: polo. The Indian and Pakistani armies of today preserve more of the ethos of Empire than any British regiment.

'People here never played cricket,' Madame Wafa'a asserted (incorrectly), 'and very few play polo today. Some members keep horses here for show-jumping. The racing, of course the racing still takes place. I have never been.' Madame Wafa'a disapproved; there was betting: addictive, impoverishing and un-Islamic. Shan Hackett had certainly found it impoverishing; his mounting debt to Ladbroke's is one of the reasons he gives for applying in 1937 for a secondment away from Cairo.

'I am glad to meet an Englishman who wants to know

about his past. If you know the past you can tell the future. We Egyptians know every moment of our past, but we do not like to talk about the time of the British. You do not want to hear my opinions. Do not make me start.' The cooling sound of watering came through the window from the cottage garden that surrounded the old clubhouse with shade, a building of an Anglo-Indian type common to hill stations. Madame Wafa'a's large assistant brought tea. She started anyway, her English slipping in her haste: 'How do you think we feel, you come here and take our house? Share with me of course, live with me, why not, but to take only? It is because there is nothing left in European countries that they come to take from other places. And the Israelis, more Europeans who come to take. They think we have no feelings? They think we have no civilization? But they cannot take our thoughts, our heart, our soul. We have a religion too, and Jerusalem is holy for us too – I tell you Jerusalem is not a place; it is an idea. It is holy for everyone, let it belong to everyone. Israel has been there only fifty years. The British were here for seventy. We have been here for seven thousand years. We can wait. The British had to leave when we took the Canal back. The Israelis will either have to leave or live with us in peace – why not live with me? Share with me?' It was encouraging to hear tolerance, albeit of a tough variety, being put forward by an orthodox Muslim as a solution to the perennial problem, but her assertions about Egypt's Jews were disingenuous. 'There were many Jews in Cairo who lived with us and shared with us. Why did they leave to become our enemies? There was no danger for them. Right now the main synagogue in Cairo is being guarded by Muslim soldiers. It has not been damaged.' As is true of most stories, hers was one with two sides. Her view of the British was equally polarized. She had once visited England, she said, and her abiding memory was of a sign in a boarding-house window; ' "No dogs. No cats. No children. No blacks," ' she quoted. 'The British never let any Egyptians into this club as members. Never.' This was not true. In January 1952 when the club was 'Egyptianized', of the 2453-strong membership 1116 were Egyptians.

For all her indignation at British exclusivity, the Egyptian members continue to discriminate against their fellow citizens without qualms; it is the nature of a club, after all, that the majority is excluded. Their list of those not welcome would read 'No dogs. No cats. No poor masses.' In the 'new' art deco clubhouse, built in 1935, the notice board for polo fixtures may be empty, but the terrace by the swimming pool retains the atmosphere of the Lido – rattan chairs and checked tablecloths below huge white parasols, liveried waiters, the whitewashed vaguely nautical wings extending from the main building that enclose the space. An old man in a grey cotton suit sat alone at a table reading the papers, a large jug of fresh lemonade in front of him. His ears stood out at right angles and from behind the lobes could be seen to wobble when he moved his head. In the pool two elderly couples stood and chatted at the shallow end. It would have been busy on the day of the races, but that week the meeting was being held at Nadi-l-Shams, another club near the airport.

🕭 🕭 🕭

It is hard to imagine a more troublesome handful of words than those contained in the letter written to Lord Rothschild by Arthur Balfour on 2 November 1917. There are 117 of them, but the 67 which really count are those Balfour put in inverted commas, expressing the Cabinet's 'declaration of sympathy with Jewish Zionist aspirations':

His Majesty's Government view with favour the establishment in Palestine of a national home for the Jewish people, and will use all their best endeavours to facilitate the achievement of this object, it being clearly understood that nothing shall be done which may prejudice the civil and religious rights of existing non-Jewish communities in Palestine, or the rights and political status enjoyed by Jews in any other country.

The British Mandate for Palestine, approved by the League of Nations in July 1922, used more or less the same form of words and gave recognition 'to the historical connection of the Jewish people with Palestine and to the grounds for reconstituting their national home in that country'. Churchill spelt out the British position in 1922 when he asserted that the Jews were in Palestine 'of right, and not on sufferance'. The resulting influx of European Jews was met by sporadic Arab violence that escalated to widespread rioting in 1929. The British aim was the gradual creation of a multi-racial, multi-lingual, multi-faith and eventually independent state and so they sought to regulate the numbers of Jewish immigrants through a system of annual quotas. After the rise of Hitler in Germany and anti-Semitism elsewhere in Central Europe, the system broke down, unable to cope with the flood of refugees. Although the quotas were increased – sixty thousand for 1935 – the majority of those fleeing persecution were forced to enter Palestine illegally. Even at the approved rate of sixty thousand a year, the Arabs calculated that they would be outnumbered in their own land by 1947. The quota was reduced to thirty thousand for 1936, but that was thirty thousand too many for the Arab Council. In May of that year they met to demand an end to all Jewish immigration, a ban on further Jewish land purchase, and an Arab majority government. The demands were accompanied by a general strike and country-wide attacks against Jewish property. Twenty-one Jews were killed by Arabs in the month of May, and 140 Arabs were killed by the British in suppressing the violence.

Of more concern to the British was the appearance of armed Arab bands from outside Palestine. The 8th Hussars were among those sent to counter this more organized threat. Still a lieutenant and in the middle of writing his thesis, Hackett was appointed liaison and intelligence officer for the Gaza-Beersheba district; his time was soon taken up with a different kind of writing. He took to composing reports in such quantity and so much detail that they were regarded almost as an annoyance. He came to be known, somewhat mockingly, as 'Hackett of Gaza', but from the reports it is evident how much relish he took teasing out the connections between the various Arab factions and analysing the internal and external dynamics of urban, rural and nomadic elements of the population.

Gaza was the quietest area of Palestine during the general strike owing to the lack of Jewish settlement in the district, but the local notables, divided into two factions, were engaged in their own squabble 'under the cloak of the general disturbance'. The Shawa and Shaba'an families were playing out the old civic drama, and at that moment the Shawas had the upper hand. The Mayor, a Shaba'an supporter, had been put in fear of his life by Shawa-sponsored bombers and had fled to the Lebanon. 'Eighty piastres is said to be the price paid for the throwing of one bomb. The people named on the above list as bomb throwers or snipers are often to be seen at the offices of the [Strike] Committee. They come for payment, it is said. A Receipt would be a very good thing for us to get, but very few are given.' Usually the bombs were set to damage only property. The Shawas seemed to control most of the guns as well, and the snipers' targets were British patrols. One Shawa was said to have brought six new rifles to Gaza from Jerusalem, but more usually firearms went in the other direction – rifles scavenged from the defeated Turkish Army in 1917 that had lain buried in orchards wrapped in oily rags. Hackett reports a slump in the market, 'the price of an old but serviceable rifle is not more than two pounds.' The local price of tomatoes, however, had gone up, indicating perversely a weakening of the strike, wrote Hackett, since it seemed that the better part of Gaza's abundant crop was being shipped out once more. Two other members of the Strike Committee approached Hackett to enquire about the awarding of the army's orange juice contracts.

The reports show an acuity and maturity that seem beyond Hackett's twenty-five years, on best display in his analysis of inter-clan politics of the Beersheba's Bedou population where his Arabist inclination comes to the fore. In the Imperial War Museum interview, Hackett remembers this as 'a really very, very interesting time', but he also recalls the frustration – absent from the reports, but one imagines not from opinions expressed off the record – he felt with aspects of the British response to the unrest.

We went up ... in the V8 pick-ups with machine guns mounted on each into the Gaza/Beersheba area, where our vehicles were very well adapted for the sort of policing role that was necessary there. There was occasional shooting ... there was the occasional infliction of a collective punishment upon a village ... which would be the blowing up by the sappers of a house after the evacuation of all of the inhabitants of the village ... I don't think it ever did any more than harden opposition.

What he had learnt from his study of mediaeval Arab tactics, based on the razzia principle of lightning raids by irregular forces that melted away into the countryside, showed him 'your only hope is to operate on similar lines'. When the Arab violence stopped abruptly, the British commanders attributed to their own tactics a cessation that had in fact been caused by political intervention from Iraq and Trans-Jordan. In consequence they failed, in Hackett's opinion, to learn this lesson, and regular troops unsuited to the job of suppressing civil unrest continued to be so deployed. Riding in the car behind that of General Dill as the 'victorious' commander made a flag-showing tour of Beersheba, Hackett had to dodge the stones aimed at the lead vehicle. People shouted at General Dill and he waved back, unaware of the 'ruderies'. '"Go Home Dill" was about the essence of it.'

Hackett also discerned a complacency in the British units that caused them to underestimate the danger of the situation. He bet a 'brother' officer in the South Wales Borders, who were guarding a pumping station, that he could slip past his sentries, through the wire and plant a 'bomb' inside their perimeter. He left an empty whisky bottle with a message round its neck right against the pump. This complacency was coupled with a sentimentality Hackett thought natural in the British soldier.

British soldiery is very bad at brutality, we use it half-heartedly or even not at all . . . [The] South Wales Borderers . . . kindly folk, they were told to do what they could to find weapons round the place, and I saw one of them at it, not beating the lights out of the little boy for information but showing him his rifle and saying 'Our lad, has your Dad got one of these?' It's very endearing, the British way of handling insurgency . . . you see the Turks took a much rougher line . . . they'd come [into a village] and as a preliminary to any negotiation they'd throw half a dozen of the leading men from the top of the minaret and, having encouraged cooperation by these means, then set about discussing the matter with the rest of the population, beating one or two to encourage the others as they went along ... Our attempt at brutality was half-hearted, unconvinced and unconvincing.

British measures against the 'habitual snipers and bomb throwers' were usually confined to demolishing their homes. Hackett's opinion in the 1979 interview, that these collective punishments merely hardened opposition, may have been proved right by the escalation of the General Strike to the Arab Revolt of 1938–9, but one of his 1936 reports states that:

> Fear of demolitions is strong, particularly in the President of the Strike Committee, Rushdi Shawa, who has just built for himself a large house of which he is very proud. He has given frequent signs of nervousness on its account ... and last week his wife told another woman that he could not sleep at night for worrying over his house. 'And if they blow it up it will kill him.'

When dealing with civil unrest, military intelligence begins to sound like town gossip.

Hackett finally delivered his thesis in early 1937 and, by the time he appeared before the Board of the Faculty of Modern History in late June for his oral examination, its members were able to congratulate him on his posting to the Trans-Jordan Frontier Force.

A cold wind had forced the tea-drinkers inside. The smell of flavoured tobacco wafted through the open door, the slapping of dominoes on the table, the tumble of backgammon dice. A red-headed boy moved among the customers with a pail of fresh coals for the water-pipes. A Sudanese hawker of sunglasses in a powder-blue galabiya leant against the door-jamb watching for passing trade. Further down the alley, just before it joins the main road there is a small printing shop, no wider than a corridor. The white-haired man behind the counter did not look up from his Greek newspaper. Fuad I Avenue was renamed in mandatory revolutionary fashion 'Twenty-sixth of July', the day in 1952 on which Fuad's son Farouk left Egypt. It has become like Oxford Street, full of clothing retailers and fast-food outlets. The evening promen-ade attracted strolling shoppers, families straggling across the width of the pavement, matrons in long colourful top-dresses and headscarves, children in Western clothes – tracksuits and trainers, jeans – the men in slacks and tweed jackets of an English cut. In the yellow twilight the shop lights seemed blue and cold, as though the stock of shoes and shirts were kept refrigerated. Taxis raced past, braking at the last minute where the road's eastward progress is blocked by the Ezbekiyya Gar-dens and it turns right into Sharia al-Gomhuriyya, the Street of the Republic (once Ibrahim Pasha Street). Turn left and it is a short walk to the site where Shepheard's once stood. It occupied the whole block north of Sharia Alfy. There stood the raised terrace, with its rattan chairs and pianist, at the foot of the three-storey facade, classical and balconied. The site remained empty for many years, a scar worn proudly by an anti-Imperialist nation. Now the plot has filled up with office blocks, the most recent of which was still under construction – all except one lot on the corner of Alfy, a petrol station.

Turning right with the traffic on al-Gomhuriyya, towards Opera Place, brings one immediately to the Continental Hotel. It was always second best to Shepheard's, but it strove to be just as exclusive; only officers were allowed into both. Hackett used to visit the Continental Cabaret – his verdict: 'rather dull'. Nevertheless it became something of an institution during the war years, its belly dancers and acrobats introduced by a pretty American called Betty. The cabaret was staged on the dance floor of the roof-top restaurant and there was also a roof garden, which was the venue for amateur concerts and shows. What passes for a roof garden today is a collection of struggling shrubs planted in old cooking-oil tins.

The hotel may have escaped the attention of the arsonists in 1952, but its recent history has been one of decline; today it is all but derelict. It remains an imposing building, occupying the whole block between Twenty-sixth of July and Sharia Adly Pasha, but its unadorned neo-classical facade is cracked in places, its louvred shutters awry, its windows showing no signs of life. The central block consists of a double loggia comprising the first and second floors, framed on each wing by a projecting tower, and punctuated in the middle by a third. At a later date a fourth storey was added whose inferior construction has since become apparent. At street level a parade of shops was added in the 1960s in a brutalist concrete box style, enclosing the carriage sweep and the *porte-cochère*, whose roof became part of a large terrace thereby. Mounted on its gable-end the hotel's sign, once garish, had faded into the jumbled shop-fronts, the single word 'Continental' in raised Arabic and Roman letters, red and blue on a yellow background. The letters 'TIN' are missing; the rest have become ledges on which dust accumulates.

Mohammed Turk led the way through the dark entrance hall. It looked shabby in the twilight, lit by single low-wattage bulbs instead of chandeliers. The marble floor had lost its shine. On the back wall, behind a dust sheet, was a large mural of heroic peasant women working in the fields of the delta. It was dated 1953, a year after the revolution. The subject seemed provocatively out-of-keeping with the lobby of a luxury hotel. The tableau stood as a lesson to wealthy visiting foreigners on what was important in modern Egypt – not the pharaohs and priests recorded on the walls of tombs, not the foreign sultans and viziers and kings who had finally been expelled, nor the pashas and beys of the Ottoman time – their titles were abolished and their land redistributed to the fellahin depicted in the mural. They were the bedrock of a republic, proclaimed on 18 June of that year, reliant on its agricultural output. The social-realist style reflected the political mood of the Free Officers, though when they seized power they lacked a coherent political philosophy. The more influential, like Abdul Gamal Nasser and Anwar Sadat, were by and large nationalists with socialist leanings, but the Revolutionary Command Council also included Marxists and members of the Muslim Brotherhood. The latter would not have approved of the mural since representations of the human form are forbidden by Islamic law. They were bound to clash with the nationalist elements and an assassination attempt by the Brotherhood against Nasser in 1954 provided him with the excuse to replace General Neguib.

The besting of the British encouraged the Free Officers to embark on a programme of nationalization, reclaiming property and trade which had become concentrated in the hands of foreigners. Despite the protests of the capitalist bloc and warnings of creeping communism, nationalization was to be the chief weapon used by newly independent and non-aligned countries against the old imperial powers, a mechanism whereby they could take control of their nation's wealth and infrastructure. Iran's oilfields, India's railways, sugar plantations in the Dutch East Indies were all nationalized in the decade following the Second World War. In Egypt the process was building to a climax of international significance, an appropriation that would see Nasser become a hero of the non-aligned movement. Along the way Egyptian Hotels Limited, the company that owned both Shepheard's and the Continental, whose shares had doubled in value during the course of the war, was also taken into public hands and renamed 'Egos'.

Mohammed Turk was one of the company's duty solicitors, on call through the night in case something happened. The Muslim Brotherhood, suppressed since Nasser's time, had found that attacking tourists was a very effective way of attacking the government – during the 1990s tourism became Egypt's second largest earner of foreign currency after the Suez Canal, but, compared to the canal, tourists are poorly protected and present a much easier target. What exactly Mohammed Turk could do from his dim office on the first floor of the centre tower should another attack occur was not clear. His desk was bare apart from an ashtray and a telephone he hoped would not ring. The only other pieces of furniture in the room were two chairs, one either side of the desk. Undulating sections of red carpet that had come from somewhere else had been laid on the floor. Once it must have been a grand suite of rooms, well-proportioned, high-ceilinged with tall windows, but, like the Windsor, 'modern' plumbing and appliances had been added without the whole ever having been renovated. One part of the room had been boxed in to make a bathroom and a hole had been knocked through the exterior wall into which a cheap air-conditioning unit, finished in dark walnut, fitted poorly. A cluster of waste pipes in one corner and the discoloured cream walls gave the room an institutional feel. Finally, said Mohammed Turk, the place had become too old-fashioned and it had closed its doors to guests in 1988. There had been talk of remodelling, and the talk went on for so long that the fourth storey had become unstable and falling plaster had made the rooms on the first and second floors dangerous. Parts were still in use though. An air marshal and a minister had offices on the ground floor and the two end towers were rented as stock rooms for the shops below. There is still talk of remodelling, of taking down the fourth storey and recreating the cosmopolitan elegance of the 1930s, but now it is more likely, said Mohammed, that they will pull the whole building down and start again.

Night had fallen. The crowds on the pavement below the roof terrace had swelled with after-work shoppers and street salesmen. Underwear was being sold to people waiting for buses from a pavement pitch that had its own light and loud-speaker. The traffic crawled past Ezbekiyya Gardens in a fog of exhaust fumes and dust, the drivers resolutely refusing to turn on their headlights. Behind Mohammed Turk the dark facade loomed, shadows filling the arches of its double loggia, now the haunt of bats and rodents and nocturnal insects. During the war the Continental had been frequented by the men in whose hands rested the future of North Africa, the Levant and Southern Europe, politicians, diplomats and sol-diers, pursuing pleasure in the midst of the mortal enterprise; Shepheard's stock of champagne did not run out until 1943, a boon for many 'trying to get over the Qattara Depression', an area of desert, below sea level, where the Afrika Korps' advance had been stopped. Some could not leave their depression behind so easily. Orde Wingate, returning from the successful 1941 campaign in Abyssinia with malaria, tried to kill himself in one of these rooms. He stabbed himself twice in the throat with a hunting knife. He was only saved because the officer staying in the next-door room, Colonel Thornhill, head of SOE in Cairo, heard strange noises through the wall and alerted the manager. Hackett, who knew Wingate from his time in Palestine, once described him as a 'puritanical, fire-eating . . . Roundhead-type Cromwellian soldier with the Bible in one hand and an alarm clock in the other'.

When asked if he knew any wartime stories, Mohammed Turk replied, 'Which war? Egypt has had so many since 1945. Even against the British.' He proceeded to list them – the 1948 Arab–Israeli War, the Suez Crisis in 1956 when the Egyptians had faced the British and the French as well as the Israelis, the Six Day War in 1967 and in 1973 the Yom Kippur War. Militarily the Egyptians had been unsuccessful in all four conflicts; though they did recapture a small amount of territory east of the Canal Zone in 1973 that had been lost to the Israelis in the Six Day War, these gains were more than offset during the Israeli counterattack. Their only real victory – Suez – had come as a result of diplomatic pressure from the United States and the United Nations rather than Egyptian force of arms. For Mohammed Turk, being in his mid-forties, talk of war could only mean one thing: war against the Israelis. His short, stout frame became animated by his sense of injustice: the illegality of the very idea of Israel; the perfidy of Albion that had let it even be contemplated; the hypocrisy of the Americans who could declare war on Iraq for invading Kuwait while supporting Israel's occupation of the West Bank; the powerlessness of the United Nations which had passed resolutions after both the Six Day and Yom Kippur wars that they could not enforce, which had set up 'safe havens' for Muslims in Bosnia they could not protect and which refused to censure Russia for its continuing campaign of repression in Chechnya. 'Do you know how much money America gives to Israel every year? Two billion dollars. Not a loan, a gift. And why? Because America is controlled by Yehudi bankers. You have read the *Protocols of the Learned Elders of Zion*?'

An abridgement of the *Protocols* was first printed in 1903 by a Russian newspaper. It was claimed they were the reports of a series of meetings between Jewish leaders and Freemasons that took place in Basle in 1897 at the time of the first Zionist Congress. The purpose of the alleged meetings was to form a plan for world domination, to be achieved by destabilizing Christian civilization through support of socialist movements in Europe and America. They were published in full soon after, and once translated were taken up unquestioned by reactionaries and anti-Semites everywhere. In America the *Dearborn Independent*, Henry Ford's private newspaper, often cited the *Protocols* as evidence of 'the Jewish threat'. In Russia they were seen to provide retroactive justification for the pogroms carried out against Jews in the 1880s and led to renewed persecution. They also confirmed for those so minded the essentially Jewish nature of Communism by revealing it to be a tool of the Zionists. It was not until 1921 that they were proved to be fraudulent, the work of a Tsarist civil servant, but for those who promulgated anti-Semitism the debunking of the *Protocols* was just another evidence of the worldwide Jewish conspiracy. In the light of subsequent events in Central Europe the credence they continue to be given in the Arabic world can only cause grave concern. Mohammed Turk, a member of the most highly educated class in Egyptian society, had sounded justifiably indignant as he listed the ways in which the world powers were failing Muslims, but the moment he mentioned that odious work he became merely a bigot. Populist Arab rhetoric is peppered with the sort of assertion that makes it easier to dismiss.

At this time of the evening in the 1930s the area around the Ezbekiyya Gardens would have been full of Europeans, men in dinner jackets or white tie, women in evening gowns and ball dresses, heading for Shepheard's or the Continental or the nightclubs nearby. Nowadays there is nothing smart about the street. Mohammed looked down on the world with an expression almost of pity, listening to the music coming from a street-level cassette shop. It was a live recording of Umm Kolthoum, timbrels and plangent strings playing in a minor key, tumultuous applause as the Nightingale herself began to sing the mournful melody, ornamented with the quarter tones of the classical tradition. In terms of the modern phenomenon of celebrity, Umm Kalthoum was an unlikely superstar, but when she died in 1975 three million people followed her body through the streets of Cairo. She had a fish mouth that turned down at the corners and a curving nose with a fleshy tip. Her eyes were distorted by thick lenses in thick black frames, and she had so much black hair piled up on her head as to suggest it was no longer all her own. But her voice . . . 'Just listen to this,' said Mohammed, 'one of her best songs, "*Enti Omri*", "You are my life".' She sang: 'Your eyes brought me back to my lost days./ They have taught me how to regret the past and its wounds . . . You are my life whose morning dawned with your light.'

'She has *shaggan*, no?' Sometimes this quality most praised in vocalists, the ability to imbue the lyric with an intense melancholic yearning, seems to encapsulate the Arab outlook on the world.

'Well, we were mechanized,' observes Hackett ruefully,

> and as one of the reasons I had joined a cavalry regiment was to have to do with horses, I seized an early opportunity [in 1936] to go away on an attachment to the Italian Cavalry, to the 4th Genoa Dragoons. I spent four months there learning Italian and learning to ride in the Italian fashion . . . Our method of warfare was fast approaching its end.

Hackett deals out some good-humoured jibes about the Italian cavalry, but he seems to have revelled in the experience, delighting in the dragoons' archaic dress – 'they wore brass flowerpots, or something that looked very like them, on their heads' – and playing up to their impression of the patrician superiority of British cavalrymen, whose 'leatherwear was always perfect'. Although they had nearly been at war less than a year earlier, Hackett could not dislike his hosts: 'They could not have been nicer.' All the while, the Italians were eyeing up the territories across the Adriatic that the Treaty of Saint-Germain had denied them. The rapprochement between the two sides was only temporary.

Learning to ride in the Italian fashion 'wasn't very popular with my brother officers'. 'They all rode with a very short stirrup . . . They were little men, and . . . they were mounted on remounts, largely bought in Ireland, which were big horses, and they found it very difficult to get up, these little Italian cavalrymen, without standing on something or without somebody to give them a leg-up. And when a squadron (this is what I used to say, completely ill-founded of course) dismounted for any reason at a halt, every man helped up the man on his left, coming to the last who then had to walk home or at least go as far as the nearest mounting block to get up.'

The recordings contain a degree of nostalgia for the regimental way of life. The regiment is a 'family unit' in which 'brother' officers extend 'a high degree of tolerance' towards each other.

In a cavalry regiment like my own . . . from the day you joined you called every senior officer . . . by his Christian name, except the colonel. And you called him Colonel. This was by way of emphasising the family nature of it. It wasn't done self-consciously. It was just the way we lived. In the mess for example the thing was run as though it were your own house as far as possible, as though it were a country house run on rather generous lines . . . the amount of respect given by juniors to seniors in the mess was exactly that expected by a younger brother to an elder brother in his home and no more. Of course at work . . . there was absolutely no question of where authority lay, in spite of the fact that orders were usually given as requests.

One cannot imagine a man with Shan's relentless energy being happy indefinitely within the confines of a country house, however generously run. His combative nature, stemming perhaps from the use of his large intellect as spiky armour for his diminutive stature, must have made him an awkward guest, and his tendency towards maverick behaviour – adopting exotic headgear and riding styles – might have seemed like showing off at times. He had advanced as a matter of course from subaltern to lieutenant, but further promotion in a regiment in peacetime moved by slow increments. It was natural for someone of Hackett's ambition to look for other opportunities in the region, especially after the mechanization of his own regiment.

In the non-colonies that the British had acquired by mandate at the end of the First World War, and for whose defence they were now responsible, they adopted a military system that had worked well in the Indian Army. Defence forces were formed whose officers were British Army regulars on secondment and whose NCOs and men were recruited locally. For ambitious lieutenants secondment to one of these irregular outfits brought immediate promotion, a substantial pay rise and more independence of action than they would ever know again. They went off to be bearers of the white man's burden and tested themselves against the Kurzian temptation to play god. Imagine being a 25-year-old acting captain in command of a squadron of the Sudan Defence Force on a two-week patrol countering slavers in the vast expanses of Darfur; plenty of lieutenants did and the Sudan Defence Force could pick and choose its officers, which made it all the more elite. Some of these forces, through lack of communications as much as strength of personality, developed into private armies. Glubb Pasha made the Arab Legion, patrolling the deserts of Trans-Jordan, so much his own that he stayed on after independence. There were other outfits from which Shan could have chosen: the Iraq Levies or the Somaliland Camel Corps: but as he 'wanted to soldier with horses and . . . get among Arabs' he applied for a four-year secondment to the Trans-Jordan Frontier Force. In 1937 he left behind his regiment, Cairo high life and his 'handsome debt' to Ladbroke's to take command of a half-squadron of cavalry, comprised of Arabs, Circassians, a Slovene and a Jew, patrolling the Jordan Valley.

In the IWM interview he remembers the CO's introductory talk, given soon after Hackett's arrival at the TJFF headquarters in Zerka, near Amman.

Myself and one other who had also just joined and who was probably the best looking young officer in the British Army – he was in the Rifle Brigade stationed in Malta . . . we were addressed by Colonel Chrystall who was an honest, forthright very likeable man . . . a man of integrity and goodwill and loyalty. He explained to us, standing to attention before him in his office, that we were now at the outposts of Empire and we had a duty to maintain some very high standards. We were expected to be ambassadors for our country with the people around us and [that] nobody joined this force for any other reason but to extend his services to King, Country and Empire.

Well, as one of my reasons for being there just then was to have the opportunity to pay off a handsome debt owed to Ladbroke's, and knowing that one of the reasons that this beautiful young man standing alongside me was there was because, as the Mediterranean fleet based on Malta was frequently at sea, a series of minor embarrassments had arisen out of this godlike young creature's being let loose among Naval wives . . . suggesting that his absence from his battalion for a space was desirable. I knew that was one reason that he was there and he also knew all about my reasons and we listened with very grave faces to what Colonel Chrystall was telling us, which was of course also to a very large part true.

They were indeed at the outposts of Empire, an empire at the stage in its life cycle where it has ceased to expand through direct conquest, and seeks instead to make the rulers surrounding its possessions its clients. The model for this type of indirect administration came from India, where a controlling influence was brought to bear on the 'independent' rulers of the Princely States through the office of the British Resident. When Abdullah son of Hussein, King of the Hejaz, marched north in 1921 with the intention of aiding his brother Feisal, who had just been expelled from Damascus by the French, the British defused the situation by installing the brothers as client rulers in two newly created states, Iraq and Trans-Jordan. No unified kingdom had ever existed in the area assigned to Trans-Jordan, and its creation, taking its name from the old Crusader fiefdom of Oultre Jourdain, effectively closed the biblical lands of Edom, Moab and Gilead to Jewish settlement.

During Classical times the area had thrived. The northern half was part of the Decapolis, Amman, or Philadelphia as it was then known, being the federation's southernmost town.

The southern half was the territory of the Nabateans, builders of Petra, who controlled the rich trade with Arabia Felix. The Romans unified the two as Palaestina Tertia, but made no attempt to control the vast area of desert to the east that now lies within the country's borders. The Muslim conquest laid open the settled lands to raids by the nomadic Bedou inhabitants of that desert and under Ottoman rule the area was so insecure that many villagers moved west across the Jordan. Circassian garrison-villages were established along the *Darb el-Haj*, the Pilgrim Way, to protect Mecca-bound caravans, which were both preyed on and guided by the Bedou. The building of the Hejaz Railway in 1908 took away that source of income, and the Bedou were more than happy to help Lawrence and the British attack it. Once the railway had been rendered inoperable and the Turks had been defeated, their raids were again directed at the villages of their settled neighbours.

It soon became apparent to the British mandatory authorities that the gendarmerie they had raised to police the country, the Arab Legion, would not be able to cope with more organized raiding from the south. Tribesmen from the Nejd, inspired by loyalty to the House of ibn Saud in their fight for control of Arabia, and by puritanical Wahhabi doctrines, mounted expeditions into Amir Abdullah's territory. His father's Kingdom of the Hejaz came under renewed attack in 1924 and a force of five thousand 'Brethren' invaded Trans-Jordan. They were met five miles outside Amman by an RAF squadron and four armoured cars from the airfield and lost five hundred men. There was a clear need for a force to counter external threats to the security of the mandated territories, so the Palestine and Trans-Jordan Frontier Force was raised in 1926. It was under the command of the RAF and funded by the Palestine government, even after its headquarters moved to Zerka in

Trans-Jordan. The 'Palestine' in its title was dropped, but the men from the Palestine Gendarmerie incorporated into the TJFF remained, contributing a Jewish element to the racial mix.

From the start, such a cosmopolitan outfit had an air of glamour about it, the romance of a foreign legion. The majority of the soldiers were Arabs, whether Christian or Muslim of one shade or another. The next largest group were the Circassians and associated Caucasians – Chechens and Dagestanis – who had, according to Hackett, 'a natural tendency toward the carriage of arms'. Under the heading 'other' fell the former subjects of the Ottoman Empire: Turks; Kurds; Armenians; Assyrians; Greeks and other Balkan types. The British connection brought in men from Egypt and Sudan, but there were some troopers over the years – Javanese, German, Afrikaaner – who had landed up in Zerka like migrating birds blown off-course.

'Arabic was the common language,' Hackett recalled,

and had to be learnt by all British officers up to an adequate standard, and at the end of six months the officer was tested in his knowledge of Arabic. I remember one splendid officer, who was called Dozy Willis, he wasn't over-quick at learning Arabic and when his turn for examination came up he was taken on to the barracks square by . . . Taweel Smith, Smith the Long. Taweel Smith said 'that recruit walking across the square, tell him to come over here' so Dozy shouted [come over here in Arabic] and the soldier obediently doubled over towards him. Dozy was then told by Taweel Smith, 'Now tell him to stand over by the third tree from the right by the water trough standing outside 'C' Squadron's stables, and Dozy, who was a man of great resource if of limited command of Arabic, at once walked across [to the spot] and from there shouted at the top of his voice 'Soldier, come here'. He was put back for further instruction.

The Briton abroad has always found it difficult to resist the allure of native costume. Whether a nobleman on the Grand Tour posing for his portrait in full Albanian fig, or the colonial administrator in his sola topi, all find it quite natural to adopt some piece of local attire. The dressing-up game became institutionalized in the Indian Raj whose army was uniformed in a hybrid fashion that spread, as did khaki, to other locally raised forces throughout the Empire. The results could be more than a little whimsical, bringing military precision to bear on such arcana as the folding of the turban or the fastening of a sarong, but often they were striking and worn with pride by local troopers and British officers alike. The Trans-Jordan Frontier Force wore theirs with a certain elan, the badge of their elite identity, and it was considered by them the smartest in the Middle East. An officer's dress uniform consisted of black butcher boots, black breeches and frock coat that buttoned up to the throat like a 'Nehru' jacket, a black belt over a red cummerbund from which hung a sword, and a black kalpac, the traditional round hat of the Caucasus made of astrakhan, with a flash of red on which was mounted the regiment's Pegasus badge. Their day-to-day business was conducted in khaki, and the kalpac was exchanged for a keffiyeh in summer, but so great was their pride in the distinctiveness and innovation of even their dress-down uniform that, when it was claimed the woollen V-necked sweater with reinforced elbows, popularized by Montgomery, had been invented by the Desert Rats, letters of correction were written to *The Times*.

At the beginning the regiment was divided into a camel squadron based at Ma'an and three mounted sabre squadrons at Zerka. Each squadron was commanded by a British major and divided into two half-squadrons, each of those being led by a British officer with the acting rank of captain and two local officers. After the reorganization in the 1930s of the Arab Legion, the TJFF's responsibility for patrolling the desert passed to it, and their own camel squadron was replaced by two mechanized ones. The headquarters staff brought the British contingent up to twenty-six in Hackett's day, in command of some three thousand men.

The threat from the south to the mandated territories passed with the Saudi victory over the Kingdom of Hejaz. Of greater concern was the worsening situation in Palestine. Arab riots broke out in 1929 and it was inevitable that the TJFF would be drawn into the conflict, being the only local force that could operate on both sides of the river. By 1930, two of its sabre squadrons were continually stationed in the Jordan Valley, as the unrest rumbled on through the early years of the decade and built to a peak once more in the General Strike of 1936. They remained there until the outbreak of the Second World War, though the strike was called off early in 1937. It was during this lull that Hackett joined the regiment and was put in command of a half-squadron encamped near the ruins of a Crusader castle north of Beisan, one of the cities of the Decapolis.

I was interested to see that the form of the camp behind its barbed wire, its perimeter fence, was really virtually identical with the form of the castle the Franks called Belvoir, but the Arabs call Kaukab el-Hawa, Star of the Air, which crowned the great bluff above the Jordan Valley looking down on Jisr el-Majamie . . . some tactically-eyed sapper who'd probably never heard of Kaukab el-Hawa took the same form, with its defences at the angles of a square enclosure, as Kaukab el-Hawa up the hill.

For the TJFF it was a lightly held forward camp from which to mount patrols into the hills of Samaria. In the early summer of 1937, while a Royal Commission investigated 'the question of Palestine', the patrols were uneventful.

In July, the report of the Peel Commission was published. It recommended the partition of Palestine into two states. It was the first official admission by the British government that their attempt to create a Jewish homeland within a single multi-racial, multi-lingual, multi-faith state was failing. Both sides, Jewish and Arab, considered the plan to be breaking the promises made to them by the British, though the Jewish Agency was prepared, reluctantly, to accept the principle of partition. It was also the first official mention of a Jewish state. Both sides accused the British of bias, the Arabs charging Whitehall with being pro-Zionist in all its policies, and the Jews claiming colonial administrators in Palestine showed overt favouritism towards the Arabs. Moreover, in trying to control the influx of Jewish migrants, the British earned further opprobrium from the Arabs for letting immigration continue at all and from the Jews for imposing limits at a time when persecution of Jews in Europe was becoming systematized. In August a limit of eight thousand was announced for the eight months till March. In September, the District Commissioner of Galilee, Lewis Andrews, was assassinated on his way to church in Nazareth by a gang of Arabs. Andrews had organized the Peel Commission's practical aspects. A new wave of violence swept over 'Palestine' that did not end until the declaration of war in 1939.

During this turbulent decade the Trans-Jordan Frontier Force displayed a remarkable impartiality. Its strength lay in its cosmopolitan make-up, with no one tribal faction having the upper hand, and in its foreign officer corps whose command was untainted by local rivalries. The force developed a strong esprit de corps, based not only on their elite self-image, but more importantly on the trust that existed between the officers and the men. When Hackett's half-squadron was ordered to counter the incursion of Arab irregulars and protect Jewish settlements, there was no scintilla of dissent from the mainly Muslim men under his command, many of whom were from the districts in which they were operating.

I would take my half-squadron out into an area where it was thought there might be bands moving, or where if they did move they might receive support . . . a fortnight out and a fortnight in. A fortnight in to bring the horses back into condition after a very hard fortnight's work. I had no wheeled transport, of course, but no pack transport either – the only pack animals were those carrying the Hotchkiss guns of the machine-gun troop. I lived entirely upon what was carried on my saddle. We used to receive our forage for the horses . . . rather barley for forty-eight hours, at points on a main road where we would make a rendezvous and this would be delivered by lorry from squadron headquarters at Jisr el-Majamie. We had no rations and no money furnished to buy rations. We lived in effect on the country. This was by no means unwelcome because we were Arabs, or if we were not Arabs we were soldiers operating in an Arab mode, and Arab hospitality insisted that if we visited a village we should be housed and fed. So approaching a village towards the end of a day's march I used to send somebody ahead, an Arab officer . . . He would come to the *mukhtar* of the village and say, 'In two hours' time sixty men and sixty-five horses will be arriving here and what we would like is sixty chickens and some *tibn*,' that's to say chopped straw which is to be fed in bulk to the horses. This was invariably produced and very likely there would be a sheep killed for the officers . . . and as one sat on the floor of the *mukhtar*'s house and ate [mutton] off the great brass dish, sitting around there would be without any doubt sympathizers, possibly even active operators, on the other side. . . .

There were many skirmishes during 1938 and 1939 in the area known as the Triangle, whose points were the towns of Nablus, Jenin and Tulkarm. Occasionally shots were fired and sometimes Hackett would lead his half-squadron in a charge – 'I may myself be,' he told his interviewer, 'the last person you will ever meet who has used a drawn sword in action on a horse's back' – but more often the bands withdrew as the TJFF approached. When they did manage to engage the Arab irregulars, it was their speed and manoeuvrability that brought them within range. Again Hackett had cause to despair of cumbersome British military planning in response to hit-and-run razzia tactics. He resented taking part in fruitless operations laid out with pins on maps by staff officers in Haifa, who were acting on stale intelligence and sending regular formations of troops against long-vanished guerrilla outfits. Hackett tells the story of one that succeeded more by luck than good planning, when his squadron, en route to its assembly point for a drive against a band Hackett knew had evacuated the area, bumped into another band that had just reached the village of Yamoun. Two Gladiator biplanes were using their machine-guns on it. As Hackett's squadron engaged, he found himself pinned down by a rifleman who had singled him out, shooting from behind a boulder:

So, something had to be done about this man and I stalked him in and around the stones and got onto the boulder behind which he was sheltering and dropped onto him. If you get close enough to a man with a rifle he can't do much about it provided you can get control of the weapon, and I did. I managed to grab his rifle and the man holding it acknowledged that he was caught. I could point it at him which he hadn't been able to do to me. And then, with I didn't quite know what intention, he began fumbling about inside his clothes. I thought he was looking for a knife and made threatening [motions] with his rifle, but no, he brought out a crumpled piece of cloth with inside it two rather ill-used cigarettes of which he offered me one. I didn't accept it because the situation as it was between us made my acceptance of his hospitality a very dangerous thing. I had to hand him over and in due course he was charged with bearing arms against the Crown, which was a capital offence. He was convicted and sentenced to be hanged. The execution had to be performed before witnesses and the police officer to whom I had handed him over asked me if I wished to be, as the person principally concerned [in his capture], a witness at his execution. I declined. I hadn't accepted his offer of a cigarette but I couldn't forget the gesture.

Since the TJFF was under Royal Air Force command they worked closely with the squadron of Wellesleys and Gladiators stationed at Amman. Both types of aircraft were effective against the highly mobile Arab bands and the slow-flying Gladiator with its forward-pointing machine-guns was especially feared. Hackett reports local opinion: ' "that father of one wing was a terrible thing, but that mother of two wings, she was the cursed one." ' These air-to-ground tactics were well suited to Britain's mandated territories in the Middle East. Faced with large areas of desert and rough hill country in Iraq, Trans-Jordan and Palestine, air power was seen as an economic way of asserting control over places too small to merit a permanent garrison and too remote for an expedition to be worthwhile. During the unrest in Iraq in the 1920s aeroplanes were widely used against mounted tribesmen and to great effect, but it soon became obvious, especially in the mountains of Kurdistan where there was plenty of shelter from bombs, that combining operations with a ground force was essential. The locally raised Iraq Levies, Arab Legion and TJFF filled this role, the air force providing reconnaissance information and enabling greater communication. Nevertheless, the theory that it was possible to bomb a country into submission, be it Iraq or Afghanistan, persisted at the Habaniyyah airfield west of Baghdad, especially with one Arthur 'Bomber' Harris who had been stationed there and was then still known as 'Ginger'.

Hackett himself learned to fly in 1938 after his half-squadron moved to Samakh, on the southern shore of the Sea of Galilee, near where the Jordan flows out and Jesus was baptized. As well as being the railhead for Upper Galilee and the middle Jordan, it also had an airstrip. There was generally more to do in Samakh than there had been at Kaukab el-Hawa. Bathing in the lake provided respite from the summer heat and the Huleh marsh offered wildfowling opportunities in autumn. There was even a half-decent bar in a German-owned hotel in Tiberias, some ten miles away along the shore.

Samakh lies on the natural line of communication from the Golan and northern Gilead to the Plain of Jezreel and Galilee. The TJFF did what they could to prevent armed bands from entering 'Palestine', but they were more successful in pursuit of Arab irregulars retreating to Trans-Jordan after a raid. Hackett's squadron spent much of its time patrolling the crags and wadis of the hill country within the more acute triangle: Irbid-Jerash-Ajlun. A late fall of snow at the end of February 1939 caught the half-squadron in Jerash, a Circassian village established sixty years earlier beside the Decapolitan ruins of Gerasa, a site abandoned since the time of the Crusaders. Never one to miss an opportunity to stretch his mind, Hackett used the enforced stay to make a Kabardi Circassian word list in his diary. He recalled later in his recorded interview:

> [None] of the major languages and dialects [has] been reduced to writing and I was fascinated by the vocabulary. As it wasn't reduced to writing they had no words for a pen or a book, but for a horse they had about a hundred words, not just for little horse, big horse, different noun each time, but for a little horse with three white legs and one black; that would have a noun to itself. And they didn't use adjectives very much. They used words put together. If they wanted to talk about 'red colour' they would say 'skin', meaning a superficial area, 'skin blood' or if a green, they would say 'skin grass'. I was enchanted and really rather sad when the snow lifted and we could move on.

His academic curiosity had not been blunted by active duty and his energies too remained undiminished; he managed to keep a diary all the while.

The present whereabouts of this diary are a mystery, which is odd since, as his biographer Roy Fullick observed, it some-times seems Hackett never threw away a piece of paper in his life. His files contain even such transient material as the notes scribbled on chits and dropped from aircraft in a weighted bag. Fortunately a good chunk relating to the events immedi-ately after the snow had cleared is preserved in a book by the late military historian James Lunt, *Imperial Sunset*, published in 1981.

> At 3.30 . . . an aircraft dropped a message saying that the RAF were in action at Einbe, to where an order was passed from

Henry for me to go, that the Colonel had landed at Jisr [el-Majamie] with a badly wounded pilot, and that Mark Selways would be pleased if I could dine on the 15th [March 1939] . . .

We set off at a fast trot and soon saw aircraft in the distance. When we left the Irbid-Ajlun road the going was very rough, but we couldn't slacken our pace. Reached Mazzar at 5 p.m. hoping it wasn't over, but were reassured by the sound of bombs and MG fire a few miles off . . . we went on cantering where we could over rough ground and stony hill paths (forty-seven men and fifty-four horses). Reached Einbe at 5.30, guided by breathless villagers panting alongside. Action appeared to be going on just over the hill, but it took another twenty minutes to get to it. Light beginning to fail. One Wellesley and a Gladiator [and a detachment of the Arab Legion] still in action . . . My advance guard shot at coming over rise.

Horses under cover and sent Rashid with a party on my left side to make good a parallel ridge 400 yards away. He turned out two or three men of the gang and when he was established the situation began to clarify . . . whole line advanced . . . Tricky going as you never knew what was going to pop up in the dusk. This is the fourth engagement I've had with this half[-squadron] and I've never been more pleased with them. Lost contact . . . Led the horses a mile and then rode through Einbe whose inhabitants were in a pathetic state of fright and asking for protection . . . Rode to Mazar and got the horses and men in by 9.30. Both very tired from the hard ride over rough country and the strenuous scramble up and down the wadis in the dusk.

Hackett went on almost immediately by truck to Irbid to telephone headquarters for further instructions, arriving back in Mazar at 1.30 a.m. After inspecting the horses by torchlight, and leaving orders with the guard, he turned in an hour later. The half-squadron mounted up once more at 6.30 to inspect the battlefield.

Hackett never did make his dinner engagement of the 15th, missing by two days, but the ride back to Zerka proved to be one of those experiences that always live with a person. After the snow at the beginning of the month the hills were now covered in wild flowers. 'Horses sometimes belly deep in flowers where the ground was bare as the seashore five months ago and will be again in three months more. Horses tired but looking well. Pleasant sight to ride behind half-squadron in single file, silken flanks swinging, tails waving, and the sun glinting from a row of upturned brass [rifle] butt plates.' Thirty-two years later this 'floral explosion' and other such epiphanies were still fresh in Hackett's mind, the night marches spent discussing history and religion with his two local officers, an Arab and a Chechen, 'with Sirius, the Dog Star, blazing on a frosty clear night. We used to say what a marvellous thing it was to be paid, and well paid, for doing something so entirely delightful.' Hackett was certainly not alone among the British officers in his enjoyment of this kind of soldiering. Lunt quotes the exclamation of Captain Blackden who joined the force that March of 1939: 'This is the life, I tell you – this is the life!' It was a time when it was still possible to think unquestioningly of the carriage of arms in the cause of Empire as an honourable calling.

Hackett returned to Syria on several occasions while serving with the Trans-Jordan Frontier Force, mainly to play polo in Damascus (as had Salah al-Din in his youth). During these visits, when parties and polo allowed, Hackett was able to observe the manner in which the French administered their mandate and contrast it with British policy. The territories mandated to Britain and France by the League of Nations were to be held in trust and not as colonies. The British, judging by their actions, intended to honour their undertaking to bring Iraq, Trans-Jordan and Palestine to independence. Trans-Jordan had been recognized by Britain as an independent state as soon as 1923, though matters of defence remained under British command and in finance and foreign affairs 'guidance' from the British resident was to be heeded. Iraq became independent, under similar terms to Trans-Jordan, in 1932, but British control of the country's oil reserves caused resentment to mount. Even in Egypt, a country promised independence ever since it had been occupied and independent in name from 1922, a twenty-year treaty of Anglo-Egyptian alliance was signed in 1936 that set out a mechanism by which the Egyptians could effect the withdrawal of British troops. In Palestine, Britain's intention was to create an independent unitary state, though that had to be modified under the pressure of massive Jewish immigration from Europe and mounting Arab resistance.

'The French', on the other hand, 'made no bones about it,' Hackett observed. 'They were running a colony which was going to remain a colony.' They set about dividing their part of Greater Syria, giving privileges to its minorities, redrawing the borders of the Lebanon, in order to minimize the possibility of unified resistance. The Alawis in the north and the Druze in the south enjoyed a measure of autonomy, while the old Ottoman province of Mount Lebanon, predominantly Maronite Christian, was enlarged by the addition of Tripoli (Sunni), the Bekaa Valley (Shi'i, especially in the south), the Chouf Mountains (Shi'i and Druze) and the cosmopolitan ports of Sidon and Tyre. Added to the mixture on the Christian side were Greek, Syrian and Armenian Orthodox, Armenian Catholic and a sprinkling of Syriac sects. The Christian inhabitants of Greater Lebanon were in the majority, but only just. In what remained of Syria the French pursued repressive policies in which Hackett discerned 'a distinct parallelism [with] British policy in North America' shortly before the War of Independence. Their desire to rule rather than administer was demonstrated in 1925, when an uprising in Damascus was suppressed by bombarding the city.

The last time Hackett visited Syria in June 1941 it was not to play polo, but as an invader. Since the fall of France the previous summer, the British High Command in the Middle East had been on the alert for any sign of practical aid afforded the Axis powers by those French colonies that had remained loyal to the Vichy government. French possessions south of the Sahara had almost all 'rallied' to de Gaulle's Free French, while Tunisia, Algeria, Lebanon and Syria recognized Pétain's authority. The British Navy attempted to neutralize the Vichy port of Oran, demanding the warships in it surrender and destroying several when they did not. The incident assured Vichy assistance for Germany's Middle East strategies. Arab nationalists, disappointed in their goals by the British and French mandates, had long been courted by the Nazi regime. The Grand Mufti of Jerusalem, Hajji Amin al-Husseini, had progressed during the course of the Arab Revolt from being anti-British to pro-German; after a self-imposed exile in Beirut, he spent most of the war in Berlin. In Iraq, the pro-German ex-prime minister Rashid Ali seized power in the spring of 1941, prompting invasion by a small British force from India. The most alarming aspect of this coup was the arrival, though too late to help Rashid Ali, of German military aid via Vichy-held Syria. While Turkey remained neutral, any threat from the east to the British position in Palestine and on the Suez Canal was minimized, but if Syria's airfields were delivered into the hands of the Germans the Luftwaffe would have been able to target not only the canal, but also the oil fields of Iraq and Iran on which British forces in the Middle East depended. The Allied commander-in-chief, General Archibald Wavell, was determined to forestall this danger.

The year 1941 had started well for Wavell. By the end of January the British were on the verge of capturing Benghazi from the Italians, and his new campaign to dislodge them from Ethiopia, Eritrea and Somalia met with early success. He had the troops and equipment to maintain two fronts, but when Churchill pledged sixty thousand men to help the Greeks resist the German advance into the Balkans his resources became severely stretched. The prosecution of the East Africa campaign was not affected, but in the desert the remaining troops proved unable to counter the newly arrived Afrika Korps. Their retreat to the Egyptian border was as rapid as their advance had been. For the Iraq expedition, Wavell had been able to call on Indian Army troops; for any action against Syria he would have to cobble together a force from what he could find under his own command. The force comprised two Australian brigades, one of Indian Infantry from the canal zone, a Royal Marine commando, a Free French contingent equivalent to two brigades, the mounted Cheshire Yeomanry and the Trans-Jordan Frontier Force. Its numbers fell far short of those the Vichy French could muster.

Operation Exporter began on 8 June. The Australians and Royal Marines moved north along the coast from Palestine into Lebanon, while the mechanized element of the TJFF were ordered to capture the railway line running up the Yarmouk Valley from the Sea of Galilee to Dera'a. It was vital to the plan that the bridges and viaducts along this difficult section be captured intact so that the Indian and Free French contingents advancing on Damascus could be easily supplied. Once this was achieved, the mechanized TJFF were set to disrupting internal communications, and the mounted squadrons joined the Cheshire Yeomanry on the right flank of the main column. Further to the east, the Arab Legion under Major John Glubb and the troops from the Iraqi campaign joined forces in an attack against Palmyra.

Once surprise had been lost, speed was of the essence in capturing key points before the Vichy forces had a chance to reorganize. The Allies were also hoping that the Troupe Française du Levant would offer no more than a token, honour-satisfying resistance before surrendering. Such had been the hope of the Free French when they tried to take Dakar in Senegal the previous year, but the men loyal to the Vichy regime, the legitimate and constitutional government of unoccupied France, regarded de Gaulle's followers as renegades and traitors and beat off their attack. Those who knew the 'highly professional' ethos of the TFL considered the inclusion of Free French forces in Exporter would have the same result. Major J.W. Hackett MBE was certainly not pleased to see them.

> I was inside Lebanese territory up telegraph posts snipping wires ... [when I] saw coming up the road a line of lorries, dusty, untidy, containing rag, tag and bobtail soldiery whom I recognized as Free French up [from] the Canal Zone ... I remember how one's heart sank. We were pretty confident that the introduction of Free French would turn what might have been a face-saving campaign on behalf of the Troupe Française du Levant into a civil war ... and in fact the fighting turned out to be quite severe.

As the Allied main column pushed on towards Damascus, their lines of communication became increasingly exposed. A force composed of the Groupement Druse and the Tirailleurs Tunisiens sallied from al-Suwaydah and took the town of Ezra'a, the next station north of Dera'a on the line to Damascus. The Trans-Jordan Frontier Force's official history records: 'On 17th June a strangely assorted force hastily collected and commanded by Major J.W. Hackett . . . made a spirited attack on Ezraa, recaptured it, and made prisoner more than 160 Tunisians.' He received the Military Cross for this action.

'We had to attack this place,' Hackett recalled for the 1991 Imperial War Museum interview,

which contained a garrison of Vichy-controlled troops in a little Beau Geste type fort, [with] the rather motley crowd that was assembled there. I had most probably a squadron of TJFF, a section of 20-pounders, elements of a Sikh battalion including a couple of carriers, some anti-tank weapons, a company of the Royal Fusiliers and the best part of a battalion of native troops from Lake Chad under Free French officers. Using the anti-tank guns to keep down machine gun fire from this little fortress, it was possible eventually to get in. Well, when this little fight was over, every officer on my side had been either killed or wounded and I'd been injured by a hand grenade, but we received their surrender and that was the end of that as far as I was concerned and the occupation of Syria and the Lebanon went on and I went off to hospital. Released from there in Jerusalem a little later, unfit as yet to go back to my regiment in the desert which I wanted to do, I was posted to be Secretary of the Commission of Control of Syria and the Lebanon and went up to Beirut and it was while I was walking [along the Corniche] in Beirut with my right arm in a sling I saw coming towards me in the crowd a blue kepi [above] a familiar face. Turned out to be a chap I'd known in the Groupement Druse, a French cavalryman seconded, like me to the TJFF, to the Groupement Druse. He had his left arm in a sling. I'd played polo and gone racing in Damascus with them before [the war] and I knew this chap quite well. 'Hello Jacques, where did you get that?' 'Oh, a little place on the Damascus road. Where did you get yours?' 'Oh, a little place on the Damascus road.' Well, when I got into the little fortress I did notice some dead horses lying around, which suggested to me that an element of the Groupement Druse had been there and had evacuated shortly before we arrived. It was equally clear to me now that this chap, my old friend Jacques, had commanded that lot before we took a hand in it and he said 'it must have been the same bit of bother. We'd better go and talk about it.' So we went and lunched at the Saint Georges [Hotel] which was in splendid order then, I remember so well those . . . I won't bother with what we ate and drank but it was magnificent in those days. And he ran through this battle in Ezra'a and he said 'Were you in charge on the other side? Now let's go into this; why did you do so and so?' 'Well, I couldn't think of anything else.' 'And then why did you do this? That seems to be in defiance of normal tactical manoeuvres.' 'Well, Jacques in the end we did win . . .' 'Yes,' he said in typical French fashion, 'and that is the least satisfactory aspect of the whole squalid episode.'

On Sunday afternoon in Beirut, the Corniche is once again the place to be seen. A broad promenade runs from the headland where the shell of the St Georges Hotel stands due west into the lowering sun for more than a mile; at Ras Beirut it turns south with the rocky coast and climbs past the Luna

Park fairground to cliff-edge cafes above Pigeon Rocks. After more than a decade of Syrian-imposed peace the atmosphere is as relaxed and celebratory as any Mediterranean *paseo*. Families promenade in the warm afternoon light from one vendor to the next, ice cream for the children, nuts and corn-on-the-cob and *termis* for the adults whose attire displays a chic, cosmopolitan outlook shared by Muslims and Christians alike, as alive to Western fads as fashions. Young boys whiz past on chromed micro-scooters, those slightly older rollerblading in skate-gear and sunglasses, using the crowd as a slalom course. Even the young mother in blackest purdah, whose toddling daughter was prone to mistake foreigners for her father, achieved fashionability, within limits. Her chador and veil were of crepe de chine, her gloves silk, her pumps patent, peeping out as she sat on the railing, her dark eyes mascaraed and lustrous framed by the slit in her veil, like a fragment of a fresco. She had been married at fourteen, but showed no envy when a phalanx of comely teenaged Christian girls bladed past, tight jeans and crop-tops and navel rings, nor immodest interest in the youths in shorts diving from the balustrade and sunning themselves on the rocks below. The most daring swim out to Pigeon Rocks, two tall sea-arches standing in a cliff-lined cove, and scale the larger.

Elsewhere along the rocky berm men with long fishing poles cluster, the water so clear the shoals of small fish can be seen. The poles rise and flex like the antennae of crayfish. Further out, jet skis and water-skiers make their passes all along the coast where Beirut's northern suburbs march up the hills that rise from the shore. In the distance yachts and motor cruisers ply the mouth of Jounieh Bay, site of a small fishing harbour until East Beirut's nightlife relocated there during the civil war. The resilience of Lebanese society and its joie de vivre are everywhere apparent, but so are the signs of what the country has endured, even on the Corniche. Among the cars cruising the waterfront are old, early-1970s American automobiles, marking, like the vintage cars of Cuba, a destruction layer, a period of turbulence after which nothing could ever be the same. The old Merc passing through the Syrian Army checkpoint outside the American University of Beirut is a scene from news reports of the past. Lecturers were kidnapped from time to time during the civil war, some never to be released, and a car-bomb was exploded next to the original college building in 1991, but the university never closed, still less its private beach, connected to the campus by a tunnel under the Corniche. There are other Lidos near Luna Park and throughout the war, even after the hotel had been shot to bits, waterskiing lessons could be booked at the St Georges Yacht and Beach Club.

The hotel was once the finest in the Eastern Mediterranean, a grand place to re-fight battles with the tableware. In the 1950s and 1960s, its bar formed the backdrop to other tactical conversations, the haunt of foreign correspondents and diplomats and operatives, the Cold War adding another strand to the tangle of interests and intrigue. In the end, the battle arrived on its doorstep and it became derelict in 1975. It is set to be restored, along with the rest of central Beirut, swathed in scaffolding and plastic sheeting and red tape, but the Beach Club is thriving once more, its bathers proof that the Lebanese reputation for physical beauty is well deserved.

Turning off the Corniche at its southern end onto Boulevard Saeb Salam, it is hard to believe this is the same city so great is the ideological shift. The Muslim population of Beirut grew rapidly after independence with the influx of rural, mainly Shi'ite migrants from Southern Lebanon and the Bekaa Valley, and the housing that sprang up to accommodate them was largely unplanned. Districts like Tallet el-Khayat and Wata are a jumble of stained concrete blocks, many showing war damage and many decorated with vast murals of Ayatollah Khomeini and Sheikh Hassan Nasrallah, leader of Hezbollah. It was nearby that the few famous and many more not-so-famous hostages were held.

In an internet cafe off Rue Hamra, near the 'Green Line' fashion boutique, Jamal offered a different view of Hezbollah than that held by the Western media. He was not a natural supporter of the organization, being Sunni and originally from Tripoli, but their persistent opposition to the Israeli occupation of Southern Lebanon has earned it the respect of all nationalists. 'No one else was fighting the Israelis, not the Syrians, not the Lebanese government, only Hezbollah. The government did nothing for the south. Hezbollah kept the schools and the hospitals open. They repaired the roads and electricity lines. Only Hezbollah cared for the people, and now the Israelis have withdrawn they can say they have won.' It had been a year since Israeli forces had pulled back to the official border, a move they had made so suddenly that neither the Syrians nor the Lebanese government were able to capitalise on it. Without Israeli support, their allies the South Lebanese Army (SLA) disintegrated and Hezbollah were left in command of the battlefield. Whatever reasons the Israelis gave for their decision to withdraw, Hezbollah could justly claim victory if only on the principle of last-one-standing. A surprising peace had fallen over Southern Lebanon under Hezbollah administration as they follow the Middle Eastern paradigm of the terrorist organization maturing into government. There are even signs of a sense of national responsibility among its leaders. They were prepared to counter Syrian claims to the Shebaa Farms with force. The 'farms', an area of rocky grazing on the south-western flank of Mount Hermon, have little agricultural value, but strategically they could have been invaluable to the Syrians in any future conflict or negotiations over al-Jawlan, the Golan Heights. Hezbollah has saved the Israelis the job of securing the area.

Jamal was too young to have taken part in the war, but like every Lebanese he bore its scars. 'My eldest sister and my father were going to Cyprus for a holiday. The Israelis attacked the ferry. My sister was killed.' He said this almost with a shrug, as though his family's loss did not amount to much in comparison with the suffering of others. 'Here, look at this.' From his in-box he opened an e-mail he had received from a Palestinian friend. It contained a sequence of still photographs, taken with a long lens on grainy film. The first two showed a Palestinian driver being stopped at an Israeli Defence Force checkpoint and dragged from his van. Jamal scrolled down. The man was on the ground while three soldiers kicked him. Then he was kneeling. One soldier stood behind him with a gun to the back of his head. The last frame is lifeless. 'They must let us live. Palestine must exist.'

🔺 🔺 🔺

All the destinations in the Middle East muster at the long-distance taxi-stand in Damascus, red and white taxis bound for Baghdad, those for Jordan white with the colours of the national flag painted on the front doors. The Beirut taxis, unliveried Chevrolets that roar up the mountains of the coast and bound across the Bekaa Valley, bring a touch of glamour. Taxis for Turkey, Kuwait, Riyadh, Jeddah, Cairo, Benghazi wait to fill before setting out on the old caravan routes that brought Damascus her wealth. The road south soon passes the spot where Saul was blinded by the light and enters the area known as al-Hauran, where the dark earth and rock deadens the glare. The Hauran lies close to the line of the northern continuation of the Great Rift Valley; it was formed by a flood of molten basalt welling up between the divergent plates. To the east lie the Syrian Desert and the Jebel Druze, to the west the land rises to Mount Hermon and the Heights of al-Jawlan. An almost treeless plateau, at its heart is a solid sheet of dark purplish brown rock, the Laja, over which the ratio between stone and earth seems still unfavourable for agriculture. Yet every patch of earth deep enough to support a crop is planted with cereals and there is sufficient rainfall during the winter to harvest the grain in early May. From then until October it is better to be in the shade. In early June, the time of year Major J.W. Hackett's mixed force invested the town, Ezra'a swelters, and its inhabitants take to their cellars whether or not they are being bombarded with twenty-pounders and anti-tank guns.

Mark Twain formed a poor opinion of most things, and the Syrian village did not escape unscathed: 'the sorriest sight in the world, and its surroundings are eminently in keeping with it.' Ezra'a, though not filled with the malnourished, begging urchins he describes, would today not alter his opinion greatly. A collection of patchily rendered block-work houses of indeterminate age deserted in the noonday, it has one taxi, one cafe and one sight, the Church of Saint George to which everyone gives the visitor directions. While the town has changed above ground, it stands on ancient foundations. Jibril put his head outside his cellar door to offer coffee and cakes. It was a low small room whose walls were plastered, but the lack of a ceiling left the stone vault bare, simply made of slabs of basalt like overlong railway sleepers laid side by side. The two sofas left just enough room for his family to sit down. Almost every house had one, said Jibril, and most people spent the summers in it. Some dated back to a time before the Romans conquered Syria, when the Greek trading federation, the Decapolis, controlled the roads east of the Jordan from Damascus to Amman. Everywhere you walked in Ezra'a, he claimed, you were walking over Roman grain-cellars. The Hauran had provided the Roman Empire not only with much wheat, but also one emperor.

Though not a native of Ezra'a, Jibril knew of one old man, a former schoolmaster, who might recall the events of 1941. Jamil Gheeth was in his family's new reception room, dozing on the carpet-covered floor and resting against a pile of cushions. He wore a plain white kaffiyeh on his head, a white shirt done up to the collar under a grey jacket, and baggy Arab trousers. Behind his thick glasses his eyes might have been open or closed. A standard fan turned slowly back and forth. The worry-beads were still between his fingers. He was ninety-one, the age Hackett would have been were he still alive. He woke with no great surprise and once more the beads slipped through his hand. Jibril translated.

'Which war?' Jamil asked, 'Nineteen sixty-seven? Nineteen seventy-three?' He had seen so many; as a boy he had seen the British push back the Turks after the Battle of Megiddo in 1918. 'He says there was no battle here in 1941, just the French fighting each other for a couple of hours.' He re- membered the troops from Chad – they were the first black Africans to have visited Ezra'a – and he remembered one, two, three, four explosions, counting them off with expansive gestures, but it was not a big battle, he said. 'After that he went to be secretary to a British officer at Dera'a, someone called Foot Effendi?' There was indeed someone called Foot involved on the Allied side, Hugh Foot, Assistant District Commissioner in Jenin and older brother of Michael, later leader of the British Labour Party. He had become a close friend while Hackett was serving with the TJFF. The general remembered him in the Imperial War Museum recordings as 'travelling in the front of a motorcar in a morning coat, very properly dressed, standing up in it to assure the Arabs . . . but a shot from a Vichy French anti-tank gun put the car out of action and nearly put the future Lord Caradon permanently out of action as well.' Jamil was not surprised that Foot Effendi was dead, but he was pleased that the importance of the man he had served had been recognised, and told the story of the assault to newcomers, complete with explosive hand gestures and this time maybe with a little more pride.

Built in 1959 Cairo's Nile Hilton stands on the site of the Kasr el-Nil, the British barracks in the heart of the city. The political piquancy was not lost on Egyptians of the Nasser era, although no one at reception knew what had been there before the hotel. For Nasser, public works were not only symbolic of independent Egypt's capacity for progress, but often a chance to eradicate traces of the past as well. His grandest scheme, the building of the Aswan Dam, provided just such an opportunity. The British had built the first Aswan Dam in 1902 and added to its height over the years. It regulated the flow of the river and generated electricity, though it was not large enough to control the annual flood. Nasser gained backing for his plans from the United States, Britain and the World Bank to build a vast new dam a little way upstream, but in early 1956 that financial support was suddenly withdrawn. His response, on the fourth anniversary of the Revolution, was to nationalize the Suez Canal. He emerged victorious from the ensuing crisis having at a stroke rid his country of the British, taken possession of its most valuable asset and secured the income necessary to finance the new dam. The Soviet Union was quick to offer its expertise, and a loan, and work started in 1960. When the dam was completed in 1971, a year after Nasser's death, the lake named in his memory grew to fill the valley as far as the Sudanese border more than three hundred miles to the south and flooded the Nubians' homeland. Egypt's cultivable area was increased by 30 per cent while its electricity production doubled.

One of Nasser's projects for the capital was the building of the Corniche el-Nil, the six-lane highway which follows the eastern bank of the river. Cairo needed a new north–south arterial road; that the proposed route cut the end off the gardens of the British Embassy, blocking access to the river, and ploughed straight through the Anglican Cathedral of All Saints, built by Gilbert Scott, were more than fringe benefits. The Arab League Building now occupies what was once part of the Kasr el-Nil's parade ground, and it is dwarfed by the hotel behind, whose roof-top terrace provides a spectacular view over the Nile. (It is a view which can also be enjoyed from the window of the Ladbroke's casino a few floors below.) The eyot of Gezira lies midstream and is used as a stepping stone by three bridges. The middle of these was built as part of the Corniche el-Nil development. Its approach road runs over the altar and along the aisle of the vanished cathedral; on the other side of the river channel the road ploughs through the grounds of the Gezira Sporting Club. It was renamed Sixth of October Bridge after the day in 1973 on which the Syrians and Egyptians mounted a combined attack against Israel, the day of the Jewish feast of Yom Kippur. The other two older bridges also sport new names. The northernmost, once Fuad I, has suffered the same fate as his avenue and become Twenty-sixth of July Bridge. The Kasr el-Nil had looked out over the Khedive Ismail Bridge towards the British commander-in-chief's residence on the other side. The Nile Hilton now looks down on Tahrir (Liberation) Bridge crossing to the island, on the trailing water weed along its shore and the new Opera House. Above where the commander-in-chief once lived now rises another of Nasser's projects, the six-hundred-foot high Cairo Tower. Its building might have appeared as an unwarranted luxury to many in 1960s Egypt, but for Nasser the statement it made was invaluable. He used money loaned by the United States to buy American armaments. The result – a revolving restaurant in the shape of a lotus flower on top of a latticed concrete cylinder – looks like nothing so much as an outsized sceptre, a giant middle finger that the Americans nicknamed 'Nasser's prick'. Nasser bought his weapons from the Russians thereafter.

During the Second World War the area south of Khedive Ismail Bridge was the centre of British power in the Eastern Mediterranean. Across the road from Kasr el-Nil was the Semiramis Hotel, an Edwardian pile requisitioned as the headquarters for British Troops in Egypt, a force separate from those fighting in the Western Desert and responsible for internal defence. The hotel never recovered. It was demolished in the 1970s and replaced by the new Semiramis Intercontinental, an undistinguished structure that has aged badly. (Next door to it the Helnan hotel group has revived Shepheard's, in name alone.) Two blocks south is the British Embassy, on the edge of the locality known as the Garden City, and it was in this area of villas and mansions that they established their wartime General Headquarters. It was said that if you wanted to find out the plans for the next Allied push all you had to do was spend an hour in the Long Bar at Shepheard's, but it was beyond the Grey Pillars at No. 10 Tombolat Street that these plans were made. As the war in Southern Europe and the desert became more intense, the general staff burgeoned and more buildings were occupied. Hermione, Countess Ranfurly, describes working in the Special Operations Executive offices in her diaries, published as *To War with Whitaker*, at a time when the organization had become notoriously leaky.

Maybe it is a false impression given by her upper-class under-statement, yet the reader cannot help but feel that the conduct of the war was in the hands of amateurs. Her account of 1940 Cairo often reads like the social pages, and indeed those stationed there had a completely different experience of the war to those in London. Artemis Cooper recounts the story of a captain leaving London in the middle of the Blitz and his culture shock on arriving in a city where there were no air raids, no blackout, no rationing – silk in the department stores, butter, sugar, fruit on grocers' shelves, meat in the butchers. He was even more shocked to be told on entering the Continental in the hope of dinner that they did not serve officers in shorts. Such niceties of etiquette had been stripped away in London by the incessant bombing and by the great peril facing Britain across the English Channel, but in Cairo they persisted and those officers on leave from the front could still play polo or go to the races. Shan Hackett remarks in his Imperial War Museum recording that 'one of the sole advantages of the withdrawal to the Alamein line, which brought us to the Delta virtually in 1942, was that some of us could get in and see ponies of our own in Alexandria, and ride them, ponies which we hadn't seen for some time.'

Hackett had rejoined his regiment in 1942 after his work for the Commission of Control had come to an end. One local prosodist, with a glance at Siegfried Sassoon's *Base Details*, was puzzled by his decision to do so:

> Hackett, of course, was always bent
> On going to his regiment
> But I shall never understand
> Why he should thirst for blood and sand
> When he could drink and love and laugh
> Till ripe old age upon the staff.

His 'Ruthless Rhyme' is full of the gallows humour that war engenders and concludes with the couplet: 'A pity if they bump off Shan;/ I always liked the little man.'

Shan returned to Egypt with the rank of major, an MC and an MBE, and newly married to Margaret, an Austrian-born widow, who had two small daughters. The children were to stay behind with their grandmother in Jerusalem, and Margaret would follow after. Shan had barely recovered from the wounds he received at Ezra'a when he was wounded a second time in the fighting at Mersa Matruh and decorated with his first DSO. The 8th Hussars had been in the desert from the start and were holding the southern end of the Bir Hakim line when Hackett arrived to take up command of its squadron of light tanks. He had never fought in tanks before – he had just spent four years on horseback – and suddenly he was facing Mark III and IV Panzers.

Well, we were stood to that night of 26–27 May and [were getting] armoured car reports that what was moving around there was moving rather faster than anybody had thought and would be on us before long . . . So I got C Squadron of the 8th Hussars on the move very quickly, a very handy lot, and out we went up, I remember, a slope in this typical undulating desert country, and as I reached the top of this rise, the commanding officer was saying to me over the radio 'Report when you first see them' and I came over the top and there in front of me was the whole bloody German Army as far as I could see coming my way, so the only answer I could give to the colonel's transmission 'report when you first sight them' was 'Am engaging now! Out.' Our wireless was not too reliable and used to break down [so] you had to rely upon flags to maintain any sort of control – I put up a black flag to say 'Attack' and like a mug forgot to take it down again. Any tank carrying a flag is of course a control element and attracts fire and so I attracted all the fire there was. I suppose my tank was the first in 8th Army that day to be knocked out, which was in about three minutes of putting up the black flag.

The 8th Hussars lost both its heavy squadrons that night. Though Hackett was badly burned he stayed with the remnants which reformed into a single squadron, until he was sent to Alexandria to recuperate. When Margaret arrived in Cairo from Jerusalem, she was greeted with this news and hurried north to be with him.

By the time he got back to the front it had shifted eastward by two hundred miles. Tobruk had fallen and the Allies were still retreating. The Allies fell back to a line that stretched between the Qattara Depression, a natural barrier to the south, and the railway halt of el-Alamein on the coast. Well-versed in irregular warfare, Hackett was in his element; 'we had no regimental headquarters, no commanding officer – he'd been captured – no quartermaster, no adjutant, no stores, nothing really but fifteen tanks and a lot of good-hearted men.' The squadron of 8th Hussars still in the field had been amalgamated with what was left of the 4th Hussars 'and these old allies out of the Light Brigade at Balaclava, where the 4th and 8th Light Dragoons had figured, were joined up again in the 4th/8th Hussars and we fought the battle of Alam el-Halfa at the bottom end of the line.' This was where Rommel tried to break through one night at the end of August. It was Hackett's job to mine the lanes along which the last harrying armoured cars retreated through the minefields and it was accomplished under fire from German tanks. The Germans did break through further up the line, but the depth of the minefields had delayed the advance of the tanks and they retreated a couple of days after. And so ended Hackett's brief return to his regiment.

This was the time called 'The Flap'. Rommel had advanced to el-Alamein, some sixty miles west of Alexandria. He was expected to move on the delta any day. The smoke of burning documents rose from the British Embassy and GHQ on 'Ash Wednesday' and around the clock thereafter. Anti-British sentiment was high and some shops began to display signs in German. But the last push did not materialize. Rommel's lines of communication had been stretched to their limit and had become vulnerable to commando raids. Such outfits were already in existence: some the creation of a maverick officer like David Stirling's SAS or George Jellicoe's SBS or Popski's Private Army or even Jock Hazelton's force of German Jews; some the rump of Balkan resistance like the Greek Sacred Squadron; some fantastic like the fleet of Greek sponge fishermen with their encyclopaedic knowledge of Eastern Mediterranean coasts and the Turkish-speaking Kalpac assassins ready to strike should the Germans invade the Caucasus; some like the Long Range Desert Group and the Libyan Arab Force were the preserve of the type of independent-minded officer who would once have joined the Sudan Defence Force. There was a danger of these multifarious forces getting in each other's way, as had happened with fatal consequences during the defence of Tobruk. It became obvious that some liaison at command level was necessary, not only to prevent a recurrence, but also to increase operational effectiveness. On the strength of his experience with the TJFF, Hackett was given the job of setting up the umbrella command for 'G Raiding Forces' and promoted to colonel. He and Margaret moved to Cairo. They stayed at the Continental, then managed by a Swiss, Freddie Hoffman, whom they knew from his time at the King David in Jerusalem. Margaret got a job at GHQ and remembers this as a happy time, parties at Shepheard's and the Gezira Sporting Club, dinners at the Meena House Hotel, hard by the Pyramids on the Giza plateau.

The Pyramids used to be clearly visible from the centre of Cairo; they also used to be some distance away from its sprawl. Nowadays they appear as sandy yellow shapes in a browner haze, when they can be seen at all. It is more probable that your first real sighting will be snatched between buildings from the raised carriageway of the Saqqara road. The Meena House Hotel is still there too, now owned by the Indian Oberoi Group. It is the last of the great pre-war hotels, a khedival lodge that first opened to guests in the 1880s, at the time when the photographer Felix Bonfils was prowling the Levant. His pictures of the deserted pyramids decorate the creaking corridors, but the rooms have been stripped of atmosphere by compliance with modern five-star requirements. Of the hotel's two jewels the dining room is the least changed, its Moorish arches recalling lost al-Andalus, but today's diners are less formal than the 1927 gathering pictured on its menu, gentlemen in suits, some in tarbushes, ladies in dresses and hats. The other treasure, its garden terrace, has not fared so well. It has been enclosed in glass the better to control the climate. The barman no longer knows how to mix a Suffering Bar Steward, but the view cannot change. The sole surviving Wonder of the ancient world, the Great Pyramid of Cheops, towers over it. Evelyn Waugh remarked that 'it was like having the Prince of Wales at the next table in a restaurant; one kept pretending not to notice, while all the time glancing furtively to see if they were still there.' During the war it was less unlikely that there would be royalty at the next door table. King George of the Hellenes stayed in the hotel, and there were two other kings in Cairo, as well as crown princes and prince regents. It was said of one beautiful Englishwoman that she had dined with four kings in a week, a week when the Long Bar at Shepheard's was alive with talk of an Allied counterattack.

🝔 🝔 🝔

The battle of el-Alamein is often divided by historians into two, the German and Italian thrust in June 1942 to break through the Allied line and the Allied counterattack in November that marked the turning point of the war in the desert. It was really one long battle, waged as much behind the lines by mechanics against sand, by lorry drivers bringing supplies to the front, by the merchant marine bringing those supplies from Europe, by the munitions workers there. The Allies won this phase of the engagement, despite 'The Flap', and assured their eventual victory. Their lines of supply were as short as they could be, while such Axis convoys as eluded the Royal Navy in the Mediterranean landed their supplies at Tripoli, one thousand miles away from the action. Their trucks, mostly captured from the Allies at the fall of Tobruk, made easy targets for Allied fighter bombers and, coordinated by Colonel Hackett, raiding forces attacked their depots and airfields along the coastal road. When the Allied counteroffensive finally came, they had 1230 battle-worthy tanks; though inferior to the Panzers, the Germans only had 210 that could take the field and not enough fuel. The Axis retreat was as rapid as their advance had been and brought them ever closer to the American force that had landed in Morocco and the joint US and British force in Algeria. The pincer closed on them at Tunis, within sight of Mount Etna. Two hundred and fifty thousand Axis troops were taken prisoner.

Leaving Alexandria, the road west runs on a low ridge between the coast and the desert. On the landward habitation peters out, giving way to vast empty plains of sand and stones, but on the seaward the jumbled suburbs become a strip of holiday home developments that stretches almost unbroken for sixty miles. Cairenes have always dreamed of spending the summer in Alexandria, and these condominium villages have brought the reality, once the preserve of the rich, within the reach of those with a middling income. The land that runs down to the ultramarine water has been sold in regular parcels, separated as much by architectural styles as by fences, Moorish apartment blocks, terraced boxes in white and blue *à la Grecque*, Costa Brava *turistica*, Californian condos painted a shade of adobe. The class of each development was easily surmised from the housing density and the amount of space and water invested in vegetation. Almost every one sported a sign for the fast food franchise that had an outlet on site, and these alternated between Pizza Hut and KFC. Rare is the parcel with nothing on it, but as the road approaches el-Alamein the proportion of complexes still under construction increases, the desert side of the escarpment one long quarry, and then abruptly the development stops. The desert reclaims the shoreline. There are too many mines and bombs and shells left in the ground and in the shallows for it to be safe to build.

The War Museum at el-Alamein commands the ridge to the east of the town, a low concrete pavilion over a marble floor. The land slopes down to the sparkling wavelets on the desert shore, and to the south lies a featureless stony plain that stretches as far as the eye can see. The two armies faced each other on a front between the Qattara Depression and the sea in a theatre devoid of habitation and physical barriers, so that despite its scale the engagement resembled the pitched battles of earlier eras, and one that was settled by a decisive (mechanized) cavalry charge. The elemental nature of the desert seemed to effect the character of the whole North Africa campaign. It was a war that had no use for subterfuge, treachery or atrocity, 'a very sporting time of the war,' said Hackett. Both sides rediscovered their chivalric traditions. Those fighting under or alongside the Cross of St George mounted an attack codenamed Operation Crusade. They fought in Crusader tanks and Saladin armoured cars. The Germans wore a black cross on a white shield painted on their helmets, the insignia of the Teutonic Knights. Their highest decoration was the Knight's Cross. In the desert Erwin Rommel, brilliant commander, respected by his enemies as a man of honour and integrity, is easily cast in the role of Salah al-Din.

It is said that one of the spoils of a war is that the victor writes its history. There was no doubting who had authored the version on display in the museum. Just inside the door of the first gallery is a dedicatory stone plaque whose carved letters, Arabic and English, are picked out in gold. The Arabic is probably as platitudinous as the English – some piffle about the sacrifice of war, and Egypt, land of peace – but the translation was execrable and set an abysmal standard above which the exhibit captions throughout the museum never rose. It is scarcely remarkable to find bad English in foreign museums and these captions might have been comic on their own, but English was not the only language into which the Arabic originals had been translated. Where the English was not completely clear one could always turn to the crisp, correct Italian or German. Of course there was nothing sinister in this. Everyone speaks English so those at the ministry had done the captions themselves to save money, while the Italian and German versions had to be translated by native speakers. Anyway, they thought, the exhibits spoke for themselves, although the two table maps in the middle of the gallery were an unintelligible tangle of lines and arrows, the push-button lights intended to illuminate the action broken. There were plans and photographs, letters and orders, identification documents and pennants on the walls of the cabinets displaying the weapons, supplies and accoutrements of the desert soldiers. Artefacts are still turning up in the vicinity, and not just relatively small ones like the corroded belts of Spitfire machine-gun shells found in the shallows in 1999. Four years earlier a Canadian three-ton truck had been discovered deep in the desert still loaded with crates of ammunition and condensed milk. Though its tyres had become friable in the heat, the engineers sent to recover the truck had filled it up with fuel and started the engine with ease. No one had tried the condensed milk.

These displays were enlivened with dummies of the soldiers themselves. Here were two Tommies in the morning, one shaving in his mess tin, the other brewing up; there was an Indian soldier being taken prisoner by two Jerries, a strange-looking group. Next came the 'Italy Hall' and more mannequins in uniform, then the 'Egypt Hall', whose cabinets contained browner mannequins, pictures of Egyptian anti-aircraft crews and a vast heroic oil-painting, commissioned by the gallery, of Egyptian troops storming an Italian position at the outbreak of the desert war in June 1940. By the time the 'Germany Hall' is reached, the suavely handsome, crisply uniformed flower of the Aryan *Volk* staring out from the cabinets, it is obvious what is peculiar about the Allied soldiers in the first gallery: they are ugly. In the subsequent halls the figures are universally handsome, being shop-window dummies. The models of the Allied soldiers on the other hand were individually crafted waxworks, but the special attention was not flattering. If one stood on any street corner in the British Isles for a couple of days one would be hard pressed to find two such ugly men as this brace of squaddies. The one shaving had the features and bristles of a ginger hog and the one brewing up looked like a corpulent caveman. The Indian soldier escaped neither the same treatment nor the handsome

Afrika Korps. He had mongoose teeth and bulging eyes. Whether or not the contrast in personal attributes was intentional cannot be known. (Equally mysterious is the provenance of these figures – a job lot from the Imperial War Museum?) It may well be that no offence was intended, but it is doubtful whether any surviving combatants or their relatives visiting from Scotland, Ireland, Wales, Canada, India, Australia, New Zealand, South Africa or Greece would be pleased to discover that the last gallery, that reserved for the Allies, was signed the 'England Hall', nor that two dashing Germans were riding a BMW motorcycle and side-car through the middle of it.

In the grounds outside a congregation of wrecked trucks and tanks, artillery pieces and armoured cars clusters round the museum building and a little way down the road is the resting place of some seven thousand Allied soldiers who lost their lives during the battle, one of a string of such cemeteries along this coast maintained by the War Graves Commission. It lies on the landward side of the ridge looking out over the emptiness of the desert, a line of pylons marking the course of the train track at the edge of the void. There is an entrance arch flanked by wings in the style that Lutyens' cenotaphs made the standard for the funerary architecture of both wars. A stairway leads to a platform above the arch from which to take the salute of the parading headstones below, so many, so bright in the midday sun. In the shaded colonnades below the names of those whose remains were not recovered are carved on the walls. A visitors' book stands on a podium in which people write things like: 'Sad', and 'Lest we forget', and 'Beautifully maintained', and even the 'old lie' *Dulce et decorum est pro patria mori*', 'Sweet and fitting is it to die for the homeland'.

116

El-Alamein was the Allies' first major victory of the Second World War, won as much because of Rommel's weakness as Montgomery's generalship. Germany's resources were being drawn into Hitler's second summer offensive against the Russians that was to end so bloodily at Stalingrad. Having lost most of his armour, Rommel had no reserves with which to resist the Allies' westward advance, the speed of which took their military planners by surprise. Once the campaign reached its successful conclusion in May 1943 there seemed to be no coherent strategy for what to do next. In his later years Hackett, who had been privy to high-grade ultra intelligence, was pleased to tell anyone (though not the IWM interviewer) that he had favoured the plan for an easterly thrust through the Balkans and along the Danube, the route taken by the Ottomans when they besieged Vienna. Such an attack would have threatened not only Germany's 'soft underbelly', but also its armies' route of retreat from Russia. The first step in this plan was an airborne assault on the German stronghold on Rhodes.

The British were slow to learn the lesson, paid for at such high cost on Crete, about the usefulness of airborne troops. 'In fact, had there been a parachute brigade to put down [to Rommel's rear] none of the Afrika Korps would have got away after Alamein.' In planning an offensive against Southern Europe such troops were to be given a role in establishing beach-heads for the seaborne invasions. The 1st Airborne Division was to fill this role. It was comprised of three brigades, two of which were sent out from England, one parachute brigade and one glider-borne, and the third was to be another parachute brigade raised locally. Hackett was offered the job of raising it and became a brigadier at thirty-two. 'And that was how I was to spend the rest of the fighting part of the war.'

Hackett mustered his men in the Canal Zone before taking them up to Palestine to train. His brigade was formed of a newly raised battalion, one from the Royal Sussex regiment and a British battalion from the Indian Parachute Brigade. His headquarters were at Nazareth and one training exercise involved his staff dropping on Zerka airfield.

This caused great excitement amongst the Trans-Jordan Frontier Force soldiery who saw these stone-coloured parachutes, of which mine was the first, and they clapped as they saw these things coming down. At the end of the stick all the parachute bags had been roughly bundled together into an untidy mass which was attached to a red cotton container parachute, the sort of thing used to drop supplies. This was roughly thrown out of the door of the aircraft and came floating to earth in all its splendour, and all the soldiery on the ground clapped again. I was by then standing amongst them and they said, 'There he is, without a doubt that is the brigadier at the end of the red umbrella.'

In June 1943, the three brigades of the 1st Airborne Division were brought together in Tunisia for the invasion of Sicily. Hackett may have objected to the choice of target, but the two other brigades had more cause for complaint in the way the operation was executed. While Hackett's brigade was held in reserve

the glider-borne brigade and [the other] parachute brigade set off with the gliders being towed by Troop Carrier Command, American aircrew, almost all civil airline pilots who'd been trained on Randolph Field in Texas. They were flying Dakotas that had no armoured protection for the flight crew and didn't even have self-sealing [fuel] tanks, so they were not the most

confidence-inspiring of vehicles [in which] to go into a shooting war. The wind was blowing offshore and they were still
some way out over the Mediterranean when flak started
coming up. Unhappily a great number of tug pilots had too
much and pulled the plug and went back home to North
Africa. The gliders couldn't reach land and went down in the
drink. We had some hundreds of troops drown.

The seaborne element of the Sicily invasion was more successful and the island was in Allied hands by the middle of
August. Plans were made for the landings on the Italian mainland at Salerno, Brindisi and Taranto; Hackett's brigade was
given the responsibility of securing the last of these. There
were, however, no aircraft available and so his parachute brigade was to be landed from ships.

Off we went on HMS *Penelope* and USS *Boise*. Early that
morning [2 September] from the bridge of the HMS *Penelope*
I'd watched the Italian battle fleet steam out of Taranto under
guard of HMS *Howe* and HMS *KG5*, so we [sailed in and]
tied up at the quayside and bundled ashore. I don't think the
Germans were expecting something so idiotic, so they weren't
ready for us and we managed to get over to the Customs
House and establish ourselves. Well, I was trying to handle
this battle as it rolled on, when a stentorian voice came out
of the mast on USS *Boise* saying, 'Will General Haddock
kindly step up. Will General Haddock kindly step up.' So I
strolled back to USS *Boise* by the quay and went aboard, very
untidy, you can picture the sort of state one was in, very dirty
and a bit torn. I went down to the wardroom and it appeared
that the Italian general had turned up and wanted to surrender
and he'd only surrender to the senior officer present. Here
was this Italian general who was as old as God and as thin a

pipe cleaner, with immaculately polished black boots and a little drawing-room sword which he wanted to hand over to somebody. So there he was saying '*Dove Generale, dove Generale?*' and this rather scruffy figure was propelled in his direction and somebody said '*Ecco Generale, ecco Generale*' and he looked at me with a mixture of surprise and contempt, '*Ma, e juvene*' (he's a kid). However, he handed over his sword and I handed it duly to the American officers of the USS *Boise* to put in their collection and I went back to the battle.

The 1st Airborne Division was withdrawn from the Mediterranean theatre soon after to prepare for an operation that would hold less potential for comedy, the Arnhem landing. Hackett's wife and two adopted children went with him, but his career in the East was not over yet. He returned in 1947 to take command of the Trans-Jordan Frontier Force.

The ending of the war in Europe brought an almost immediate resumption of hostilities in Palestine. As the magnitude of the Nazis' crime against the Jews of Europe became apparent so agitation for the creation of a Jewish state in Palestine became more militant. The situation that existed before the world war, when the Jewish Agency and Jewish settlers cooperated by and large with the mandatory authorities, was reversed and British targets were attacked by the Stern Gang and Irgun, then led by future prime minister Menachem Begin. The Haganah, a Jewish defence force whose existence had long been tolerated by the British, took up arms and its efforts to take control of the Galilee brought it into direct conflict with the TJFF. Hackett found the Force under fire from the Jewish press, which accused it of deliberately shooting up Jewish settlements, and bombarded by Syrian radio with calls to join the 'Arab Army of Liberation', offering rewards for those who came over with their weapons. However impartial its conduct in the field (the settlements it was accused of attacking were the same ones it had defended against Arab raids in 1938–9), however loyal it remained to its commander, the Force could not defend itself against propaganda and it lost the trust of both the mandatory authorities and local leaders. When in November 1947 the United Nations announced its plan to partition Palestine, creating both a Jewish and an Arab state, it became obvious that the TJFF would have to be disbanded. Hackett was asked to prepare a plan for doing so ahead of the end of the British mandate in May 1948.

I remember being sent for by Kirkbride [then British Minister in Amman] and [he] said that there was information . . . that revolt, mutiny and massacre were imminent in the Trans-Jordan Frontier Force. We could expect a mutiny and a mass-acre of British wives and families and what was I going to do about it? Well, I said to him you can only play this two ways. You can play it by going on as if nothing were happen-ing, make no gestures, take a few simple precautions like making sure that arms were secured, but not withdrawing them, keeping a watchful eye on any dissident elements, but not evacuating the British wives and children and playing this in terms of high confidence and trust. You could do that or you would have to go to the other extreme. You would have to surround . . . the Trans-Jordan Frontier Force and disarm it by what would have to be force. And I was going to play the first way.

Hackett had managed to negotiate terms that looked generous, but, he said, 'weren't as much as I wanted'.

The gratuities were to be paid out at once over the pay table.
I think we paid out a quarter of a million pounds in one day
in gratuities and the whole thing passed off without incident.

'It was a sad day,' said Major Tawfiq. He remembered the
parade at which the Order by the Force Commander was read
out, announcing the disbandment and the terms offered by
the Palestine Government and the Colonial Office. He
remembered that a schedule detailing the rates of the gratuities
was distributed to every man. 'But for me it was the start of
a new career.' He had stayed at Zerka and transferred to the
newly formed Royal Jordanian Air Force, which had not been
greatly involved in the war that started after the British left.
He ended thirty-three years in uniform as a soldier once more
in the Emirates, having left the RJAF after it was destroyed
on the ground by the Israelis in the Six Day War.

The house on the crest of Jebel al-Taj caught what breeze
there was. The hill was the site of one of the original Circassian
villages established around Jebel Amman to protect the Pilgrim
Road. Around the sitting room photographs of Major Tawfiq
wearing the various uniforms of his career were interspersed
with those of his wife and children, and their children, commissions, graduations, weddings and other festive occasions,
the history of the family's new life since his grandfather had
fled from the Caucasus. His wife and widowed daughter
brought out coffee and returned to the kitchen to prepare
lunch. Two of his granddaughters, born in America, had been
sent to live with him after their parents' divorce eight years
previously. Jennifer, a pretty 17-year-old, spoke English con-
fidently, though no longer like a native. Her younger sister,
six when she left the States, fought shy of talking it. Major
Tawfiq, wearing a brown checked shirt and grey flannel
trousers, sat in his customary armchair, sipping his coffee and

Captain J.W. Hackett, Trans-Jordan Frontier Force, c.1937.

The German colony of Haifa, the Templers' first settlement, founded at the foot of Mount Carmel in 1868. From an engraving by J. Schuhmacher, 1877.

Postcard of the Jerusalem Hotel in Jaffa, 1917. This was where Richard Grossmann worked when he arrived in 'Palestine' in the 1890s.

Members of the largely German Jaffa Sports Club, c. 1892. Richard Grossmann is standing second from right.

Templer cemetery, Haifa.

Tiberias: the lake shore, photographed by Richard Grossmann before 1900.

Hotel anfang 1894

The beginnings of the Hotel Tiberias, 1894. The writing is that of Frieda Grossmann, née Ruff.

Hotel Tiberias and citadel from the minaret of the mosque, 1913.

Tiberias: view over the town and the mosque of Daher al-Amr from the roof of the Hotel Tiberias, c. 1910.

ABOVE The widowed Frieda and her three children: from left, Dore, Richard (Rix) and Fritz, c. 1920.

ABOVE Frieda and Richard Grossmann's wedding day, 1904.

RIGHT Margaret, Fritz and Rix skiing on Mount Hermon, 1938.

BELOW Hotel Tiberias, c. 1934. The two figures on the terrace are Fritz and Margaret.

The Feingold party, 1938: a mixed group of Jewish, Arab, British and German dinner guests.

The last picture of Fritz Grossmann at the Lido with his two daughters,
Brigitte (nearest) and Liesl, June 1938.

Rix reading *Esquire* magazine in Tunis shortly before its capture by the Allies, 1943.

Frieda's brother Alfred Ruff (back, far left), his wife Anna (front, far left) and their daughter Elfride (back, second left) in Tatura internment camp, Victoria, Australia, 1945.

Frieda on the hotel terrace revisiting Tiberias in 1969.

The former Hotel Tiberias, today's Meyouhas Youth Hostel.

adjusting his hearing aid. Jennifer sat by him to boost the signal and translate when her grandfather's English failed him.

Tawfiq Mousa Ahmed joined the Trans-Jordan Frontier Force in 1939 and out of the draft of 138 all but two of the recruits were Circassians. He had trained at Zerka and then joined the mounted squadron at Samakh. He produced a picture of himself as a recruit in his TJFF uniform, home on his first leave. He cut a handsome figure in his black kalpac. 'Look at my new moustache – I was only a little older than Jennifer.' Remembering the days of his youth, the spark of his adventurous and excitable character shone in his eyes. He remembered his first big parade at Samakh, when a general came up from Jerusalem to inspect their drill, and said 'very good, very good'.

'Here, I will show you how we did it.' Tawfiq took an Indian cutlass from its stand on top of a bookcase and began to perform an arms drill. Jennifer ducked. 'Of course we used sabres.' He looked at the dull weapon contemptuously. 'This sword is a souvenir from when I was in Dubai.'

In 1940 he was stationed at Beisan, a time when everything was peaceful in Palestine, and when Captain Hackett was attending staff college in Haifa. The officer in command of Tawfiq's squadron was called Sullivan, and on one moonless night, he remembered, returning to Beisan from a patrol in the hills of Samaria, the captain had called him forward. ' "Tawfiq," he said, "you lead us to camp." I didn't know where we were and it was too dark to see the right road. There was a fork in the path and I didn't know the right one, so I let the horse decide. The horse knew.' Jennifer said she had heard the story several times before.

During Operation Exporter, the 1941 invasion of Vichy Syria, Tawfiq had been with the bulk of the TJFF cavalry on the eastern flank as the Allies marched on Damascus. Their targets were the positions of the Groupement Druse around al-Suwayda and they came upon a force of cavalry some ninety strong at Umm al-Walad. George Sullivan led 'B' squadron around one side of the village, as 'A' squadron went round the other, while 25-pounders bombarded the Vichy position. After a brief fight the Druze cavalry broke out through a gap in the attacking line. The TJFF adjutant Captain Walter Milner-Barry watched the engagement from the command position on a hilltop some one thousand yards away, a distance that gave the battlefield, he recorded in his diary, the appearance of 'a chessboard brilliantly controlled by Monty [Lieutenant-Colonel Montgomery]'. The Force continued their march north, skirting the eastern boundary of the Laja lava field and arrived at Damascus from the side of the desert. Tawfiq said the Australians and the Indians had been pinned down on the outskirts of the city for a week before the TJFF surprised the defenders from the rear. He mimed the action of firing a rifle downwards, into a trench maybe. 'We were in Dimashq two days later.' It was the last action the TJFF saw during the war. Tawfiq's squadron spent most of it policing the region north of Aleppo on the Turkish border. 'We were camped in some orchards, and the farmer had a very beautiful daughter. When she went to town she passed by the camp, and I asked what she was going to get, a dress for our wedding?' He grinned remembering the flirtation again after sixty years.

Jennifer looked round to see if her grandmother had understood, but she spoke no English and little Arabic. She continued setting the table for lunch. Jennifer now looked at her grandfather in a quizzical way. Major Tawfiq seemed distracted as the food was served, hardly noticing the plate of rice and chicken in a walnut sauce in front of him. A thought sent him shuffling over to the bookcase in his slippers. 'I think I have a picture of him here.' His wife and daughter groaned when they saw what he was bringing back to the table. The tome was well furnished with photographs of dead patriarchs in varied garb. Tawfiq flicked through slowly, giving a brief biography of each person, while the two women cleared the lunch. His wife waited till she was on her way to the kitchen before passing comment in Circassian. 'What did she say?' Tawfiq asked Jennifer in English. She gave an unembarrassed laugh. 'She said, haven't you finished with all your pashas yet?'

PART TWO

PART TWO

The small twin prop hit turbulence over the Jordan Valley, the hot air of a June day rising into the cool night sky. The plane was in range of Israeli anti-aircraft positions. The passengers were all men, Israeli Arabs returning from a weekend visiting relatives, or Jordanian businessmen with morning meetings. No one spoke as the lights of Jerusalem passed below, close enough to see the city's contours, and the plane descended to a bouncy landing at Ben Gurion.

There is a game to be played with passport stamps when travelling to Israel: if the bearer wishes to visit almost any other Muslim country thereafter, and since the opening of border crossings, the game begins by having the right exit stamp from Jordan or Egypt. Leave via Amman's international airport and you could have gone anywhere; cross the Allenby Bridge and, the Syrian consular official will surmise, there is only one place to which you could have gone, the 'Zionist entity'. Israeli immigration allows visitors to carry their entry stamp on a separate piece of paper, though the officer may make you feel selecting this option is akin to denying Israel's very existence as she inspects the ornate Iranian and Pakistani visas on other pages. Malaysia, Indonesia, Brunei Darulislam. A complete Eastern Mediterranean set from Istanbul to Cairo, including Northern Cyprus, even a holiday in Tunisia becomes a political act at this counter. Why should Israel welcome someone who had had so much truck with her mortal enemies? From beyond the gate an agent in a khaki uniform stepped forward.

She inspected the passport again, keeping her finger in the page with the Iranian stamp. 'Why do you come to Israel?' Something in her demeanour suggested an answer of 'for a holiday' would not be sufficient.

'My mother was born in Haifa.'

She looked up from the passport. 'You are Jewish? No? Then what do you want to do here?' She was young and pretty and I would have told her everything if I had thought that was what she wanted to hear.

'I have come to find out about the history of my mother's family.' She turned back to the Iranian visa.

'And why did you go to Iran?'

'For a holiday.'

'You think it's a good place?'

'It's a very beautiful country.'

'My grandfather says so. He came from Hamadan. Did you go there?' She went to consult her superior.

An El Al flight from New York had just touched down and its passengers filled the arrival hall. As in airports everywhere, they formed more or less orderly queues at the immigration desks, a cross-section of human conditions, faces at which, individually, one would not look twice on the streets of a European capital. Even the group of Hasidic youths in dark suits, white shirts buttoned at the collar and large felt hats, even their curious ringlets would not have drawn prolonged stares in parts of London or Rotterdam or New York. But looking around I realized that for the first time in my life I was in a crowd of whom the majority was Jewish, and I began to understand what the existence of Israel means to Jewish people everywhere. My interrogator came back with my passport.

'Good luck. I hope you find what you are looking for.' A sullen taxi driver afforded ample space in the back of his chilly cab to ponder what exactly that was.

It had been comparatively straightforward to follow the path of Shan Hackett's career in the East, from the Gezira Sporting Club to the castles of Northern Syria. I had been remarkably lucky to find people whose paths had crossed his, Major Tawfiq and Jamil Gheeth; there are not many of that generation left. One person whose life had been bound to his since she had walked up the aisle of St George's Anglican Cathedral in Jerusalem in May 1942 was his wife, Margaret, my grandmother. She was ninety when I asked her about how she had come to be in Palestine. I was surprised how little of the detail I knew, an indication of the dominance her second husband exerted over all conversation.

Her father, Joseph Peter Frena, was an Austrian from the South Tirol, now part of Italy, and worked as an engineer on the Vienna-Trieste railway. He was posted to Marburg, now Maribor in Slovenia, where he met his wife. They had two children, Richard and Gisela, before moving to Graz, the next major station on the line to the north. Margaret was born there in January 1910 and her mother was still living in the town in 1971 when my brother and I were taken to visit her for the first time. She was the oldest person I had ever met. My mother spoke to her in a different language as I explored the house, its cool floors and dark furniture. She was small and wrinkled, her grey hair in a bun. Jars of preserved fruit filled her kitchen shelves. She had won the trust of the blue tits in the garden. Hold out your hand like this and they will fly down from the trees and perch on your fingers to eat the food in your palm. She lived to be ninety-four.

Margaret followed her brother and sister to the local school. Richard went on to Graz's technical university to study chemistry. After retiring he had concentrated on perfecting a plum schnapps that made my father gasp. Gisela had done a two-year business course after leaving school and then worked as an accounts clerk for a construction company. Margaret too enrolled on the business course, but on completing it aged twenty-one went to Switzerland to study further. It says much for Joseph Frena as a father, his liberal practicality, that his daughters' education and careers were so encouraged and supported. Margaret arrived in Luzern in September 1931 to study hotel management. There she met a young German man, Fritz Grossmann, and they fell in love. Soon they were inseparable.

A year and a half older than Margaret, Fritz had already completed the hotel management course; indeed his family owned a hotel. But the hotel was in Palestine, run by his widowed mother, and he returned there for Christmas. Margaret's course ended in December, and she stayed on in Switzerland to take another in French in Geneva. If she intended to look for a position at a European hotel her school French needed some polish. She and Fritz corresponded the while, and then came an invitation from Fritz's mother, Frieda Grossmann, to visit them in Palestine and work in the hotel for the summer. In April 1932 Margaret sailed for Haifa. The hotel was in Tiberias on the Sea of Galilee and Margaret's lasting memory of the place from that first visit was of toiling over the accounts in the heat. She confesses the experience of that summer nearly put her off the whole idea, but she returned to Graz in the autumn engaged to be married. The wedding was set for May the following year. In the intervening period Margaret started to learn English since that was the lingua franca of Palestine. They were married in Graz and honeymooned in Germany, avoiding the summer heat of Tiberias. Fritz took the opportunity to visit relatives in Swabia. Both he and his mother had been born in Palestine, part of a German community which had established itself in that holy corner of the Ottoman Empire during the last third of the nineteenth century.

High season at the Hotel Tiberias was dominated by religious holidays, beginning at Christmas with the influx of pilgrim-tourists that descended on Bethlehem and then fanned out over the Holy Land to visit the places of the New Testament. It ended a little after Easter. There was a steady flow of Thomas Cook's tour groups throughout the year. British administrators, army officers and their families formed an important part of the clientele. There was also a handful of elderly permanent residents. George Bernard Shaw had once stayed as had Haile Selassie and Rider Haggard.

Margaret and Fritz had their own house a little way up the hill behind the hotel, while Frieda lived in the quarters she had shared with her husband. Fritz was the second of three children. The eldest, Dore, had settled in Germany. The youngest, Richard – Rix – returned to Tiberias in 1935 after a catering course and work experience in Stuttgart. I was surprised that I had heard so little about them, and more so to discover they were both still alive. Margaret and Fritz had two children of their own, Bridget, my mother, in April 1935 and my aunt Elizabeth in August 1936.

The Galilee had by and large escaped the violence associated with the general strike of 1936 and the region remained peaceful through most of 1937. Nevertheless, the hotel's fortunes dipped during the strike, and did not improve in 1938, as bombs went off all over Palestine. 'Then came the war,' said Margaret, 'and eventually the hotel was taken away from us.' All she would say about her first husband, my real grandfather: 'By then, he was no more.' In 1938 Fritz had committed suicide. Lizzie took me aside afterwards. 'When she talks about Fritz, tears are never far away.' I had seen them in her eyes, and I had not been able to summon the impertinence to press her on such a painful topic. His grave, Lizzie said, was by the lake in Tiberias.

Britain's declaration of war on Germany did not have immediate consequences for the Grossmanns, though many German citizens in British-administered Palestine, especially those of military age, were detained. The early months of the conflict were experienced as a 'phoney war' in the Eastern Mediterranean, but when the first Italian bombing raid took place Margaret happened to be with friends in Haifa. They noticed a plane flying low over the coast and were astounded to see it drop bombs on the port. Her friends recommended she leave for Tiberias immediately. All the German 'colonists' were rounded up soon after and interned in their own settlements, which had been fenced in with barbed wire and turned into detention camps. The Grossmanns, the two women and the two girls, remained in Tiberias and free a little longer. A manager was appointed for the hotel, and they moved briefly to the German Colony in Jerusalem before they too were interned in the camp at Sarona on the outskirts of Tel Aviv. Most of the detained enemy aliens were transported to Australia, but the Grossmanns were released. They took up residence in Jerusalem once more and a year later Margaret and Shan Hackett were married.

The taxi sped towards Tel Aviv on the brightly lit Ayalon expressway. I could not know just how much evidence of these transient events remained sixty years later, or how much I would be able to find.

For a city whose nightlife had been the target of a suicide attack two days earlier, it seemed wide awake as Monday morning approached. The bars on HaYakon and the 'party hostels' on Ben Yehuda were full of people, mostly young, a crowd typical of any European resort yet so strange to my eyes, so scantily clad after months of Muslim modesty and moustaches. Where Ben Yehuda becomes Allenby there is even a red-light district, two blocks of girlie bars and Ukrainian prostitutes, testament to the freedoms enjoyed by the citizens of a secular democracy. At the corner by the traffic lights a shop selling beer has put a few tables on the pavement. In front of the drinkers a white van pulls up at the red light; the door swings open switching on a sound system. From the interior two figures emerge, backlit by flashing lights, an older man with a grizzled beard and his teenaged son, both dressed in white shirts and dark trousers, a prayer shawl around the waist, and ringlets hanging below a yarmulke. They dance energetically on the pavement to the pop music. When the traffic light turns green, they jump back in and the similarly attired man behind the wheel drives off.

'They were Habadniks,' said Akia, 'a kind of Hasidic sect. That is how they worship.' The bar below the Gordon Inn was quieter being off the main road, but still it stayed open till two. It had a CD juke-box, a pool table and Guinness on draught. Akia was out for the night with her childhood friend, Yitzhak, who had moved to the States to study and they had dropped in for one last drink. She worked as a junior reporter on the Hebrew tabloid *Yediot Ahrenot*. 'Small local stories mostly, but sometimes they get bigger if they run for a long time, like the plans for the old German settlement. There's talk of restoring the buildings. You won't find the name Sarona on the maps. It was changed after independence to Hakiriya, when the new Israel Defence Force took over the camp. Sure you can go and look, but don't take any pictures. Mossad have their headquarters there.' Yitzhak wanted to discuss other local events, the bombing in particular, but all Akia would say was that terrorism must not be allowed to win by making Israelis change the way they live. Yitzhak wanted to take it further. His eyes were slightly unfocused despite his glasses. He said the new intifada showed that the Arabs did not want peace, even though Israel had offered them land. 'Either that or they are just stupid. You know how many Arabs there are in total? Say two hundred and fifty million, and there are fourteen million Jews in the world. How many Nobel prizes have the Arabs won? Not many, you are right. In fact they have won seven. There have been one hundred and thirty Jewish winners. What does that say?' Akia looked embarrassed by her friend's popular wisdom.

The pattern of conversation about Israel/Palestine, it seemed, was the same on both sides of the Jordan, its purpose the rehearsal of 'evidence' proving the legitimacy of one side's claims or disproving those of the other. Yitzhak was a business student and was using his statistics in a business-like way. In the intelligence market, these figures proved, Jews outperformed Arabs; their product was more highly valued. Therefore, with this superior brain-power at its disposal, it was self-evident that the policies and claims of Israel must be more considered, more reasonable and more valid than those of their uneducated, undemocratic neighbours. Of course there are counterarguments to be made about the differences in educational opportunities and cultural values. 'Well, let's look at a situation where Jews and Arabs have had the same opportunity. Here in Israel. What was the country like before the creation of Israel? Barren and poor. And what is it like now? Fertile and rich.' Yitzhak opened his hands in a gesture with which there was no arguing and launched into Golda Meir's old argument that there was, in fact, no such thing as a Palestinian people, there never having been such a place as Palestine until the British invented it. Consequently there could be no such thing as a Palestinian nation-state – they were Arab settlers and there were plenty of Arabic lands where they could settle again. 'Here's a joke. Sharon and Arafat were talking one day – no, that's not the punch line. Arafat was going on about stolen land as usual, and Sharon said, "I'll tell you a story about stealing. One day Abraham and his sons were looking after their flocks. It was hot and they decided to bathe in a pool nearby. While they were in the water a Palestinian came and stole their clothes." "Wait a moment," says Arafat, "it couldn't have been a Palestinian. There were no Palestinians here then." "Exactly," says Sharon.' When Abraham's name is mentioned in this context scriptural legitimization is not far behind, the notion of a particular covenant between God and Abraham's descendants, the choosing of a people, the promise of a land. It is hard to see how this proof, relying on religious legend, could carry any weight in a secular, scientific world, but science too has been recruited to the cause. Israeli archaeological efforts in the occupied West Bank centre on proving the serious claim behind the Sharon joke, that the Jews were there first, and therefore Judea and Samaria are an inseparable part of Eretz Israel. Just how political archaeology in the region has become was made more than apparent by the assassination in 1992 of the American professor Albert Glock, head of that department at the Palestinian Bir Zeit University.

Science is not of itself partisan, though its practitioners sometimes are, and good science can be used for bad ends. If it can provide a mandate for continued Jewish settlement in the Occupied Territories, it can also be employed against those settlers. Only the day before I had heard science used to prove that there was no such people as the Jews; a Palestinian doctor in Amman had cited a medical study that had found no substantive genetic difference between Ashkenazi Jews and other Central Europeans, and none between Sephardic Jews and the

137

Muslim peoples amongst whom they were found. He argued that if the Jews were in fact heterogeneous followers of a religion rather than a homogenous ethnic group then their claim to be a nation, to statehood, was nugatory. This is how it has been ever since the writing of that letter to Lord Rothschild, back and forth, a game of words.

'The real tragedy is,' said Akia, paraphrasing the Israeli writer Amos Oz, 'that both sides are right.'

It is telling that, once the looting of artefacts had been put on a scientific basis, the first major archaeological digs in the 1880s set out to prove the truth of ancient legends, as though bringing a new rationalism to folk stories about the past could change them into historical facts. Both Schliemann at Troy and especially Evans at Knossos ultimately interpreted their finds in relation to those legends; the reconstruction by Evans of the palace of the Minoan kings is the work of an imagination formed by a classical education. Moreover, Schliemann's excavation of Troy suggested that archaeology could bring scientific truth to an ancient text. Religiously minded academics saw in this type of investigation a chance to reverse the erosion of Christianity's authority in Europe by science, to employ the weapons of science in their own cause. If the concrete truth of the *Iliad* could be dug out of the ground, so too could that of the Bible. While practitioners like Flinders Petrie developed Schliemann's meticulous method of strata analysis into an objective science during his dig south of Jerusalem, those who followed, sponsored by Christian organizations or religious philanthropists, used his methodology, often with less rigour, to prove the literal truth of a collection of Hebrew legends, a truth that till then had been a matter of belief. The idea that what the ancients had written about their world could be taken at face value was further strengthened by the discovery of Tut Ankh Amun's tomb. Egyptologists had read of his existence in papyrus scrolls and on the walls of other tombs, and then suddenly there he was, the boy pharaoh's splendid accoutrements and shrivelled body, hidden for so long. The legendary treasures of the past were merely awaiting a similar discovery. That was the theory behind Nazi attempts, fictionalized by Steven Spielberg, to find the Ark of the Covenant and the Holy Grail. This school of archaeology has survived to modern times, exemplified by American 'biblical archaeologists' and the expedition to find Noah's Ark on Mount Ararat.

In the 'Holy Land', even when the most objective excavators are at work, it is hard to escape these biblical resonances. Those who followed W.F. Albright were saddled with his definition as 'Israelite' of a style of artefact and architecture which appeared in the record between 1200 and 600 BCE. The main aims of Mary Kenyon's masterly 1956 excavation of ancient Jericho were not only to establish the period of the earliest settlement, but also to ascertain the date of its sack by the invading 'Israelites', moving into promised Canaan from east of the Jordan River. She may not have set out to prove the literal truth of Joshua, that the trumpets blew and the walls tumbled down, yet her assertion that the destruction layer she discovered around 1400 BCE was caused by such an invasion has modern political consequences.

It had occurred to me that in a very small way I was undertaking my own archaeological expedition, trying to wring some kind of truth from what remains of the past, from memories, stories, texts and photographs, artefacts and buildings and graves. Similarly I was open to the hagiographic bias of the biblical archaeologist, the danger of setting out to look for evidence of a received truth rather than to discover what was actually there. Yet an objective investigation was not without perils of its own. What if my discoveries contradicted my family's received history? It had been so once before, on the day that I discovered Shan Hackett was not my real grand-father. The mystery of Fritz's suicide suggested a truth darker than they might like me to tell. What would I do if I came across such information?

'Do you want the good news first or the bad news?'

I had called Professor Alex Carmel from a pay-phone on shady Dizengoff Avenue. During my researches in London I had visited the Palestine Exploration Fund's curious premises tucked away behind a piano showroom off Marylebone High Street. Dating from the early days of archaeology the Fund sponsored expeditions to the Holy Land and still provides a forum for archaeological papers on the Levant through its meetings and its journal. Despite the computer terminals its reading-room has retained the atmosphere of Victorian acad-eme and until recently its basement contained cardboard boxes of artefacts thousands of years old. The librarian had given me Professor Carmel's card, citing him as the leading authority on the German settlements in Palestine.

The professor had received my fax, but he had been busy with researches of his own in Switzerland and Germany. He asked me if I knew how many such enquiries from curious descendants arrived per week. I did not. Reminded of the relevant family names – Grossmann and Ruff, Frieda's maiden name – the brusque, impatient voice posed the question about which kind of news I wanted to hear first.

'The bad.'

'The bad news is I don't have much information about your grandfather, but his cousin Karl Ruff was the head of the Nazi Party in Haifa. He was a real shit. I have lots of material about him.' My silence prompted him to add, 'I'm sorry to have to tell you this.'

'And the good news is?'

'The good news is I do not think the Grossmanns were Nazis. I have a carbon copy of a letter that Karl Ruff wrote to his superiors in Berlin about Richard Grossmann, saying that he was not a suitable candidate for the party. Richard was Fritz's brother? Yes, if you come you can see the letter, but look, you don't know much about the German Templers, do you? I don't have the time to tell you everything about them. You will have to find out for yourself. You speak some German? Then you could read my book.'

I replaced the receiver slowly still not quite believing what I had heard. I was standing on a street corner in the city where they had hanged Adolf Eichmann. That old man sitting with his paper at a cafe table might have a number tattooed on his forearm, and I had just discovered I was related to someone complicit in the most evil mass-crime of the previous century. I felt ashamed of my very presence. Until that moment I had accepted a piece of the cultural shame every European should feel for the centuries of anti-Semitism that led to the Holocaust, that continues to this day. I did not think of myself as particularly blameworthy, but in the days before I thought at all about what I was saying, when scotching plans and welching on deals bore no racial load, I do remember having admonished people I thought were being stingy by saying 'don't be such a Jew'. One can attempt to unlearn received prejudices, but no amount of political correction was going to undo the fact that my grandfather's cousin was a Nazi. While that seemed a fairly distant relationship, the professor was not certain that the taint did not come closer still. I sauntered past the entrance to the Israel Defence Force/Mossad compound trying to look nonchalant and feeling guilty as hell.

There was not much to see beyond the walls and fences that front Sha'ul HaMelekh Road and the security on the gate did not encourage peering within, but a block to the south stood three new towers, one square, one round and one triangular. At the top of the tallest, the round Azrieli Tower, there is a viewing lounge and two security checks to clear before stepping into the express elevator. At 160m it is the tallest building in Israel, indeed the tallest in the Eastern Mediterranean, which sparkles beyond its strip of sand, dappled with the shadows of clouds that sail past at head height. It was on these dunes north of Jaffa that Arthur Ruppin envisioned the founding of a modern all-Jewish city. The first buildings were erected in 1909 and by the outbreak of the Great War there were two thousand inhabitants. This number had grown to two hundred thousand at the time of Israel's war of independence in 1948 and today the city has expanded to swallow Jaffa and conurb with its satellites. The Jewish metropolis, its high-rises and lower flat-roofed blocks spread out around the tower, now has a population of nearly one million. Nestling amongst trees at the foot of the tower and in the shadow of antennae and dishes on top of IDF headquarters is an anomalous collection of red-tiled pitched roofs belonging to the buildings of a settlement that predates Tel Aviv by thirty-eight years, the German colony of Sarona. This was where my mother, aunt, grandmother and great-grandmother were held by the British as enemy aliens. From ground level the stone buildings, still surrounded by barbed wire, show signs of neglect, the lanes between them thronged with 20-year-olds of both sexes in khaki fatigues, automatic rifles slung over a shoulder. It is not a place to linger.

The Grossmanns were inmates of the camp for ten months, but Margaret does not remember it as a bad time. The conditions may have been cramped, and the internees may have been subject to a curfew, but they were still relatively free. They could even leave the camp and receive visitors, fiancés among them. My mother remembers little about Sarona, but more about the time after their release on licence in 1941, the year of her sixth birthday. She remembers the cool stone building – the Fast house in the German Colony – where they stayed, and the large garden near Jerusalem's railway station, the daily walk to the British Community School, and how once Lizzie had got lost on the way back through the Old City. Lizzie remembers stopping for a moment and then taking hold of a hand that did not, when she looked up at the face, belong to her grandmother.

'I cannot comprehend,' wrote Mark Twain on first setting foot in the Holy Land, 'that I am sitting where a god had stood . . . and am surrounded by dusky men and women whose ancestors saw him, and even talked with him, face to face, and carelessly, just as they would have done with any stranger . . . It seems curious enough to us to be standing on ground that was once actually pressed by the feet of the Saviour. The situation is suggestive of a reality and tangibility that seem at variance with the vagueness and mystery and ghostliness that one naturally attaches to the character of a god.' Twain may have been more sceptical about Christian beliefs than some of his companions (the lack of capitalization and the indefinite article in 'a god' are the indicators here) but he does echo the sentiments common to all Victorian visitors. Coming from a background of nineteenth-century industrial progress they found a country they considered so backward that they presumed it to be unchanged since the time of 'the Saviour'. By illustrating the setting of the Bible the images they relayed to Western Christianity confirmed its gospel truth. Even today, entering the Muslim Quarter through the Damascus Gate, when one has been deposited outside the eastern walls of Jerusalem's Old City by a nervous Israeli taxi driver, knowing that these fortifications were built by Suleiman the Magnificent between 1537 and 1541, it is hard not to recall the events of the first Palm Sunday, to shake the thought that this was where those Feet really did walk in ancient times. It looks so right. The stone steps have been polished by the passing centuries; the sempiternal market just inside the gate is stocked with the first figs of a new season. The mediaeval wynds and covered alleys seem to tally with the detail of Christ's story, to explain the action and make it more believable. Did you ever wonder about the body of Lazarus being lowered through a skylight? In the northern lands of high rainfall and pitched roofs it is hard to imagine, but peer into one of the vaulted caverns of the shops along the Khan el-Zeit, noting the rectangular hole giving access to the flat roof, and all becomes clear. A little further along, on the corner of the Via Dolorosa, is the Seventh Station of the Cross, where Jesus fell for the second time.

Confronted with such tangibility one realizes just how much Judaeo-Christian background noise is transmitted alongside secular Western culture, a received familiarity with places one has never seen. It is like visiting America for the first time after years of watching its films and TV programmes, the surprise to discover that it really does resemble its on-screen image, that steam really does come out of New York pavements. It is an experience that encourages the future suspension of disbelief. So pilgrimage to holy places long imagined acts as a confirmation of belief and eliminates doubt, to see the very spot where miracles happened, but first these sites must be identified. For this contribution to religious tourism Christians have to thank St Helena, mother of the Emperor Constantine. She had been converted to Christianity by her son and in 326 made a pilgrimage to the Holy Land. There she commissioned the building of churches on the reputed sites of the Nativity and the Crucifixion-Resurrection and gave the religion's two most important festivals a concrete geography, altars at which the rites of winter and spring could be performed. She soon became credited with 'finding' not only Christ's tomb, but also the rock of Golgotha in which three post holes had been cut and, in a grotto nearby, the very cross on which He had suffered. With the passage of the centuries the number of sites she was alleged to have found grew. Twain remarked: 'She travelled all over Palestine and was always fortunate. Whenever the good old enthusiast found a thing mentioned in her Bible, Old or New, she would go and search for that thing and never stop until she had found it.' Her good fortune was augmented, he noted, by the remarkable number of sacred events that had taken place in caves.

Helena's Church of the Holy Sepulchre stood for more than six hundred and seventy years. It lost its roof to fire in 614 when the Persians captured Byzantine Jerusalem and was spared conversion to a mosque after the Muslim invasion twenty-four years later through the foresight of Omar, the conquering general. On a tour of inspection of the church the time for midday prayers arrived and the Greek Patriarch invited him to pray where he was. Omar declined, warning that if he were to do so the church would be lost to Christians. He stepped outside to pray and the Mosque of Omar was raised on that spot. His considerate act is still cited as an example of the tolerance Islam extends to other faiths. What is not usually added in that context is the church's complete destruction in 1009 by the mad Fatimid Sultan of Egypt, al-Hakim (whom the Druze believe to be divine). It was rebuilt first by the Byzantines and then by the Crusaders, though the new building was less than half the size of the original.

The courtyard is much as it was when those armed Frankish pilgrims left bloody footprints across it, but another fire gutted the church in the early nineteenth century and most of the interior dates from the restoration of 1810. The Crusader facade is the most intact feature, though some of the finer carving is now in the Rockefeller Museum in East Jerusalem. One of its doorways was blocked up after Salah al-Din's reconquest, and the imbalance is accentuated by the jumble of chapels that cluster around it. The centuries of damage suffered by the fabric of the church and the confusion of accretions and architectural styles present an obvious metaphor for the state of ecclesiastical matters within where the various sects and schisms guard their stakes with the wary eye of a forty-niner. A pair of Orthodox priests with snowy beards, dressed in long black robes and pill-box hats, had stopped to talk on the threshold. Their church controls the most important shrine of all, the Holy Sepulchre itself, as well as the largest congregational space, the central aisle. They also have the Monastery of Abraham, the Chapels of St James the Less, the Forty Martyrs, St John the Baptist, and St Mary of Egypt, of the Exaltation of the Cross, of the Angels, of St Longinus, of the Crowning with Thorns, and a half share with the Roman Catholics in the Chapel of the Finding of the Cross. The Latin Church was especially bitter about the Greek prominence in the 1810 restoration when objects important to those of their creed, like the graves of their Crusader kings, vanished. Their holding was reduced to the Chapel of St Mary, those of the Agony of the Virgin and of the Nailing to the Cross, and the altar that marks the Thirteenth Station of the Cross. The

Armenians, who have the Chapels of St James, St Helena and of the Parting of the Raiment, run a close third. The Syrian Jacobites and the Copts have a niche and a chapel each, while the poor Ethiopians, like the miner who lost his claim in a poker game, sold their place in the main church and have to make do with a chapel up some side stairs and a monastery on the roof. Johnny-come-latelies like the Protestant denominations have found no room at the inn.

The competition between the sects can be childishly intense. Little girls are not the only people to have lost their way in Jerusalem. Fist-fights have broken out between rival priests over such mundane quarrels as a trespassing rug or a broom disturbing a different denomination's dust. There were three services going on at once. From behind a curtain drawn across the entrance to the Chapel of St Mary came the familiar sound of a European hymn sung to the accompaniment of an organ, but this was drowned out by the stout voices of the Armenian all-male choir. Thirty young men in black cassocks and each carrying a candle and a psalter followed a mitred priest in procession from their Chapel of the Parting of the Raiment along the south aisle, and clustered around him outside the Chapel of the Crowning with Thorns, where he swung a censer with some vigour towards its closed Greek doors. Pausing at the base of the rock on which the crosses were raised, and at the Stone of Unction commemorating the anointing of the body of Christ, they processed around the baroque strong room the Greeks have built over the mother lode, the Sepulchre itself, and assembled to one side, filling the rotunda with Armenian plainsong. The Greek priest standing guard at the entrance to the two tiny chapels within affected not to notice them. He was dwarfed by a spinney of candles each the size of a sapling as he waited for tips. Inside the Holy of Holies, dimly lit by brass oil-lamps, there is room for two people to kneel at the altar over the empty tomb. A golden fresco of the Virgin and Child flanked by angels looked down on the weeping Russian penitent. Around the back of the cenotaph, tending a small shrine that looks more like a match-seller's stall, a conspiratorial Coptic priest offers the passer-by a shufti at a fragment of the *real* tomb. Their Chapel of St Michael lies just outside the main door. Before its altar four dark priests leaning against their staves chanted mesmeric responses. Stepping over the threshold a woman shrouded in sackcloth knelt and touched her forehead to the floor.

While the tradition surrounding the site of Calvary and the Tomb remained firm over the centuries, there have been many different versions of the Via Dolorosa. The current alignment is mediaeval, Roman Catholic and dependent on the belief that Pontius Pilate's manual ablutions and Jesus' condemnation to death took place in Herod's fortress by the north wall of the Temple. Modern classical historians have asserted that the Roman governor would have stayed at Herod's palace on visits to Jerusalem, putting the first Station of the Cross near the Jaffa Gate on the other side of the Old City.

'But if it was not here', said Varouj, 'that Jesus called out "Daughters of Jerusalem, weep not for me" then it was not far away. What does that matter?' Varouj, in his seventies, liked to sit outside his photographic studio near the Eighth Station and watch the world go by, firm in the belief that the Messiah would return as promised. He had lived all his life in the Holy City, immersed in a pool of faith; the Armenians adopted Christianity at the beginning of the fourth century and established a presence in Jerusalem soon after. Famed for their entrepreneurial acumen, even their priests have an eye for a commercial opportunity. As tourism and the demand for images of the Holy Land increased in the late nineteenth century, the Armenian Patriarch of Jerusalem established a photography school in his palace. Varouj was the inheritor of that proud tradition and of a large archive of old prints, though some looked like re-photographed book plates, including the famous 1914 image of a Zeppelin over Jerusalem.

'Your family was German? Here, I have some pictures of the Kaiser's visit taken by another Armenian, Krikorian.' The Kaiser's ridiculous up-turned moustache is clearly visible as he rides, mounted on a white charger at the head of his entourage, as Frederick Barbarossa never did, through Old Jerusalem decked with flags and bunting in his honour. He is dressed in a spiked helmet and a white cloak, which make him identifiable in the crush in the doorway of the Church of the Holy Sepulchre and in the group outside the Lutheran Church of the Redeemer which he had just dedicated. 'You know they knocked down part of the Jaffa Gate so he could go through it without getting off his horse.' Varouj did not have any pictures of the German Colony, but at the mention of the name Fast he got down another box of prints and started flicking through them. 'Fast, like the Hotel Fast, no? Here it is. It used to be just outside the Jaffa Gate. I used to work in a little studio just there.' He pointed out one shop-front opposite the three-storey, stone-built hotel that occupied a triangular site by the Old City's westernmost wall. The rooms facing the street had access to the two balconies above the main door. 'Do you recognize it now?' It was another photograph of the same building, but most of the facade was hidden by a vast flag hanging from the top balcony: a black swastika in a white circle on a red field. The photograph still has the power to shock, the symbol of Nazism writ so large in the Jewish City of Holiness. Varouj produced a photocopy of a newspaper article from 1938 reporting the flying of the flag at the hotel in honour of a group of important German tourists. After the war of independence the hotel was demolished and the modern Dan Pearl stands in its place.

Since its adoption by the German National Socialists in 1920 the swastika, the *Hackenkreuz*, the cross of hatchets, has been in the European context an unambiguously anti-Semitic symbol. How an Indian sign denoting prosperity and long life came to be used by the Nazis is bound up with their pseudo-scientific theories about the Aryan master race, and on 15 September 1935 the banner of the Nazi Party became the national flag of Germany. From that time until 1945, whatever your political convictions, if you were a German citizen there was only one flag you could fly. Looking at the 1938 picture of the Hotel Fast bedecked with that flag, it is hard to see past the atrocities committed thereafter, and consequently almost impossible to disassociate anyone who flew it with complicity in those atrocities. To ask, especially in modern Israel, whether a patriotic pre-war German could fly his national flag without being both a Nazi and a collaborator in genocide, is akin to heresy. Non-Jewish Germans born before 1928 are not eligible for a visa on arrival.

There was no room for such nice distinctions in the pageant laid on for the Museum Live event in the old German Colony, purportedly an exploration of the area's German past. Among the crowds that filled the shady lanes wandered youthful performers dressed in a confusing variety of costumes, some looking like southern belles and antebellum gentlemen, while others could have stepped out of the chimney-sweeps' chorus from *Mary Poppins*. A couple were giving a recital of British music-hall and Great War songs. There were stalls selling cakes and candyfloss, beer and kosher *knockwurst*, and on the street by the disused railway station some chairs had been laid out for the performance of a historical tableau. A figure representing General Sir Alan Cunningham, the last British High Commissioner for Palestine, dressed in a red military tunic, was accosted by another in a sombre suit who introduced himself as Ludwig Buchhalter. Their conversation was interrupted by the impromptu and anachronistic appearance of Theodor Herzl, father of political Zionism, looking more like Abraham Lincoln in a stove-pipe hat and stuck-on beard. The discussion bounced back and forth in Hebrew before reaching a dramatic conclusion, Cunningham stretching out an imperious arm and an accusing finger and declaiming in English, 'Go. Go to Australia, you Nazis,' to general applause.

Nili Hod, chief architect for the Municipality of Jerusalem, was chatting to one of the society's organizers who was mustering a group for a tour of the colony. Her job gave her responsibility for the conservation of the colony, but her appreciation of the simple style of the German buildings made her interest personal as well. She was happy to point out some of the landmarks: the meeting hall set back amongst a grove of pines which had been taken over as an Armenian church and the school behind it, now derelict, the pretty stone houses with their louvred shutters and biblical inscriptions in Gothic letters above their front doors. 'Emeq Refa'im has become a very desirable area in recent years.' A frown clouded her generous features when I asked whether the Germans living here had been Nazis. 'Of course they were. This Buchhalter was the head of the Nazi Party in Jerusalem and in the school *Mein Kampf* was part of the curriculum. That was why the British put them in a camp, and after the British left there was a lot of Nazi material found in the houses. There can be no doubt.' It seemed extraordinary that these buildings had been allowed to stand, that the new Israeli state, with the Holocaust such a recent event, had not bulldozed the colony, wiping out all trace of their enemy's presence and starting afresh. 'You say your mother lived in the Fast house? Well, here it is, number nine Jan Smuts.' It was a building like the others, a modest house with climbers growing up the facade and a shady garden behind where Bridget and Lizzie had played. 'Theodor Fast was a remarkable man. He was a surveyor who made topographical maps of Jerusalem – I still use them. He was the agent for a shipping line and taught in the German school. Thanks to him this was the first district of Jerusalem to have running water.' She suggested I visit the municipality archives to find out more. 'Or you could try ringing the radio station. They have a programme, '*Khipos Krovim*', 'Looking for Relatives'. Don't forget that the families of almost every Israeli came from somewhere else. We want to find out about our history as well.'

The crowds dispersed after dark and the guest house on Lloyd George Street had few people staying in it, a Jewish American family who came every year to show their solidarity with the state of Israel and the three Australian women I had seen at breakfast. They had been huddled together over a map, with a miniature cassette player whispering a chant over their silent studies, until the one who seemed to be their leader, a hard-faced woman in her late fifties, started upbraiding the oldest member of the group, a small, meek, white-haired 70-year-old, in a dry monotone while the youngest, big-limbed woman had looked on accusingly. They seemed much happier now, having returned from a day trip to Bethlehem and they were discussing their visit excitedly over coffee in the dining room, the hard-faced woman, Joanne, doing most of the talking. 'I had a vision last night about a baby born in the spirit and Jesus made me remember it at breakfast and I said, "Gosh, we've got to go to Bethlehem." But everyone said the border is closed, that we couldn't go into the Palestinian Authority, so that's what we were doing this morning, travelling there in the spirit.' She laid her hand on the map that was spread out on the table again. 'That was a blessing in Hebrew on the tape, and I was praying that Jesus would find a way for us to get through the border.' They had found a taxi driver who was willing to take them to the checkpoint. 'When we got there he said, "Closed, see?" thinking he'd get double fare for taking us back again, but I said just put us down here and there was another taxi on the Palestinian side, so I put up my hand and he came over. We jumped in and he took us all the way to Manager Square. He was called Moses. The Lord knows we women like that kind of thing! The first person we met was a born-again guide and he said, "Do you want to pray?" He hugged us and he took my Bible from me, took the headship, and we prayed in the spirit – yes, Jesus!' The younger woman closed her eyes and held up her hand in a silent hallelujah. The old woman's head was bowed over her Bible, the pages fluorescent with highlighted passages. Joanne nodded in her direction and mouthed the word 'praying', but the old woman's posture suggested she had gone to sleep.

Joanne was older than she looked, and the younger woman, Kerry, was her daughter. 'I'm sixty-nine you know. When I was thirty-five my father was put into an asylum, suddenly, so I prayed that I would do anything for the Lord if He changed him – I was a Catholic then – and one day he just came home. Then when I was fifty-six I heard the call in the shoe shop in Melbourne where I worked. It was the Lord calling in the promise and he told me what he wanted. Six months later I was in the snow in Russia on a train to St Petersburg with no permit and a suitcase full of Bibles. The Lord told me to be very quiet getting off the train and there were all these KGB men checking papers. Then I saw them parting in front of me, drawing aside, and the Lord said "Now!" so I walked out of the station. Then I walked up and down in the snow for eight hours until a man came up to me. He spoke no English, but I went with him and he took me to the man who needed the Bibles. It turned out that this man had called out to the Lord to send him some Bibles at the very moment that I had heard the call in the shoe shop!' Kerry raised her hand again and let out a low 'Yes, Jesus!'

'Since then I've been all over, in underground churches in China, everywhere. We call ourselves the Housewives for Jesus. Housewives have a very special relationship with the Lord. I've had a difficult life because of what the Lord tells me to do, but oh, the miracles!' She told a story about a young man she and her husband had met on the street in Melbourne. 'I could see he was troubled. I started to say a blessing in tongues under my breath and he went wild so I made a sign to my husband to hold him and my husband started crying and the lad started crying too. Then a couple of months later the lad got in touch with us and said that he had been really depressed when we met because he was dying, but when my husband held him he had felt the joy of the spirit enter him and he had been cured of the AIDS! Yes, Jesus!' Her voice broke into a high-pitched keening, a tuneless chant of half-formed words.

'She's singing in the spirit,' Kerry explained. 'Do you feel it getting hot around you? That's the spirit. That's spontaneous joy.'

Joanne came back to herself. 'Oh, the miracles! It's all there in the scriptures, or else we'd be whackos.' And then the question I had been dreading. 'Do you believe in Jesus? No? Well, you do really. There are angels behind you right now. You are blessed and blessed and blessed and you have a blessing. Here, I'll give you a hug.' And as her arms enfolded me she let out a stream of sounds deeper than her speaking voice. 'There! That's spontaneous love, a blessing in tongues! I can only do that when the Lord tells me, otherwise it would be vanity, wouldn't it?' Joanne led her followers off to 'walk around and worship', but the old woman came back with a question of her own. 'Do you know Croydon?' she asked wistfully. 'That's where I grew up before the war.' Her reminiscences were cut short by a sharp voice calling from the stairs. The born-again harpies set off looking for people to hug.

At the mention of the German colonists the woman surrounded by old ledgers in the municipal archive looked up sharply and listened to the conversation I was having with the assistant archivist, who spoke only a little English, before joining in to help.

'What was the family name? Grossmann of the Hotel Tiberias? You need to look in the Tiberias municipal archive. Besides, weren't they paid for the hotel?' She called over to the man photocopying pages from a file and asked him a question in Hebrew.

'Reparation,' he said. 'That's the word. Didn't they receive reparation for the hotel?'

'Some,' I said, 'much later.' Lizzie had bought her first car with money her mother had received in the early 1960s as Fritz's share. There was a note of suspicion in the woman's question, as though she was trying to head off any claim I might make on my family's former property. 'Actually I am looking for information about my grandfather's death. His suicide.'

The man left the photocopier. 'Well, there should be something about it in the newspapers. Have you checked the *Palestine Post*? They have a complete set on microfiche at the National Library. I am driving out to Giv'at Ram in a moment. I could give you a lift.'

He introduced himself as E'ond and his battered Renault 4 suited his dishevelled look, jeans and a T-shirt, bushy beard and a mop of hair. He was in his late thirties and researching a doctoral thesis. 'Don't mind what that woman said. She's doing her Ph.D. on the war reparations treaty between Germany, Israel and Australia, so of course her first thought is about the compensation.' His thesis was on the activities of the Nazi Foreign Ministry in Palestine before the war. 'There was a lot of pressure on the Germans living here to work for the Nazi Party. Do you know why your grandfather killed himself?' I told him the version of the family legend that attributed Fritz's suicide to his unwillingness to spy on his British clientele. 'That's not so unlikely. I know of three similar cases. Two suicides and one murder. Of course you won't find that out from the *Palestine Post*. Do you know Professor Carmel? You might try asking him.' E'ond had met him several times. 'It was his doctoral thesis that started the interest in the German settlers. It was published in 1970 and you can imagine how unpopular it was to say that the early Jewish settlements were following the example of German Christian fundamentalists. People did not want to believe that the early development of the country was due to their efforts, but in the last ten years there has been a lot of work done on their history and on restoring their houses. You should see the German Colony in Haifa. It's all thanks to Carmel. I'm sure the library will have a copy of his book in German.' E'ond helped me fill out the reader's ticket application and made sure the librarian knew what I was looking for. He had a seminar to give elsewhere on the Hebrew University campus and he left me sitting at a microfiche reader in the airy hall, waiting for the rolls of film, six months to a box. I plunged into 1938.

I knew the year Fritz had died, but I had no idea as to the month in which it had happened. There was nothing for it but to start on 1 January and work my way through, consoling myself with the thought that context was as important as events. The front pages were full of global unrest, syndicated Hemingway reports on the Spanish Civil War, the Anschluß of Austria leading to riots in Graz, 'Heil Hitler!' written in neon lights on the flanks of Mount Vesuvius. How could anyone have thought that another world war was avoidable? The local news too was full of trouble, small incidents at first, 'Stones Thrown at Jewish Omnibuses', 'Arabs Destroy Orange Groves', building through May and June to 'Haifa Bomb Kills 25 Arabs'. The courts were full of those charged with possession of illegal firearms, for which the penalty was death. The daily column '24 Hours of Crime' reported incidents of sniping and damage to property. There were strange portents – 'A child with two heads and six fingers was born to a Yemenite woman yesterday. The monstrosity lived for 1½ hours . . .' – and comic accidents, 'Milk Lorry Skids into Ditch'. Tiberias did not escape the unrest. In May a bomb exploded in the market place and a riot broke out during a funeral, young Arab men pelting the police with stones. In June a bomb went off during an Arab wedding. The editorial pages discussed the plans for partition that had been put forward the previous year by the Peel Commission, whose practicality was then being explored by Sir John Woodhead. The features pages ranged over subjects as diverse as recipes for 'Four Marmalades Without Oranges' and a brief history of the Trans-Jordan Frontier Force, their 'magnificent record of unswerving loyalty and unfailing success'. In the world of the small advertisements life went on as usual, announcing the films showing in the cinemas, concerts at the King David Hotel, the healthful properties of Spinney's mineral water, even one placed by the Czechoslovak Tourist Information Bureau promoting a break in that country's mountains as 'the right place for your tired nerves', the mountains that were overrun by German troops that autumn.

As the film spooled into June, the last month on the first roll, I began to despair of finding anything about my grandfather in the first half of the year. Or maybe I had missed the report already. The prospect of reeling through another six months was not appealing, although I would have been able to follow the rest of Australia's cricket tour of England; they had knocked up 700 runs against Cambridge University, but in the Trent Bridge Test Match England had declared on 658 for 8. Another sporting item caught my eye, the King's Birthday Cup polo match played between the Palestine Club and the Trans-Jordan Frontier Force. Shan Hackett's name was not on the TJFF team list, but playing for the Palestine Club was one W.L. Milner-Barry, my late godfather. The twenty-nineth of June came and went – nothing – and I was resigned to hearing the film click out of the spool and flap free in the projector, but then, Thursday, 30 June, lead story, page two (from a special correspondent):

HOTEL-KEEPER FOUND DEAD
CORONER RETURNS VERDICT OF SUICIDE

TIBERIAS, Wednesday . . . The owner and manager of the Tiberias Hotel and the Lido Cafe-Restaurant, Mr Fritz Grossmann, was found dead this morning in the bathroom of his flat with a bullet through the brain. His licensed revolver was found at his side.

At the Coroner's Inquest, held this afternoon, a verdict of suicide was returned.

Mr Grossmann, who was 30, was the son of the founder and previous owner of the Tiberias Hotel and was a native of Tiberias. His family and his friends are at a complete loss to understand his motives in taking his life, as he had given no sign of being in any trouble.

In fact, up to the time when he went to his room in the

Hotel, where he apparently read and smoked for several hours, he was with his friends who suspected nothing.

Grossmann leaves a wife and two small children.

The funeral took place in Tiberias this afternoon and was largely attended by friends from Haifa and district.

Among those who attended from Haifa were Mr and Mrs Charles Boutagy, Mr Jeffries, Mr Nassar, Mr Hermann Teitz [sic], Mr Farajallah, Mr Pross and others.

Dust motes swirled in the light of the projector. A wheel squeaked on a trolley moving unseen among the stacks. Keyboards tapped. Pages turned. Whispers. Nobody else had heard the shot. My grandfather was dead, 'with a bullet through the brain'.

I do not know how many times I reread the article, the bald and inaccurate reporting of a domestic tragedy. 'His family and his friends were at a complete loss . . .' and so was the special correspondent; it happened in his house and not in the hotel. Nevertheless, the piece did contain some hard facts. Grossmann had a hotel, friends, and a licensed revolver. He was a husband and a father. He smoked. He had been born in Tiberias in 1908. Further, one could deduce that the town's morgue had no refrigeration facilities, that the afternoon of Wednesday, 29 June 1938 was hot, that Palestine's internal communications were good – news of his death had spread quickly and his friends were able to reach Tiberias in time for his interment. Was it possible to know more? What had happened the day before? What happened next?

On Thursday, 30 June Donald Budge beat Bunny Austin in the men's final at Wimbledon.

Professor Carmel was right, I did not know a great deal about the German settlers, the Templers, before arriving in Israel. When I had first heard the term I had imagined an association with the Knights Templar, some sort of latter-day revival of the chivalric order, but I was soon relieved of that notion. The German Templers were, according to a guidebook entry for Haifa, members of a 'religious reform movement' who had first settled there in 1868, but further searches for information on them turned up nothing, until my visit to the Palestine Exploration Fund library shortly before I left London. There I had found a copy of the German edition of Alex Carmel's book, *Die Siedlungen der württembergischen Templer in Palästina, 1868–1914* (*The Settlements of the Württemberg Templers in Palestine*). A cursory glance at the index, however, had failed to convince me at that time of the book's relevance to my own research. There were no entries for either the Grossmanns or the Ruffs. Tiberias itself only rated three mentions. It was not until the 'Conclusion' that any reference was made to the hotel, and then only in passing in a list of the Templers' achievements: 'Tourists . . . found for the first time hotels of a European standard . . . which the Germans had opened in Haifa, Jaffa, Jerusalem, Tiberias, Nazareth and Ramle.' The amount of pertinent material hardly seemed to justify the strain it would have put on my school German to plough through such boulder-strewn expanses as the section entitled '*Das Verlangen nach zusätzlichen landwirtschaftlichen Kolonien*' ('The desire for additional agricultural colonies') or such dusty tracts as '*Die Lockerung der religiösen Bindung der Templer in Palästina*' ('The loosening of the religious ties of the Templers in Palestine'). Besides, from what I could gather from my grandmother, the Grossmanns had not been members of the Temple Society. Luckily the book was well illustrated, and there opposite page 176 was a photograph of the 'German hotel in Tiberias' from

1925. It was the first picture I had seen of the building. Now that Professor Carmel had confirmed that my great-grandmother's family, the Ruffs, had been Templers their history became bound up with my own.

The word 'fundamentalism' has become almost indivisible in the West over the course of the last thirty years with the word 'Muslim' and the two together synonymous in the Middle Eastern context with 'fanaticism'. Yet it is surprising to discover that the term 'fundamentalism' was coined by certain denominations of American Christians in the early twentieth century to describe their own beliefs. The term was intended to signify a return to the 'fundamentals' of belief, a stripping away of the corrupted rituals and dogma of established religion to reveal a pure doctrinal basis on which a community of faith could be built. The cornerstone of such an edifice is the literal truth of scripture. Those opposed to these groups characterize their beliefs as reactionary, seeing in their rejection of many aspects of the modern world, its science, its laws, a return to mediaeval ignorance. This is true equally of American Creationists or the Egyptian Salafiya movement, or even of Eastern European Hasidism. Those within such communities on the other hand regard themselves as reformers, as presenting a new way forward.

Christian Protestantism has its origins in such beliefs, in the 'Reformation' of the early sixteenth century. On 31 October 1517 Martin Luther is said to have nailed his manifesto, 'The Ninety-five Theses', to the door of the Castle Church in Wittenberg. It contained all the elements of 'fundamentalism': rejection of the religious orthodoxy of the established church; criticism of its hierarchy and insistence on the absolute authority of the scriptures. Combined with these revolutionary ideas were notions of a more personal and mystical relationship with the deity and aspects of nationalism implicit in the rejection of the Pope's temporal authority. Of course human society is such that the rejection of one hierarchy leads to the creation of another, which is then rejected in its turn by other non-conformist groups. So Luther's break with Rome opened the way for the formation of a plethora of sects, usually coalescing around a charismatic preacher, each claiming that the beliefs of the previous groups were wrong and that they alone had access to truth. Anabaptists, Calvinists, Mennonites, Methodists, Quakers, Shakers, Baptists, Hutterites, Rappites, Presbyterians, Unitarians, Disciples of Christ, Jehovah's Witnesses, Evangelicals, Pentecostals, Congregationalists, Universalists, Adventists, Mormons – this list could be much, much longer. Persecution of such groups merely confirms for their members the truth of their beliefs, turns them in on themselves and leads to the formation of exclusive, isolationist communities. Many saw emigration to the New World as a chance to find the space and freedom to establish communities of the righteous. The best-known example, thanks to Hollywood, is the Amish community of Pennsylvania, a Mennonite splinter-group who have maintained their separate identity into the twenty-first century.

Tied up with the desire to establish a community of true believers are mystical beliefs about the End of Days as set out in the Book of Revelations. The growing corruption and decadence these groups perceive in the world are seen as signs of the imminent birth of the Anti-Christ and the final struggle between Good and Evil. The return of Christ and his ultimate victory will usher in an era of peace lasting a thousand years during which the righteous will rule the earth. The unrest that swept across Europe in 1848 was seen by many as the beginning of the final struggle. One such believer was Christoph Hoffmann, an Evangelical preacher in the Kingdom of Württemberg.

Christoph Hoffmann's father had founded the Evangelical Community of Christian Brethren in Korntal, an agricultural settlement near Stuttgart, and he grew up with a belief in a practical Christianity where hard work was equated with worship. Though he studied theology at Tübingen his inherited beliefs turned him against the abstract spirituality of the State Evangelical Church and he decided against becoming a minister. Instead he taught philology and history at a pietist Christian institution in Ludwigsburg, and wrote radical articles for the *Süddeutsche Warte* (*South German Sentinel*) newspaper. His views were widely supported in the rural areas and in 1848 he put himself forward as a candidate for the German National Assembly in Frankfurt with high hopes that the revolutionary movement in Europe would lead to the creation of a Christian state. His disappointment that such a state could not be brought into being through political means caused him to resign from the Assembly after only ten months.

He returned to his teaching career and the *Warte*, becoming its sole editor. He also published many pamphlets and in one, 'Voices of Prophecy regarding Babylon and God's People', he outlined what Christians must do to escape the approaching cataclysm and prepare for the Second Coming of Christ. 'Mere prophesying, alleging and sermonising' were not enough. Practical action had to be taken. 'A community has to be founded, whose conduct of life will be a testimony to the truth of the Word of God and will demonstrate that by believing in Jesus Christ people become wise and just, holy and happy.' Moreover, since biblical prophecy pointed to Jerusalem as the scene of Christ's reappearance on earth, the goal of all true believers should be the gathering there of God's people in preparation for the establishment of the Kingdom of God. 'Is it impossible to establish such a community with the means He won for and bequeathed to us? If this is incredible the unbelievers are right, and the Christian faith is no better than the religions of the heathens.' The circulation of the *Warte* fell, but Hoffmann's views remained unshaken. 'Not the approval of a majority of brothers, but the concordance with the essence of the teachings of Jesus Christ, are the touchstone of our actions,' he wrote in the paper. 'Thorough examination of God's expectations of us will be a surer way to certitude and true righteousness than listening to opinions voiced by men.' The attacks he made against the state church and its clergy left him and his followers increasingly isolated. Even the community at Korntal was wary of his views. When he applied to return to the settlement in 1854 its council would only allow him to reside there if he gave up writing and renounced his intention to bring God's people together in Jerusalem. The experience convinced him that rather than try to convert evangelical groups to his way of thinking he should form his own and in this he was aided by Georg David Hardegg, a Ludwigsburg merchant.

While Hoffmann preached a practical Christianity, Hardegg had the organizational and commercial experience to turn it into a going concern. He formed the Committee of the Friends of Jerusalem and the Society for Bringing Together God's People in Jerusalem which had grown to a membership of five hundred by the end of 1854. He raised money and contributed generously himself. While Hoffmann drafted a 'Constitution of God's People', Hardegg set out the next steps the Committee should take. Rather than rush to Trieste and board a boat for Palestine, it was decided to send a commission to the Holy Land which would report on the type of conditions God's People could expect to encounter when they arrived, and investigate the possibility of acquiring enough land on which to live. In the meantime, a community constituted along the lines Hoffmann envisioned was to be established in Germany as both an experiment to see if such a thing were possible and a training camp for those who would make the journey to Jerusalem. In January 1856 the Committee purchased the Kirschenhardthof estate near Marbach am Neckar, some five miles northeast of Ludwigsburg, where they sought to institute 'a way of life according to God's will'.

Once the community at Kirschenhardthof had been established, the urgency of settling in the Holy Land seemed to recede. A three-man commission was dispatched to Palestine in 1858: Hoffmann, Hardegg and an agricultural expert called Bubeck. They reported that the prophecies of the Revelation were coming true, that the Holy Land had been reduced to a desolate state, but they concluded that its foretold restoration was also possible if the German people would heed the call. To spread the word Hardegg set up a 'School for Prophets' at Kirschenhardthof and missionaries were sent to Mennonite communities in Russia and America. Meanwhile, Hoffmann's increasingly vituperative attacks on the State Evangelical Church and his insistence on performing baptism, communion and confirmation services himself, even though he was not an ordained minister, caused his and his followers' expulsion from that church. During an assembly at Kirschenhardthof in June 1861 the Friends of Jerusalem declared themselves to be an independent religious society under the name 'the German Temple', alluding to their intention to raise a spiritual temple in Jerusalem whose building blocks were to be the true believers. But still no plans were formed for their emigration, and the delay caused dissent among Hoffmann's followers. Some families left the society altogether, while others settled in Russia and America. Some more impatient young members even attempted to establish a community in Palestine on the edge of the Plain of Yizre'el. Of the twenty-five Templers that arrived in Palestine between 1865 and 1867, fifteen had died by 1868 and the remainder had settled in Nazareth.

The delaying of the departure of the Templers was due in part to the political turbulence of the 1850s and 1860s. While the threat of popular revolution had receded, conflict between the Central European states loomed. As a direct result of the Piedmontese involvement in the Crimean War, the Italian principalities revolted against Austrian rule and achieved both unification and independence, giving impetus to the national cause in the northern German states, led by Prussia. Austria and Prussia combined in 1864 to drive the Danes out of the duchies of Schleswig and Holstein, but the two states were already on course for conflict between themselves. Bismarck's attempt to extend Prussia's influence south of the River Main in the face of an alliance between Austria, Bavaria, Saxony and Hanover could only end in war. It broke out in 1866, lasted seven weeks and was won by Prussia. It resulted in Austria's exclusion from the German Confederation and the loss of Venetia to Italy. Prussia's preeminence was confirmed by its subsequent victory over France in an opportunistic war started by Napoleon III. The result was a unified Germany ruled by a Prussian emperor, Kaiser Wilhelm I. In these struggles the Templers detected the approach of the apocalypse. On 6 August 1868 the two heads of the society, Hoffmann and Hardegg, and their families, some thirteen people altogether, began their journey to the Holy Land.

In preparation for their departure the Templers had sought to gain the backing of the North German Federation for their enterprise and were assured of the support of its representative in Constantinople. For good measure, Hoffmann and Hardegg travelled via Vienna to enlist Austrian support as well. Their plan was to proceed to Constantinople and apply in person at the Sublime Porte for a *firman*, a licence from the Ottoman Sultan that would smooth their way with local officials and guarantee their safety. They applied for a lease on three square miles of state land at the foot of Mount Carmel, with an option to purchase it some time in the future. Frustrated by the slow workings of the Porte they continued to Beirut after waiting six weeks for a reply, and without the *firman*. There they joined up with other Templers from Germany and Russia and set out on 30 October for Haifa where they intended to spend the winter. Finally in December they received a reply from the Ottoman government. A lease on the land would only be granted to them if they became Ottoman citizens. This they declined to do and circumvented the stipulation by purchasing the land outright through an agent.

The Templers were not the first Protestants to settle in the Holy Land. Apart from various missionary organizations that had set up shop in Jerusalem, a group of 156 American settlers arrived in Jaffa in 1866 equipped with prefabricated houses. They were followers of the 'Church of the Messiah' whose purpose was much the same as that of the Templers, to hasten the End of Days by establishing a community of true believers and preparing the country for the return of the Jews. They built a settlement on the outskirts of Jaffa and the local inhabitants, once they had overcome their initial surprise, saw in their arrival an opportunity to relieve the Americans of their money and goods. When Mark Twain's tour group reached Jaffa a year later, they found the settlers in a sorry state. 'The colony was a complete *fiasco*,' he wrote. They took on board the *Quaker City* some forty settlers who wanted to go home. '[Their] prophet Adams – once an actor, then several other things, afterward a Mormon and a missionary, always an adventurer – remains at Jaffa with his handful of sorrowful subjects.' Some of the settlers had died, 'others had deserted before . . . Our forty were miserable enough in the first place, and they lay about the decks seasick all the voyage, which about completed their misery, I take it. However, one or two young men remained upright, and by constant persecution we wormed out of them some little information. They gave it reluctantly and in a very fragmentary condition, for, having been shamefully humbugged by their prophet, they felt humiliated and unhappy.' One of Twain's munificent travelling companions gave the American Consul in Alexandria sufficient funds for their repatriation to Maine. By 1869 G. J. Adams himself had had enough of the Holy Land and the Templers were able to purchase the abandoned settlement. Not only did the property give the Templers a second base in Palestine, but it also provided them with employment, comprising a steam-powered mill, a saw mill and an oil-press. The purchase also included a nineteen-room hotel which Hardegg's son Ernst took over and ran as the Hotel Jerusalem.

With such an example of failure before him Hoffmann had good reason to proceed cautiously in the Templers' venture. He was at great pains to restrict the number of new settlers from Württemberg and even stipulated the sort of applicant he would accept. In his analysis the chief reason for the failure of the Adams Colony was that it did not have a broad enough agricultural base. In order to avoid repeating that mistake, he did not allow more people to emigrate than the Templers' land could support, and was especially desirous that the newcomers should be farmers. Nevertheless, the Templers' first seasons as cattle-breeders and wine-growers on Mount Carmel were hard, and the settlement in Jaffa had very little cultivable land. It was decided that a purely agricultural settlement should be established and in 1871 an area of land an hour's walk from Jaffa was acquired and divided into eighteen lots. The foundations for Sarona's first buildings were laid that autumn. The site near the Yarqon stream consisted of rough grazing and some swampy ground where malarial mosquitoes bred. The settlers suffered from disease and not a few died, but, learning from the French in Algeria, they planted eucalyptus trees to drain the swamps and the new agricultural technology they brought with them, especially the deep-plough, soon turned Sarona into a healthful and prosperous community. The settlers in Sarona adapted well to the climate, growing winter wheat and vegetables, establishing vineyards and a dairy herd and planting orange groves. Those in Haifa and Jaffa became increasingly involved in trade and commerce, importing German goods, and bringing new skills to Palestine in the fields of medicine, education, architecture, construction, engineering, surveying and metal-working. They were also well placed to take advantage of opportunities in the nascent tourist business and took it upon themselves to develop the country's internal communications, improving the track from Haifa to Nazareth into a road that could take wheeled transport and operating the first passenger service on it. One Templer, Mathhäus Frank, built the first steam mill in Jerusalem in 1873 and the German Colony at Emeq Refa'im grew up around his business. The Templers had achieved what no one thought they could. Carmel concludes: 'For the first time since the Crusades, European Christians had succeeded in establishing a foot-hold in the Holy Land and laying the foundations of a modern settlement in that long-neglected country.'

The 1870s and 1880s were the era of Germany's 'Great Depression'. Almost two million people emigrated in the course of those two decades, mainly to America, but the Templer settlements received very few new settlers – many of those who had been so enthusiastic were put off by reports of the difficult conditions in Palestine. As in previous (and subsequent) times of economic hardship some of the frustration felt by the urban and rural poor of Central and Eastern Europe translated into anti-Semitic violence. The pogroms of the

1880s in the Ukraine were the worst examples. While the renewed persecution of European Jewry was the 'push' factor in the rise of a new quasi-nationalism that would eventually be called Zionism, there were other 'pulls' drawing both secular and religious Jews towards Palestine. Not least among these was the example set by the German Templers. They had shown that it was possible to think about Judaism's promised return – 'Next year in Jerusalem' – in practical terms. While there had always been religious Jewish communities in Palestine, most notably in Safed and Tiberias, the 1870s saw the foundation of a new type of agricultural settlement modelled along the lines of those of the Templers. The first of these, Petah Tiqva, 'the Gate of Hope', was established in 1878 near Sarona and like the Templer communities it would not have survived its early years without continued backing from Europe, coming mainly from Baron Edmond de Rothschild. The French philanthropist realized the practical experience of the Templers could be of great use to the newly arrived and largely urban Jewish settlers, and he engaged a Templer from Haifa, Dr Gottlieb Schumacher, to draw up plans for the building of wine cellars at Rishon Le Tzion and to survey and divide the site of Zikkron Ya'akov near Haifa. Relations between Templers and Jewish settlers were more than cordial, Templer schools taking in Jewish pupils while the Jewish settlements provided an important market for Templer dairy produce. Nevertheless, as Jewish immigration increased so did land prices, which was a hindrance to the expansion plans of the less well-funded Temple Society, and the Germans had to reconcile themselves to the fact that their numbers in Palestine would never be as great as their influence on the country's development.

Relations with the Arab populace and the Turkish authorities were more mixed. Templer businesses in Haifa and Jaffa relied on Arab patronage and were frequently conducted with Arab partners, but in rural areas Arabs who had sold their land to German farmers were often prey to envy, seeing the fertility to which it had been raised. Theft was commonplace as were acts of vandalism, like driving goats onto wheat fields when the new shoots made for sweet fodder. Despite the consolidation of their achievements there were still many who doubted that the Templer communities would survive into a second generation after Hoffmann's death in 1885. (Hardegg had died in 1879.)

Though the Templers had thrown off the authority of Germany's established church they remained staunchly patriotic both to their home state, Württemberg, and to the German Reich. Their loyalty was repaid with practical support, financial and diplomatic, and when in 1898 Kaiser Wilhelm II decided to make a pilgrimage to the Holy Land the Templers were singled out for special imperial attention. A new landing stage was built in anticipation of the arrival of the Kaiser's yacht *Hohenzollern* in Haifa. A continuation of the main street of the German Colony, with plans drawn up by Gottlieb Schumacher, was executed by the Beilharz brothers' firm. On 25 October a German emperor set foot in the Holy Land 670 years after Frederick II had landed his army at Acre. A reception was held in the garden of the German consulate at which the Kaiser pledged his continuing support and protection. The imperial party proceeded down the coast on horseback, camping overnight at Burj el-Khail and visiting Sarona en route to Jaffa. There the imperial couple took the first floor of the Hotel du Parc, owned by the Ustinov family, while many of the grafs and generals stayed at the Hotel Jerusalem.

'You know the whole of the Kaiser's journey was organized by Thomas Cook?' Alex Carmel's smile was as square as his jaw. 'How about that? How about if your queen visited

Turkey on a Neckermann package?' He liked the idea of monarch as tourist. It appealed to his egalitarian view of the world. He sat behind his desk, piled with files and papers, in shorts and a T-shirt. He was tanned and muscular and looked much younger than his seventy years. His grey hair was cropped short and he was handsome in a virile way one does not associate with academia. He nodded to a woman sitting at a table in the corner of the book-lined room who was studying papers in a box-file. She was dressed in the conservative manner of the ultra-orthodox Jews, her hair obviously a wig. 'When she came in she didn't believe I was the professor,' he said conspiratorially, 'because professors don't wear such clothes, she said. Now she wants me to translate everything because she doesn't speak much German. I really don't know what she's doing here. Every day these people come to waste my time.' The telephone rang and his assistant answered it. 'Here, look at my book while I take this call. You said you understand German?'

The Kaiser's visit had given new impetus to German efforts in extending their influence in the Eastern Mediterranean. The Templers in Palestine, who numbered 1343 in 1898, were regarded not only as a shining example of what Germans could achieve, but also as a bulwark against French colonial ambitions in Syria and Lebanon. More funds became available to them and were used to purchase more agricultural land. New colonies were founded in both the north and south of Palestine, one some six miles east of Jaffa called Wilhelma in honour of the King of Württemberg, and two on the road between Haifa and Nazareth, Waldheim and Betlehem (not to be confused with the alleged site of Jesus' birth near Jerusalem). As German citizens the young men of the colonies were required to return to the Fatherland to do their military service, and when the Great War broke out they were called up as reservists, fighting on the Western and Russian fronts. Although the Ottoman Empire quickly became embroiled in the conflict the war seemed distant from Palestine, even after an ineffectual Turkish assault on the Suez Canal in 1915. The Turks enjoyed notable successes elsewhere, capturing the British expeditionary force in Mesopotamia and beating off the Allied assault on the Dardanelles, though their campaign against the Russians in the Caucasus faltered during the winter of 1915–16. Late in 1916 British, Australian and Indian forces began an assault on Turkish positions in the Sinai while the Arab revolt, fostered by Lawrence, grew in strength, capturing Aqaba in July 1917. Templer men were then pressed into service with German and Austrian units fighting in southern Palestine, and their colonies provided supplies and transportation. General Allenby had assumed command of the Allied forces and pushed northward in the autumn of 1917, breaking through the Turkish defensive line between Gaza and Beersheba. Jaffa fell on 17 November. Sarona, which had been used for a time as the German-Turkish command post, was occupied by Australians and New Zealanders, some of whom broke into the cooperative's wine cellars and paraded through the streets playing musical instruments they had liberated from the settlers' clubhouse. At the end of the month a counterattack was launched against British positions near Wilhelma, many of its buildings being destroyed in the bombardment, but it was not successful. On 5 December Allenby entered Jerusalem through the Jaffa Gate, on foot.

'Of course it was a deliberate contrast to the Kaiser's visit.' Carmel was off the telephone. 'Everyone knew that the Kaiser rode his horse into Jerusalem, and here was the victorious Allenby, who had just beaten the army of this vainglorious man and his oppressive allies, humbly walking into the holy city. But it's all propaganda, you know? The Kaiser was much criticized for having part of the city wall torn down so he could ride in. Actually the Turks did it without being asked and the Kaiser was embarrassed by what they had done, but that's not such a good story. That's the problem with history in this country; everyone has their own version of events and it's the one that suits them.' Carmel had encountered a great deal of opposition when he had started challenging the assumptions Israelis made about the German Templers. His pioneering work was eventually rewarded with the creation of a professorial chair, the Gottlieb Schumacher Institute and Chair for Research into the Christian Contribution to the Reconstruction of Palestine in the Nineteenth Century.

The autumn of 1918 saw Allenby's final offensive against Turkish and German forces, routing the Turks at the Battle of Megiddo, and sweeping through northern Palestine to Damascus and on to Aleppo. (When Lawrence arrived in Damascus he stole the iron wreath, bearing the legend 'From one great commander to another', that the Kaiser had left on Salah al–Din's tomb; it is now in the Imperial War Museum.) The Ottoman government capitulated at the end of October. Most of the German settlers in Palestine were deported to camps in Egypt, one at Sidi Bishr near Alexandria and the other at Helouan outside Cairo, and that was where Carmel's book left them.

'What happened next? You can read about that in Paul Sauer's book, *Uns Rief Das Heilige Land*. There's even an English translation, *The Holy Land Called*. Basically the British allowed them to return from Egypt in 1920 and some of those Palestine Germans who had ended up in Germany came back in 1921. There was a lot of reconstruction to be done, but within a few years the settlements were profitable again.' He called to his assistant who brought him a slim file marked Grossmann. 'I told you I didn't have much on your family, but this was something that turned up recently when they were renovating the Ruff family house here in Haifa. There were lots of papers and photograph albums in the attic, a lot of personal stuff, so I got in touch with the Ruff family in Germany to let them know I had it, but I heard nothing back. I even sent them the photograph albums. Still nothing. I am in touch with many relatives of the Templers there, but the Ruffs were not interested.' The telephone rang again. 'Here, you look at this while I answer this call.' He passed me the file, and launched into a voluble German conversation about his last trip to Switzerland and the Temple Society archive in Stuttgart.

The file contained two typed sheets of crinkly thin paper, carbon copies whose ink had turned purple with age. It was a letter written on 11 January 1938 to the '*Wehrbezirkskommando Ausland, Berlin*', the Overseas Military Command, in response to an enquiry concerning Richard Grossmann: '*Auf Grossmann moechte ich wie folgt ausfuehren . . .*' It was written on an English typewriter and so lacked umlauts and the double 's' character '*ß*'. It ended '*Heil Hitler!*'

Richard Grossmann, born in Tiberias, has been known to me since his earliest childhood. His residence there and his subsequent schooling in Nazareth and Germany have meant he has had little contact with the other Germans of Palestine, a state of affairs he naturally much regrets.

He comes from a good family. They own a large hotel and beach cafe in Tiberias which it appears they run in a good and orderly fashion.

Only two German families live in Tiberias, one of which is the Grossmanns. Other Germans, employees of these families, only ever stayed there a short time because of the hot climate.

Grossmann spent his earliest childhood in this isolation

without contact with different surroundings. This may account for his earnest demeanour, especially as his father died in the summer of 1916, and the unfortunate outcome of the war resulted in our deportation and the not always friendly rule of the English.

He had a good schooling in Nazareth together with his two siblings and five other children from that town. A very competent German schoolmistress, born in Nazareth, had set up a private school there and gave the children of the area the chance to gain an education somewhat superior to that we offer in Haifa.

After attending school in Nazareth he went to secondary school in Germany and then on his mother's advice he became an apprentice chef. This was her express wish because of the nature of their business in Tiberias. The isolation of Tiberias and his discontentment with his job led him, it would seem, to try to change his lot.

Grossmann is of a very earnest character. He is most reserved as a result of his undoubted shyness. He is companionable and home-loving and he shows a pronounced affection for his mother and a particular propriety towards women. In personal matters he is stubborn, though not quarrelsome; in fact through his youth he has been on balance quiet and lacking in self-confidence. Grossmann has little sporting ambition although his large build and well-proportioned frame enable him to compete easily above the average. He is a good swimmer and good at water polo and tennis.

He is also very reserved in political matters; though he is German in outlook he is immature and inexperienced, again due to the solitude of his existence in Tiberias.

The Grossmanns' relations with the Semitic population are not yet strained. They treat the diverse inhabitants of Tiberias with tact. The family is held in high regard by the general population for its honesty, industriousness and, in a word, decency.

Grossmann's talents can be characterized as mediocre.

Grossmann has not yet had to worry about his living or the future.

Grossmann's sister Dore is married to Dr Vorster, a gynaecologist in Göppingen, and four children have come from this marriage. His brother Fritz is married here and that union has produced two healthy children.

I hope I have served you in supplying this information and I am certainly ready to report any other details so far as I know them.

Heil Hitler!

'Well? What do you think of that?' I had not noticed the professor replace the receiver. 'Certainly not a glowing report, which is good news for your uncle. One part that puzzles me though. Here: ". . . his discontentment with his job led him, it would seem, to try to change his lot." What does he mean that Richard is trying to change himself? And has that got anything to do with the reason that Berlin asked for information about him? You see what I mean? Obviously Berlin had no interest in Fritz, didn't know much about him, so why are they asking about Richard? Something for you to think about. Anyway, in general terms the letter shows how the Nazis before the war were trying to build a network among the Germans here, so that story about your grandfather's suicide may be true. The person you should speak to though is Elisheva Ballhorn in Tiberias. She was the municipal archivist there for many years. She told me a different story. A love story. Here's her number.'

The professor had an appointment to keep and two pictures to take to his car, large framed prints of Haifa's German Colony. I offered to carry one, a view from Mount Carmel done by Gottlieb Schumacher's father, Jakob, executed with a surveyor's eye. It showed the orderly stone houses set on either side of the main street running from the foot of the hill to the sea with fields and trees on either side. In the bay sail-steamers lay at anchor and on the far side was the town of Acre. The other was a more intimate version of the same view, painted from a position lower down the hill a little above the level of the red-tiled rooves, a small enclosed garden in the foreground, an orange and a lemon tree, the main street lined with dark green cypresses and silvery olive trees. 'This one's by Gustav Bauernfeind. You should look out for his work. He sold sketches to tourists and now they're pretty valuable. Most hotels sold such views to their guests, either watercolours or photographs by Bonfils or Frith or the American Colony. I believe your great-grandfather was something of a photographer too. I have seen his pictures in several archives.' He ran me down the hill, past the Baha'i temple, to the spot where Bauernfeind had sat and left me there with more leads than answers. 'Let me know what you find out. Send me a postcard.'

In his novel *Altneuland*, published in 1902, Theodor Herzl, the first true leader of political Zionism, imagined a Haifa of the future where 'huge white liners rode at anchor', pictured the slopes of Mount Carmel covered with 'thousands of white homes and the mountain itself . . . crowned with imposing villas'. He had seen Haifa from the sea in 1898 as he sailed past on his way to Jaffa in the hope of meeting the Kaiser. He had come from Constantinople where he had failed to secure an audience with either the Kaiser or the Sultan, and now he was racing to join a Jewish delegation that intended to waylay the Kaiser on his journey from Jaffa to Jerusalem. During that interview Wilhelm expressed his support for the Zionists' aspirations and offered them his protection, though in practical terms that was largely meaningless. As Carmel points out in his essay *Der Kaiser reist ins Heilige Land* ('The Kaiser's Travels in the Holy Land'), Wilhelm was two-faced in his attitude towards the Jews. It suited his foreign policy to have German- or Yiddish-speaking Jews settle in Turkish Palestine as a means of extending German influence in the Levant, but his personal feelings are revealed in a letter he wrote to his English mother, Queen Victoria's eldest child, on his return journey:

Jerusalem is very much spoilt by the large quite modern suburbs which are mostly formed by the numerous Jewish colonies newly erected by Rothschild. 6000 of these people were there, greasy & squalid, cringing & abject, doing nothing but making themselves obnoxious equally to Christian[s] and Muslims by trying to fleece from them every farthing they manage to earn. Shylocks by the score!

In 1927, almost a decade after he had been deposed, he wrote with glib prescience: 'the press, the Jews and mosquitoes . . . are pests of which mankind must rid itself one way or another . . . gas would be best.'

Looking at Haifa from the sea today, Herzl would see much of his vision realized. White houses do climb up the slopes of Mount Carmel and the town has spread along the coast to surround the old Arab fishing port. There are no liners in the harbour, but cargo ships are tied up by the quayside below the lading cranes painted red and white. The houses of the German Colony are about the only thing he would recognize, ranged either side of the wide road leading from the harbour to the foot of the hill, but they would not be the first things he noticed. Rising above the colony is one of the most extraordinary buildings in all Israel, the Shrine of the Bab, the centre of the Baha'i faith. A grand stairway leads up the steep slope through an exquisitely landscaped garden of rills and fountains, cypresses and palms, to a shining golden dome. The whole effect is more reminiscent of the sensuality of Samuel Taylor Coleridge's poem than to a faith that has its origins in the austerity of Shi'ism, and far removed from the nervous group of Baha'i refugees I had met in a Turkish bus station on their way to a new life in America, escaping persecution in Iran. In 1844, Mirza Ali Mohammed, the son of a Shirazi merchant, declared himself to be the 'Bab', the 'Gateway' to the hidden imam, the messianic leader whose return would usher in a golden age of righteousness. He was executed for his heresy six years later. The faith he had started did not die with him; in 1867 one of his followers, Mirza Husayn Ali Nuri, exiled from Persia to Constantinople, proclaimed himself to be the Baha Ullah, the *imam-mahdi*, the Divinely-Guided One whose coming the Bab had foretold. He was banished to Acre and died there in 1892. The Baha Ullah's claims may have drawn on Shi'ite beliefs for their legitimacy but the faith he preached was universal, that all the world's major religions taught the same truth. His work was to free that truth from dogma and ritual and thereby unite humanity. His creed of a universal brotherhood of man, without racial, class or religious differences, a code of ethics rather than a religion, has attracted an international following, especially in America. It has become a rich organization. The gardens around the Shrine of the Bab are reputed to have cost US$250 million.

Mount Carmel seems to have always drawn the religious to it. Egyptian texts from 1600 BCE refer to it as a sacred mountain and it was a centre for the worship of Baal, until the prophet Elijah challenged his priests to a fire-lighting contest. In Crusader times barefoot Carmelite hermits lived in huts and caves on its slopes and sects on the fringes of Islam have not been immune to its allure. Further up from the Shrine of the Bab is the 'mosque' of another messianic cult, the Ahmadiyah, whose Indian leader proclaimed himself to be not only the *mahdi* and a *buruz*, 'reappearance', of the Prophet Muhammad, but also the returned Christ and an incarnation of Krishna. In contrast, the millennial beliefs of the German Templers seem as level-headed and orderly as their civic architecture. The clean simple lines of their buildings have been newly restored, and homes with pious mottoes over their doors, like 'Let the Lord direct your course and trust in him; he will make all well' and 'Blessed are those who obey His commandments and follow the path of righteousness', have become bars and restaurants. The Templers' Community Hall is now a museum and art gallery where Alex Carmel's own collection of photographs is on display, groups of bearded elders in sombre suits, some affecting a tarbush as did Christoph Hoffmann, ladies in bonnets and leg-of-mutton blouses, school children in pinafores and miniature naval uniforms, a group of Templer conscripts on the eve of war in 1914, picnics and street scenes. Their businesses and farms were also pictured, molten metal glowing in the dark interior of the Wagners' foundry, the olive press and drying racks in the Haifa soap factory, the Ruffs' joinery workshop, boxes of Sarona oranges being loaded onto camels for the journey to Jaffa, a team of oxen deep-ploughing and a threshing machine – scenes reminiscent of 'sod-busting' in the American mid-west. Almost all of these pioneers are now dead, and not a few rest in the Templer cemetery, a shady grove in the shadow of the Dagon grain silo, screened from the noise of the highway by trees and oleanders. There lie Hardeggs and Hoffmanns surrounded by the families of their followers: Blaich, Beilharz, Beck, Bitzer, Herrmann, Heselschwerdt, Unger, Keller, Lange, Imberger, Lämmle, Pfänder, Müller, Pross, Fast, Sus, Stutz, Schumacher, Wurst, Wagner, Paulus, Rohrer, Schimdt, Haar, Ruff, Tietz . . . and how many of these were my relatives?

I became aware I was not alone in the graveyard. A man was peering from behind the bushes some way off and what he saw gave him the confidence to emerge from the undergrowth pushing a wheelbarrow, empty apart from a hoe and a rake. He introduced himself as Adran, a thirty-something park-keeper who tended the graves and the nearby war memorial as his father had done. He spoke a little English, and told me the cemetery had very few visitors nowadays, and mainly they were local youths who came here to drink. He followed me around pointing out the damage the 'alcoholists' had done, kicking over gravestones, decapitating angels, smashing crosses. He repaired what he could. If they were Jewish graves, he said, there would be big trouble. As it was, 'the police, the newspapers just relax.'

⚗ ⚗ ⚗

The bomb in the nightclub queue had been followed by a lull in the violence. No one thought it had stopped for good. No one thought there was a hope of it stopping. People were just waiting for the next outrage, wondering where it would happen and what the target would be, while trying to carry on with their lives and not let vigilance tip over into paranoia. Finding myself outside the American consulate in Tel Aviv I hurried past on the other side of the road, or walking through the Muslim Quarter in Jerusalem behind an Israeli plain-clothes-policeman wearing a bullet-proof vest, a yarmulke and a side-arm I dropped back some distance. Buses have proved to be perennially popular targets and most of Egged's fleet have bullet-proof windows and blast-proof floors. Travelling back from Acre it was not hard to see why buses are attacked. Soldiers ride for free and most of the passengers were in uniform, young men and women who scrutinized me with intense suspicious stares as I got on. Suicide bombers have tried to disguise themselves as backpackers often enough. I passed the test and they settled back into the weekend atmosphere, chatting across the aisle, texting and listening to Walkmans. They could have been on a university outing, apart from the uniforms, berets tucked into their epaulettes, and the automatic rifles, muzzles sticking up through the seat-back handles that double in Israel as gun racks. You might be encouraged to feel secure, surrounded by so much fire power, until you recall that you have just boarded a moving military target.

For the journey to Tiberias I caught an Arab-operated minibus from the junction by the oil refineries in the Qishon Valley east of Haifa. In the gathering dusk it skirted the northern edge of the Plain of Yizre'el and climbed up into the dry hills of Galilee. Somewhere to the north of the road was the old Templer settlement of Betlehem-Waldheim, on land once controlled by the Teutonic Knights. It was dark by the time we reached the Nazareth crossroads and continued to climb into the night, wafts of tobacco smoke and plaintive *oud* music coming from the front seat. And then the road began to descend, gently at first, the lights of Tiberias' upper town hazy in the night air and drawing a line across the middle distance that suggested we were approaching the edge of a cliff. The road plunged over the drop. The engine whined into a lower gear, our lights sweeping round switchbacks, flashing over a sign that announced we had passed sea level, and still we descended deeper into the depression. The luge ride ended in a whiff of ozone at a set of traffic lights where the driver indicated I should get down.

The sodium lights seemed to be giving off heat, glowing like coals in the thick air. There was no one about and the traffic signals changed unheeded. The orange light turned the low concrete blocks into a jumble of rectangles above which rose the dome and minaret of a mosque. Across the street was a fragment of the old town wall, large dark blocks, and behind a tall building in the same stone whose end wall allowed only a narrow pavement between it and the road. I tripped on an uneven paving stone and fell heavily on my knee. I limped up the steps beyond the wall's end and into the Meyouhas Youth Hostel, formerly known as the Hotel Tiberias. Having anticipated this moment for so long, now that I had arrived what I felt most was the pain in my leg.

Tiberias is peculiar among the towns of the Jordan Valley in that it has no history before the beginning of the Common Era. Both Beisan and Jericho stand on sites that were occupied for thousands of years before the birth of Christ. Tiberias was the purpose-built capital of Galilee constructed in lavish Roman style by Herod Antipas, the Herod of the New Testament, between 17 and 22 CE and named in honour of the Emperor. It hardly rates a mention in the Gospels. There was a small settlement to the south by the hot springs at Hammat and its inhabitants had long used the steep uncultivable site as a burial ground. Consequently the new town was shunned as unclean by the more religiously minded Galileans. Herod drew settlers in with offers of free housing for the poor and tax exemptions for the rich; freed slaves and released criminals accounted for a sizeable proportion of the population. Nevertheless, after the destruction of the Temple in the first Jewish revolt (66–69) and the expulsion of Jews from Jerusalem as a result of the second (132), Tiberias became Judaism's spiritual capital and home to a succession of brilliant rabbis. The deliberations of the juridical schools of Akiva, Meir, Simeon (who purified the city from 'the contamination of the dead' with an offering of lupines), Judah ha-Nasi and Gamaliel codified the oral laws supplemental to the Torah into a written collection, the Mishna, and compiled the Gemara commentary, bringing the two together into the authoritative 'Jerusalem Talmud'. Their tombs are places of pilgrimage to this day. Not only was Tiberias the seat of the Sanhedrin, the supreme Jewish council, and the centre of Talmudic scholarship, but also where the definitive edition of the Old Testament was compiled in the ninth century and a system of representing vowels with diacritical marks to ensure correct pronunciation was developed that became the standard Hebrew notation. That such an achievement should be realized while Tiberias was under Arab rule bears witness to the tolerance and wisdom of the first lords of the Islamic Empire.

Tiberias was captured shortly after Jerusalem fell to the Crusaders in 1099 by Tancred de Hautville, a scion of the Norman family that had wrested Sicily from the Arabs. He built his castle just to the north of the old town and assumed the title Prince of Galilee. As Crusader knights and kings tended to be short-lived, property and titles were often passed on through their widows and daughters. Eschiva, Princess of Galilee, made such a dynastic match with Raymond of Tripoli, the most brilliant soldier and statesman of his day. He had twice been regent of the Kingdom of Jerusalem and had negotiated in person with Salah al-Din the truce which Reynald of Châtillon, Lord of Oultre Jourdain, broke by attacking a Mecca-bound caravan. In the summer of 1187 Salah al-Din marched into Crusader territory with the intention of provoking a fight, and in order to draw the Latin army out of its strongholds he laid siege to the castle of Tiberias with Eschiva inside. After his decisive victory at the Horns of Hattin, Salah al-Din returned to Tiberias and destroyed the town at his leisure. The ruins were left more or less undisturbed for five hundred years.

Galilee languished under the rule of the Mamelukes and their defeat by the Ottomans in 1516 did little to improve its situation. The focus of Judaism in 'Palestine' had transferred to Safed, a little to the north from Tiberias, and though various schemes were dreamed up for the rebuilding of the town, including the establishment of a silk industry, nothing came of them. There was a glimmer of a revival in the early seventeenth century when the Druze emir Fakhr al-Din carved a fiefdom for himself out of Ottoman neglect, but that was extinguished by his execution in 1634. Another hundred years passed before any serious attempt to rebuild the town was made. Daher al-Amr, a Bedou sheikh, bartered, intrigued, married and fought his way into a position of supremacy over Galilee. He rebuilt the walls of the Crusader citadel and at his invitation the grandson of the last rabbi of Tiberias, Hayyim Abulafia, re-established a Jewish community in the town. Three times Daher fought off the army of the Pasha of Damascus, but like Fakhr al-Din's before him his sheikhdom did not survive his death in 1775. Tiberias itself was brought low by an earthquake in 1837, yet it continued to attract Jewish settlers from both Europe and North Africa. At the time of the earthquake Jews made up a quarter of its population of four thousand. Most of these settlers were supported by donations from Europe and America rather than by their own industry, and visitors from those two continents were prone to compare unfavourably the indolence of the Jews with the agricultural activity of the Arab landlords of the Tabari family. Mark Twain calls it a 'stupid village'. 'We went into the town before nightfall and looked at its people – we cared nothing about its houses.

Its people are best examined at a distance. They are particularly uncomely . . . Squalor and poverty are the pride of Tiberias.' Most of the visitors who followed recite the folk tale about the 'King of the Fleas' holding court there. It is no wonder that they preferred to stay in tents outside the town, as did Thomas Cook's mounted tourists. The town had no medical facilities until the arrival in 1885 of Dr David Watt Torrance, a Church of Scotland missionary, and no hotel worth the name before Herren Grossmann and Krafft, the latter a hotelier from Haifa, established the Hotel Tiberias in 1894. Elisheva Ballhorn told me there were pictures of it under construction in the municipal archive.

◊ ◊ ◊

I had spent an unhaunted night in a narrow room made narrower with two bunk beds, the air conditioner drowning out all external sound, washed in the male communal bathroom, descended the stone staircase and breakfasted in the spartan dining hall on hard-boiled eggs and yoghurt. There was time to walk round the outside of the Meyouhas Youth Hostel before Elisheva was due to arrive. I descended the steps and walked away from the building, without looking round, towards Dr Torrance's Scottish Hospital on a cobbled path between parterres planted with palm trees. When I could bear the suspense no longer I turned. It was true, what I had only been able to glimpse the night before, the exterior of the hotel was almost completely unchanged from the 1930s. Ground floor and two upper stories nine windows long and six wide, a lower ground floor by the road where the slope fell away towards the lake and a taller block with a pitched roof above the kitchens at the other end. The dark grey basalt masonry was set off with white pointing and windows, a white course between the floors and up the corners of the building, linking with the white parapet around the flat roof. An area of the ground floor terrace had been enclosed; a small roof built over the steps, another over the top balcony where the hotel sign had once been attached and a larger one erected over the broad first floor veranda that ran between the entrance and the dining room. Air conditioning units projected from the windows. Yet anyone who had visited Tiberias in the mid 1930s would recognize the Meyouhas Youth Hostel instantly as the Hotel Tiberias. It had been the Grossmanns' home and business for forty-five years, where my grandfather had grown up, where my mother had spent the first four years of her life, where the tragedy had occurred that had changed its course, changed her name and her nationality, and without which I would not have been conceived. I sat down to wait for Elisheva on the small covered terrace outside the front door, feeling somewhat shaky. The heat of the June morning was already extreme. Workmen were moving slowly around the Scottish Hospital where a major reconstruction was under way. Across the road, above a window in the ugly concrete supermarket against which were piled rolls of lavatory paper, was a sign announcing ample stocks of both milk and honey.

Elisheva came up the steps slowly with the aid of a stick. I could not see her face for her floppy white sun hat. She wore beige slacks and a striped cheesecloth shirt buttoned at the wrist, her hand on the railing revealing the pallor of her skin. She did not look up until she reached the top step and her pale features creased into a smile when she saw me standing to greet her, slightly self-conscious that I had been watching her progress. 'So, I hope I have not kept you waiting.' She spoke almost perfect English, but with a German accent. We settled onto the bench.

'Yes, my family came from Germany in 1933. My father

was a painter and he must have had an idea that evil times were ahead because he left behind his career, his family and friends and came to Palestine with his wife and two small children and we settled in the *moshav* at Kinneret near the southern end of the lake. It must have been very hard for him. But we are not here to talk about my family, and we do not have so much time.' She looked at me in silence for a moment as though considering how much to tell me or what I wanted to hear. 'First I must tell you what is not true. There are two mistakes about the Grossmanns and the hotel that appeared in the first Hebrew history of Tiberias and they have been repeated ever since. First, they were not Swiss. I think that mistake was made because *Schwaben*, Swabia, sounds a bit like *Schweiz*, Switzerland. The second thing is that Theodor Herzl never stayed here. I don't know how that came to be written, but there are so many legends about him, so many places he is said to have visited. It is always like that with heroes. A journalist from the *Jerusalem Post*, Helga Dudman, wrote a book in English about the history of Tiberias and I helped her with it. That is much better. There is a copy of the book in the municipal library. We will go up there in a moment.'

There was something ominous in the way she had prefaced what she had to say by correcting these errors. I was unsure of her motives for doing so. Maybe the atmosphere of para-noia, intrigue and conspiracy that pervades the Middle East had infected me too. I was loath to disbelieve this kindly 80-year-old woman who had gone out of her way to help me, but her opening remarks made me suspicious of what was to follow. I wanted to believe her – after all she might have been able to tell me things that my own family could not, for one reason or another – but I could not help feeling I was being set up for something. Was she trying to convince me

189

of her truthfulness in admitting these small errors of fact so that I would not later question more serious contentions? I decided to play my own cards close, not to prompt her with what I had already discovered or correct any further errors I might notice, until I had found out what she thought she knew to be the truth.

She told me about the building of the hotel in 1894. 'It must have been your great-grandfather? Richard Grossmann senior. It was built by Arab workmen and German craftsmen. There were only three or four rooms for guests at first. You will see the pictures. He took many photographs. He dug a cellar and a well and over time he added to the building. He married a German girl from a Templer family – Pauline she was called.' (I did not interrupt, though I knew her name was Frieda.) 'He made a contract with the British firm Thomas Cook and soon many tourists were coming to Tiberias. The Grossmanns were then the town's biggest employers, very important for the development of Tiberias. Not just the staff in the hotel, but also boatmen for tours on the lake and after the First World War drivers to bring guests to Haifa and Nazareth and the ancient sites to the north. They were also the biggest buyers of local produce and many of the early Jewish settlements sold vegetables and meat to the hotel. They bought fish from the Arab fishermen and milk and butter and cheese from the Templers at Betlehem and Waldheim. Richard died during the First World War, of tuberculosis I think, but his wife carried on running the hotel. Under the British many civil servants and army officers came here with their families or to drink in the bar. In the late twenties and early thirties business must have been very good and when Richard's son Fritz, your grandfather, took over running the hotel he decided to build a Lido down by the lake. They already had a private bathing beach next to the gardens of the Scottish Mission and there he built a harbour for small boats and a restaurant. There was even a tennis court, I think. It was the first development of its kind on the lake and it was the beginning of Tiberias as a resort town, not just a base for exploring other sites. The original building is still there, though the place is built up now. But then the trouble came, in 1936 and after, and then there was the suicide. Do you know why your grandfather killed himself?' I deflected the question by mentioning what Alex Carmel had said about a love story. 'Well, of course when someone kills himself for no apparent reason there is much speculation, and when it is such a well-known local person there is gossip, naturally. Suicide was a big scandal in those days. Fritz could not be buried in consecrated ground. His grave is in the gardens of the Scottish Mission. I believe it is still there.' She had heard the story of a love affair from an old Arab who used to work at the hotel. He had moved to Acre after the Arabs were expelled from Tiberias and had died there in the late seventies, so there was no way of hearing his account at first hand, hearsay though it was. 'There is a picture in the archives of the guests at a dinner party given by Mrs Feingold in early 1938. The Feingolds started a big hotel in the 1920s called the Elizabetha. I have often wondered if the "other person" is in the photograph. Do you know anything about this?' I didn't; it is hardly the sort of thing upon which one's grandmother might elaborate. She had actually said even less than the *Palestine Post* report about the reasons for Fritz's suicide. I told Elisheva what my mother had said, that he was depressive and had financial problems, having borrowed a great deal to build the Lido and being unable to repay the loan since business had dried up during the civil unrest. I told her what my aunt had suggested, that his creditors were using the debt to force him to spy for the Nazis. Mostly, I was angry that I did not have any more solid information to counter the old Arab's account, and angry that because I had been told so little I half believed it myself.

Elisheva nodded at the debt and depression scenario and muttered 'It could be,' in a conciliatory way, yet on the subject of Nazi coercion she was more definite. 'But they were Nazis themselves.' For her it was a matter of fact. She must have seen the surprise on my face, surprise at the force of her assertion rather than its content, because she took a more measured tone: 'You must realize that for many patriotic Germans Hitler was a national hero in the beginning. Don't forget he had British admirers too. He put an end to unemployment, he stopped the advance of Communism and he gave the country back its pride after the First World War. Germans everywhere loved him. I'm not saying that the Grossmanns were anti-Semitic, but I have seen Pauline's diary and there was lots of '*Heil Hitler!*' She writes about celebrating the Führer's birthday with other Templers in Haifa.' I did not mention the letter that Alex Carmel had shown me nor the conclusions he had drawn from it about the Grossmanns' political persuasion. For me the most extraordinary part of this news was that Frieda had kept a diary and it had survived. Elisheva explained how she had come to see it. 'It is in the possession of a lady in Jerusalem. She's a historical researcher too. It was found there in the German Colony, but I don't know how it came into her hands. She wanted to do something with it, maybe publish it, so she got in touch with Alex Carmel and he told her I had some photographs in the municipal archive. So she came to look at them. She showed me a few photocopied pages, but she wouldn't let me see the original. She was very jealous of it, thinking that someone would steal it from her. Anyway, she looked at the pictures and went away again and I heard nothing more. This is perhaps ten years ago. I wrote to her a few times, but I received no reply, and when I called her she was just rude, so I don't know what has happened since. She did ask me not to tell anyone about the diary, and I suppose I have broken her confidence telling you, but I can't tell you her name. I promised.' I did not want to press the point, but I had an ominous feeling I was being drawn into a long Levantine game of negotiation via intermediaries.

I was curious as to how the Grossmann family photographs had come into Elisheva's possession. 'Well, the Grossmanns must have left Tiberias in a hurry because they left everything behind. The hotel continued to operate throughout the war, but afterwards, when the war of independence started in 1947, the British Army took it over as their headquarters. This is a very important strategic position, you see. The road coming down the hill is the main road to the coast and this one running past the Scottish Hospital is the main road from the railway at Samakh to the north. If you control this position you have effective control over all of Upper Galilee. When the British left in 1948, Arab forces took the hotel and all the lower town and the Haganah had the upper town. The Jewish settlements in the north were cut off. There was very heavy fighting as the Haganah tried to take the lower town, and it was especially severe around the hotel. The Haganah lost many fighters, so you can imagine when they finally took the hotel they were pretty angry and not just with the Arabs, but also with the British who had given the position to them, as well as with the Germans in general. They threw everything out of the windows, everything, beds, furniture, china. People took what they wanted. A few years later, after I had started a small museum, a man came to me with the photograph album that he had saved, and when I retired all that material was moved to the new town hall, Yad Shitreet, up the hill. But I have to tell you not all the photographs are there anymore. After my husband retired from the police he worked as a tour guide. This was in the 1960s. One day when he was showing a group around he met another guide. She said that in her group were two old women who said that they had lived in Tiberias and were asking about the hotel. It turned out to be Pauline Grossmann and her daughter Dore. So my husband met them and they talked about Tiberias. When he came home that evening and told me, I realized who they were and that I had some of their property. I felt embarrassed about how I had come to have their photograph album and I didn't want to meet them, but I took the personal pictures out of the album, the ones showing the family, and made a package that my husband could pass on to them anonymously. He said they were so happy to have them they were crying. But the other pictures I kept in the archive. They are very important for the history of Tiberias. Because Richard Grossmann took photographs to sell to his guests and to make into postcards there are many pictures of the early Jewish settlements in Galilee and these are important to the history of Israel. They have been reproduced often in history books. Maybe we should go up to Yad Shitreet now to see them.'

The only redeeming feature of Tiberias' modern concrete town hall is the view it commands over the Sea of Galilee and even that was tarnished by dirty tinted windows. At least the library was cool and while Elisheva and Yehudit Cohen, the archivist who had replaced her, went to fetch the photographs from the strong-room I was left at a table with Helga Dudman's book *Tiberias*. It came as no surprise to find that this popular history of the town was in fact a Jewish history. This slant had led the author on a twisted path when it came to Christian European endeavours in the nineteenth century, so while Dr Torrance's medical achievements are grudgingly acknowledged, they mainly provide an opportunity to lament the fact 'that European Christians could do what the Jews could not' and detail how Jewish physicians subsequently rose to that challenge. Dudman's bias is even more marked in her potted account of the town's nascent tourist industry. The chapter entitled 'Hotels and Guests, Mandate Style' also provides a digest of local events under British rule. While it is entirely proper to deal with the subject of the town's hotels in one place rather than dotted about in her otherwise chronological history, I could not get away from the impression that she had delayed its introduction until after the chapter dealing with 'The Great War' specifically so that she could open with the establishment of a Jewish hotel rather than a Christian one. 'The most glamorous event of the decade in Palestine, and certainly for the Tiberias social season of 1929, was the festive opening of the Hotel Elizabetha, the largest and most luxurious in the Land.' It may sound like sour grapes to point out that this is not where the story of the European-standard hotels of Tiberias actually starts, and if there were a decent description to follow of the Hotel Tiberias, already in business for more than thirty years when the Elizabetha opened, then one might call the account balanced. But there is none. For four pages we are told about the opening night and the Feingolds' history and the Bar Mitzvah of Rabbi Abulafia's eldest son, until Dudman concludes: 'Still, it brought the town into the era of modern tourism. Until Feingold built his Elizabetha, there had only been one establishment in town deserving that name – the Grossmanns' Tiberias.' That might seem the perfect opening to recount the history of the earlier hotel, but first we must hear about a 'Tiberias widow' who 'opened a four-room hospice [in 1910], which closed during the war in 1917', and about 'another tiny establishment serving Orthodox Jewish travellers . . . opened at about the same time by a Tiberias rabbi; it, too, closed soon after' and about 'another widow . . . and her daughter [who] tried their luck with another four-room hotel in 1916' and further about the opening of the Guberman Hotel in 1914, before, finally, Dudman brings her apparently unwilling pen to write about the Hotel Tiberias. What she has to say is brief:

By far the most famous and best known, until Feingold's appearance, was the Hotel Tiberias. A massive black stone building in the traditional Tiberias style, it was in its day a beautiful example of modern facilities, the only conceivable choice for European (and American!) visitors, and recommended by the prestigious English tour operators, Thomas Cook.

The Hotel Tiberias takes us back to 1896 when a German family, the Grossmanns, opened their establishment, not far from the Scottish Mission buildings. The name Grossmann has a Jewish sound, but the Grossmanns, far from being so, were ethnic Germans and descendants of the Templers who had settled in the Galilee village of Wilhelma. Herr Grossmann is said to have come to Tiberias in search of a cure for a lung condition: it was a wise move, and 17 years later he was still in the best of health.

In 1916, not a good year for tourism, the hotel was made available to German officers by the Grossmanns. A European civilian, the then famous Swedish travel writer Sven Hedin, enjoyed his stay at the Hotel Tiberias in 1916. The hotel, Hedin noted, had brought the Grossmanns 'a small fortune', but the high cost of everything during the war had seriously reduced it. Host Grossmann is described in Hedin's book *Jerusalem*, published in Germany in 1918 and dedicated 'with reverence and gratitude' to the Turkish ruler Jemal Pasha. No neutral Swede, Hedin wrote his book with passionate German patriotism; his introduction, on England's vicious war aims, concludes with the cry: 'The one thing which can free the world from this vampire (England) is Germany's victorious sword!' Hedin (whose ancestry was partly Jewish) became pro-Nazi later in his life – at about the time the Grossmanns disappeared from Tiberias when World War II began because, as was widely suspected, they too were Nazis. With England's victory, it was back to business as usual for the Grossmanns' hotel, managed by an Arab.

And that is all.

Elisheva and Yehudit returned to find me flicking through the rest of the book looking for other references. There were a few: a note that 'Richard Grossmann (1892–1922), Fritz Paul Grossmann (1908–1938) and Pauline Grossmann, infant' were buried in the garden of the Scottish Mission; another that the Imperial Airways flying boats used to land on the lake, dock at the Lido, and the passengers check in at the Hotel Tiberias, later described as 'the one enemy hotel' in town. It was time for me to make a few additions to Elisheva's list of 'errors': Richard's wife was called Frieda, not Pauline; Richard could not have been born in 1892 – he opened the hotel aged four? – and that Wilhelma, far from being a Galilean village, was a Templer settlement near Jaffa. I was not in a position to challenge the assertion that they were Nazis – here confirmed by the fact that they 'disappeared', implying that they slunk away in shame, when in fact such adult Grossmanns as were left at the outbreak of war, Frieda and my grandmother Margaret, were interned as enemy nationals – because Elisheva's confirmation of it was based on material I had not seen. Moreover, just as denying or diminishing the Holocaust is illegal in many European countries (though not specifically Great Britain), so in Israel questioning whether all Germans were Nazis is likely to be cast as a type of anti-Semitism.

Without access to Frieda's diary I could only hope that pointing out these sloppy errors to Elisheva, who had shown herself so scrupulous about the truth when we had met, would make her re-examine what else she was presenting as fact.

The camera, at least, does not lie as easily, and Elisheva opened the ring binder whose plastic pockets contained the pages of my great-grandmother's photograph album. 'You can see Pauline, I mean Frieda, made her album in some sort of accounts ledger.' There were four pictures to each page of yellowing red-lined paper with Frieda's captions in blue ink. Hebrew annotations and catalogue numbers on round white stickers had been added. 'It was in a bad condition when I got it and after I took out the pages to give back to her it fell apart. Here, look, here is the hotel under construction.' Two faded pictures marked '*Hotelanfang 1894*' show the modest building backing onto Daher al-Amr's old town wall, two windows either side of the entrance on the ground floor and a lower ground floor where the slope falls away towards the road three windows wide. In one there are figures on the flat roof and Arab children in the foreground; the other is empty of people. The flag on the roof hangs limp in the still air and the sign above the door announces the Hotel Tiberias open for business – in 1894. Another easily verified fact that Dudman had got wrong. At the bottom of the page were two muddy photographs of the hotel in 1915 looking down the slope from the other end of the building and showing the addition of another storey and a pitched roof. 'You see how the hotel was built against the old town wall? There used to be an archway over the road. There it is in 1904 and you can see the hotel already has a second storey and a sloping roof. Here it is again, in about 1910, in a picture Richard made into a postcard. By the time of the next expansion, when the building was extended on the side of the hill, Frieda writes

"Gate arch already fallen down". In fact the whole section of the old wall next to the road has gone by the 1920s and has been replaced by more rooms. Also here, on the hillside, they are beginning to build over the kitchens. The final expansion must be in the late 1920s or early thirties, when they built another storey and made the roof flat and the block over the kitchen reached its present height.' The final form of the Hotel Tiberias was shown in a postcard published by the Eliahu Brothers of Tel Aviv. The roadway is paved and a row of taxis cabriolets parked stern-in lines the wall in front of the hotel. The drivers stand around chatting, a tyre is being mended, and in the foreground are some figures looking at the camera, a man and a boy in Arab dress, a youth in a European flat-cap and jacket, his tie too short to reach the waistband of his trousers, a teenager in shorts with a rag in his hand, a man in the mid-morning shadows wearing a homburg.

Elisheva had not removed all the pictures of people. There was a group of three employees, Joseph, Sliman and Fuad in Arab robes and tarbushes, and two pictures of Fräulein Paula Klotz, the children's nanny, one on her own and one with an Arab maid, Sabha, Dore as a little girl with a boy's haircut, dressed in a smock and carrying a broom, and standing on the wall next to Sabha was Fritz, four years old maybe, in shorts and sailor's jacket, his hair a mess. The two children appeared again, this time with their father, in a picture of the hotel's courtyard, '*Vaterle m. Dora & Fritz*'. (Frieda always wrote Dore with an 'a'.) Richard's face is shaded by a pith helmet. A dovecot is fixed to the old town wall and a pigeon watches from its perch. Other pictures on that page show the new well being bored and the interior of the little pump house. Dore also sneaks into the front of a group on the steps of the hotel comprising German visitors, two Ehmanns, a Ruff, a Beck and a Schafer. There was a page of interior scenes, the entrance hall set with two small tables at one of which sat a man in a suit and tarbush, Amin Faris, looking over his shoulder into the lens, a view of the stone staircase and iron hand-rail beyond. The spartan dining hall of today's youth hostel was recognisably the same room as that in three photographs from 1911, but not nearly so welcoming as that pictured, the long tables spread with crisp white cloths, the simple wooden chairs. On the walls were various sets of animal horns, a large stuffed fish, a display cabinet full of small archaeological artefacts, pictures of Galilee and one of the Kaiser, whose imperial shield and flag were also given pride of place in the corner of the room screened off for family use. From the ceiling hung petrol lamps and a stuffed bird of prey with outstretched wings. In the other corner stood a large, dark wood dresser whose shelves were well stocked with bottles.

There was no date in these pages later than 1915, although a couple of the pictures must have been taken after that, and presumably after the Great War, since they showed developments absent in the dated images. It made me wonder how much more photographic material had been lost when the hotel was sacked in 1948. The pictures of the Jewish agricultural settlements did not interest me, and certainly had little artistic merit, groups of scruffy shacks and tents in an otherwise featureless landscape, but I was not blind to their historical importance. The barren land around the settlements made me think of Disraeli's other dictum from *Tancred*, 'the East is used up', an impression held by nineteenth-century imperialists that was to have murderous consequences for this part of Ottoman Syria. And then, right at the end of the folder, there were two pictures of the Lido, one an 8×10 that must once have been tacked to a hotel notice board – the holes at the centre of a circular depression showed where the drawing pins had been. In fact the picture had been taken before the construction of the Lido, showing a palm tree and an open-sided *cabaña* beside the ruins of one of Daher al-Amr's corner towers. Out on the water was a four-engined bi-plane flying boat. Someone had written on the picture in large capitals: 'Private Bathing-Beach of the Hotel Tiberias': and then smaller: 'Free-Tickets for Customers of this Hotel.' Something after that had been blacked out and correction fluid had been used under the 'hing' of 'bathing'. The second picture was another Eliahu Bros. postcard of the 'Casino "Lido"'. I had never heard of gambling at the Lido, but maybe the word 'casino' was being used in another sense, that of a 'public music or dancing room'. There is a small motor boat in the foreground tied up at a stone wharf on which stand a group of men in tropical uniforms. On the shore are some other figures and rising from a lush garden a three-storey building, not large, white and stepped up to provide two sun terraces on the first and second floors. The luxuriant growth of the garden and the uniforms suggest that the picture was taken during the Second World War, after the Grossmanns had left Tiberias.

'So,' said Elisheva, 'now you have seen everything, except the Feingold picture, and Yehudit says she cannot find that at the moment.' We parted on the steps of Yad Shitreet. 'You probably have a lot to think about. Call me if you have any more questions.'

I limped back down the hill into the heat of the lower town, hardly noticing where I was going. The hostel, empty that morning, was now full of ghosts for me, and had been overrun by two parties of school children, one Jewish, one 'Israeli Arab'. They chattered noisily in separate groups in the entrance hall where Amin Faris had been sitting, ran up and down the stairs and along the corridors, out into the courtyard where the pump had once stood. The pump house had made way for a lavatory block. The manager of the Meyouhas stuck his head out of his office to shout a few well-chosen words. Avi Eylon was in his late forties and had a suave look that seemed out of place in a youth hostel. I had not told anyone about my family connection to the place. I did not know how the information would be received. I had not expected incredulity.

'Really?' Yes. 'Really? You are telling the truth? But you are British and the people who built the hotel were Swiss.' German. 'No, no, they were Swiss. Come in. I know all about it.' And he proceeded to repeat the other 'errors' Elisheva had warned me about. At least if he believed they were Swiss he did not think they were Nazis. I let it go, though I did try to correct him when he stated that it had been called the Eliza- beth. 'No, you are wrong. See, here is a postcard.' He had a copy of the Eliahu Bros. card in a frame on his bookcase, but this one had a double caption, reading 'Hotel Tiberias' at the top and 'The first class "Elizabeth Hotel"' at the bottom. 'I know what I know.' He told me that this room next to the dining room had been the original office and the reception desk and office used to be the bar. I realized I was sitting in the room where my grandmother had worked on the accounts through the hot summer of 1932, hardly bearable without air-conditioning. He told me there had been another office in the basement room on the corner rented by Imperial Airways.

Avi gave me the key to the door to the roof. My mother remembers sleeping up there on summer nights and my grand- mother that it always leaked during the winter rains. They had been sleeping up here on the night of a lunar eclipse when the town reverberated with the banging of pots and pans to ward off evil spirits. They would still recognize the view to the east over the Scottish Hospital and St Andrew's Church to the lake, but to the south the old town of Tiberias has completely disappeared under concrete. Almost the only old building left is the Grand Mosque of Daher al-Amr, dwarfed by two modern hotels on the southern side of the town, the Moriah Plaza and the Carmel Jordan River. An Israeli flag flying from a pole at the corner of the roof rose and fell in the fitful afternoon breeze.

The name has not been changed, but the Lido was almost unrecognisable. It took a moment to get my bearings. The stone jetties I had seen in the postcard in Yad Shitreet were no longer in evidence. I walked out onto the new concrete dock where a large tour boat was just tying up and looked back towards the land. To the right was a circular bar-nightclub, to the left a long mole projected into the lake on which was an open-sided restaurant. Straight ahead was a broad area of tarmac where the tour bus was waiting for the passengers to disembark, and in between the concrete jetty and the car park was a shallow harbour for small boats, the landward wall of which was made of large basalt blocks. The bus departed and now I had a clearer view of the building behind, overgrown with creepers. It was the original Lido restaurant, and still standing outside, the old date palm whose fruit my mother and Lizzie once used as projectiles to be shot from the neck of a shaken soda bottle – until one got stuck up Lizzie's nose. The restaurant's two sun terraces had been enclosed, and an extension had been built to one side, but the ground floor facade facing the lake, its arched windows, was unchanged, and now it became clear what had happened. The lake level had dropped by twenty feet. The basalt harbour wall was in fact the old outer jetty, a mere eighteen inches above the water in the old photograph. Now its foundations were exposed and the old harbour behind had been filled and lay below the car park. Israel is a thirsty land, but nothing illustrates more graphically the intensive water abstraction on which its agriculture is based than this irreversible fall in the level of the Sea of Galilee, water that is locked away in the crisp fresh herbs on British supermarket shelves.

In the open-sided restaurant the staff were setting up for the evening. It was a beautiful space, wooden floor and a long wooden bar, tables looking out over the water spread with fresh white cloths, the roof was rigged like a sail and had awnings that could be rolled down to keep out wind or sun or rain. It would not have looked out of place on Sydney Harbour. The staff were equally beautiful, young men and women full of the sun-kissed confidence of secular Israeli youth, and at the bar sat a young man with Bollé sunglasses on top of his crew-cut head, studying a weather map of the Eastern Mediterranean on his laptop. He introduced himself as Ino Gross, son of the Lido's owner. We were both struck by the similarity of the names Gross and Grossmann and he stood me a beer on the strength of it. He managed the restaurant for his father, but his heart was not really in the business. 'That's where I want to be,' he indicated the weather map. The family chartered yachts to Israeli clients that sailed around the Greek islands and the Turkish coast. He did not know much about the history of the Lido, only that his grandfather who came from a family of Bucharest bakers had bought the place in the 1960s when it had been in a terrible state. 'We kept the old building, but of course we renovated and added. We can go and see when you have finished your beer.' The sun had left the water, but still shone on the steep hills of the farther shore, the kibbutz of Ein Gev just visible. To the north of the settlement was the cliff over which the Gadarene swine plunged. Hard by the mole, in the shadow of the western shore, stood the old tower of Daher al-Amr's wall. The old poster advertising the hotel's private bathing-beach had shown it standing some way out into the water, but now its foundations were dry. Behind it were the gardens of the

Scottish Mission. 'We used to climb over the wall when we were kids and play around in there. Yeah, I think there are some graves, but I haven't been in there for a long time. My dad's been trying to buy their beach for years, but they're not selling.'

His father stood in the reception area of the old Lido building, talking earnestly with some employees. Ino introduced me, and Mr Gross looked at me suspiciously as he shook my hand. 'Sure, have a look around,' and he returned to his conversation. The ground-floor dining room was empty, the tables laid for the evening's sitting. It was easy to imagine that the room had not changed much, ceiling fans turning slowly, the light coming through the windows green from the creepers growing over them. 'This is where we feed the bus parties. They have a set menu, chicken or fish. You have tried the fish from the lake, the St Peter's fish? Sure, go upstairs. I'll be outside.' I wandered around the place for a while, the house my grandfather built. It had been his idea to develop the hotel's beach, his dream and maybe his downfall, but I had no sense of his presence in the modest building. Outside, another coach-load had arrived, their aimless milling curtailed by the tour leader ushering them towards the boat and their sunset cruise. Once the boat had left the quayside, the music started, loud pop blaring out over the calm waters of the Sea of Galilee.

Unlike Ino I could not just climb over the wall of the Scottish Garden. Luckily there were other means of entry open to me. I made an appointment with Fred Hibbert, the Church of Scotland minister. 'Be punctual,' he said in a very un-Scottish accent, 'or the guards won't let you in.' The metal gate was opened by a burly Israeli with a side-arm who beckoned me in. Fred was busy and his wife Diana greeted me at the top of the steps of the mission house. She explained the air of nervousness that hung over the building. 'We've

205

had all sorts of threats recently from the ultra-orthodox Jews, all because of the redevelopment plans.' She showed me an architect's model of what the Church of Scotland were proposing to do with the old hospital and the three residences alongside it. The hospital had ceased to function as such in the 1960s and had been converted into a guesthouse. Now the plan was to upgrade it into a luxury hotel, turning the three houses into further accommodation for guests, and to build a large modern annexe on the sloping gardens above the road to the north. 'Of course the mission will continue in this building, which was the old hospital staff quarters.' There had been problems from the outset, objections not just to the development, but also to the continuation at all of a Christian mission in Judaism's second holy city, whose original aim had been the conversion of the Jews. When ancient graves were discovered by the workmen preparing the site for the new building, matters rose to a head. They had tried to keep the discovery quiet until the department of antiquities could determine exactly who was buried there, but the news leaked out and awakened all the old taboos surrounding the foundation of the Roman city that had been dormant since Rabbi Simeon bar Yoha'i's purification. The news had been taken up by the local and national press and the furore intensified. 'They are planning a demonstration next week and in the meantime work has stopped.' If the department of antiquities concluded they were Jewish graves work would stop all together. Diana was clearly shaken by the vehemence of the protests and glad that their five-year tour was nearly up. They would be returning to Surrey soon.

Fred appeared from his office and after some small talk about how he became a minister, he led me out into the heat and to the garden door. On the other side of it was my grandfather's grave. The garden sloped down steeply from the high stone wall beside the road to where the lake water once lapped. Its retreat had left a wide flat area of sand and stones where weeds had gained a foothold. A large mound of basalt blocks was piled against the wall separating the garden from the Lido. 'We pulled down some out-buildings over the road. I can't tell you how many offers I've had for the stones. You can't get the black basalt anymore.' Fred hovered as I tried to take in the garden a little at a time. The slope was terraced and planted with eucalyptus in whose shade no grass grew. On the top two terraces a handful of gravestones stood in the shade. The first monument, a large Celtic cross on a plinth of rough-hewn basalt blocks, was that of David Watt Torrance himself. 'Quite a character. He was married three times. His first wife died in childbirth. His second died during a cholera epidemic and his third outlived him. The first two are buried here, as are four young children and one of his assistants.' His epitaph read, 'Bear ye one another's burdens.' Among the other headstones on the upper level one bearing the Star of David and a Hebrew inscription stood out. 'It's the grave of a child that the rabbis refused to bury in the Jewish cemetery for some small reason, a technicality. The Torrances took pity on the family and offered to bury their child here. Waifs and strays, and those who could not find a resting place elsewhere, like your grandfather.' He left me to find his grave.

On the next terrace down there were three headstones. The first was that of my great-grandfather, a dark plain stone with white letters that had left streaks down the charcoal-grey background. The inscription was in German: '*Hier ruht/ Richard Julius/ Grossmann/ geb. 26. Juli 1873/ in Stuttgart/ gest. 2. Nov. 1916/ in Tiberias/ Evangel. Joh. 10. 20.*' There was no decoration of any kind, just facts as hard as the stone, forty-three when he died, twenty-one when he built the hotel, this man with his face in the shadow of his pith helmet as he stood next to the pump, hands on hips, looking down at his two children. Would John chapter 10 verse 20 reveal any more about him? There was a space between his gravestone and the next – reserved for his wife? – which belonged to their first child, Pauline, born in October 1905 and died in May 1906. The panel of white marble let into a basalt slab was cracked across the bottom where Gothic characters pledged a reunion in the afterlife: **'Auf Wiederseh'n'.** I moved on towards the last stone on the terrace near the Lido wall, dry leaves crackling under foot, the harsh mid-morning sun diffused by the trees and dappling the dark earth, the extreme contrast between light and shade making it hard for the eye to adjust to either. Fritz's headstone was as plain as his father's and its negative image, a light background streaked by the dark letters. The inscription was in German also, in Roman characters though with a stylistic touch – the 'i's dotted despite being capitals – and equally curt: 'Here rests Fritz Paul Grossmann, born 26 November 1908 in Tiberias, died 29 June 1938 in Tiberias', and '*Ev. Matth. 11. 28.*' When eventually I looked away there was a rectangle of light engrammed onto my retinas, a thermal image of the memorial that flashed across the inside of my eyelids every time I blinked.

At my feet lay the mortal remains of my biological grandfather, the skeleton of a 29-year-old male with a bullet hole through the skull that would have set an archaeologist speculating. Already I was older than this man who had never been a grandfather to me. My real grandfather was the only grandfather I had ever known, John Winthrop Hackett, whose death I still felt keenly. And yet standing there before the grave of a man of whose existence I had not even been aware until I was sixteen years old, I did feel a sense of loss and grief, though not my own. I could scarcely imagine what my grandmother felt on that June afternoon almost sixty-three years previously when she had stood on this very spot, next to the freshly dug hole, and had watched the coffin of her husband and the father of her two girls lowered into the ground. Nor what Frieda had felt. The girls were probably too young to feel the loss immediately, but they lived surrounded by the grief of others and as a result of the tragedy they would lose their names, their home, and their nationality, part of their identity that could never be replaced by the new one they assumed when they arrived in England. I had come here not just to see for myself where Fritz Paul Grossmann had lived and died, but also as a messenger from all his family to let it be known that this man was not forgotten, had been loved, was still missed, that despite his failings, his troubles, his despair, his blood still lived.

With melodramatic timing a crow landed in the eucalyptus branches overhead and cawed in mockery of my got-up feelings of pity and sadness. I tried to think unsentimentally about the various explanations I had heard for Fritz's suicide. There are circumstances under which suicide is understandable, if a person is terminally ill or in the depths of grief, but when friends and family 'are at a complete loss', what were others to make of it? Trying to discover a motive in such a case forces one to consider what could happen in one's own life that might prompt one to end it. And how one would do it. Putting 'a bullet through the brain' is in a different category to 'cries for help' like slashing one's wrists or an overdose of pills. What would make someone do that? Something so dramatic? There would surely have to be an equally sensational reason, something like an affair, to justify such a desperate act. Certainly a cause as unromantic and pusillanimous as depression would not have suggested itself to the local populace, not on its own, whereas the modern understanding of clinical depression as a chemical imbalance in the brain shows

209

it to be a resistless force. In the 1930s this medical explanation was not available. In those days depression was regarded as having its roots primarily in external causes, the debt, the affair, the coercion, and if such circumstances were not patent, then the town gossips could be relied upon to provide them. A modern reading of Fritz's death might run: depressive nature plus circumstance equals suicide. A 1930s version would reorder those elements: circumstance equals depression plus suicide. My scepticism told me that the stories about both the coercion and the affair owed more to the need to find a circumstance large enough to fit that equation than to the truth.

I also realized it was unlikely I would ever stand in this garden again. To record my visit I set about photographing the gravestones, and it occurred to me to take some memento home for my mother, something physical from her father's last resting place 'beside the Syrian sea'. I collected a handful of eucalyptus leaves from his grave, long and curved, shaped like the blade of a scythe, and while I was doing so I noticed some small animal had been scratching at the earth and had turned up several small bulbs. I took one of these as well. It did not thrive.

Back in the mission house, Florence, the secretary, brought me a glass of iced water and when I asked produced a Bible from the drawer of her desk. Matthew 11, 28: 'Come unto me, all ye that labour and are heavy laden, and I will give you rest.' Fritz's epitaph was straightforward and apt for someone whose strength had given out under the weight of his burden. Richard's turned out to be much more problematic. The '*Evangelium*', the Gospel, according to St John, chapter 10 verse 20, reads in the King James version: 'And many of them said, He hath a devil, and is mad; why hear ye him?' I had double-checked the inscription, so I had not mistaken the chapter and verse, and '*Evangel.*' could not mean anything other than John's gospel. Just to make sure I checked the other parts of the New Testament credited to St John: three epistles, none longer than five chapters, and the Revelation whose tenth chapter ends at verse eleven. Florence suggested the mason had made a mistake in the inscription. But what was the intended text? John, chapter 20 verse 10 could be ruled out: 'Then the disciples went away again to their own home.' A more likely candidate was chapter 10 verse 28 in light of both the possible confusion between eight and zero and the sentiment of the verse: 'And I give unto them eternal life; and they shall never perish, neither shall any man pluck them out of my hand.' But what if it was no mistake? While the verse itself was a bizarre one to find on a gravestone, was there anything in the context that might explain its appearance there?

John, like Mark, has no time for angels and stars and stables, but, after a little wordy preamble, plunges straight into the waters of the Jordan where Jesus is baptized. By the end of the first chapter Jesus has been hailed as the Messiah and the disciples have assembled around him. The second chapter tells the story of Jesus' first miracle, the turning of water into wine at the marriage at Cana. By chapter 7 Jesus has driven the money changers from the Temple, performed a healing over some distance on the son of a nobleman from Capernaum, healed the lame man at the pool of Bethesda, fed the five thousand, and walked on the waters of the Sea of Galilee. Chapter 7 sees Jesus in the Temple in Jerusalem once more where his provocative preaching and inflammatory claims enrage the Pharisees to such a degree that by the end of chapter 8 'they took up stones to cast at him'. Jesus makes good his escape and on his way out of the Temple he sees a man who has been blind from birth. Jesus spits on the ground and makes a clay poultice which he applies to the man's eyes. Then he tells him to go and wash in the pool of Siloam, after which the man can see. The Pharisees are angered further by this egregious miracle and question both the man and his parents before 'casting him out'. When Jesus hears at the end of chapter 9 that the man has been cast out he goes to him to reaffirm that he is the son of God and then enters into another conversation with some of the Pharisees who were still close by. Chapter 10 contains what he said to them. He speaks in metaphors, a parable about sheep in the fold and the shepherd who enters by the door and leads the sheep out; the sheep follow because they know the shepherd's voice. Anyone who does not enter by the door is but a thief and the sheep will not follow him. The Pharisees need an explanation, and Jesus says (verse 9), 'I am the door: by me if any man enter in, he shall be saved . . .' and (verse 11) 'I am the good shepherd: the good shepherd giveth his life for his sheep.'

17 Therefore doth my Father love me because I lay down my life, that I might take it again.

18 No man taketh it from me, but I lay it down myself. I have power to lay it down, and I have power to take it again. This commandment I have received of my Father.

19 There was a division therefore again among the Jews for these sayings.

20 And many of them said, He hath a devil, and is mad; why hear ye him?

21 Others said, These are not the words of him that hath a devil. Can a devil open the eyes of the blind?

This reference to and paraphrasing of Psalm 23 reinterprets the passage through the valley of the shadow of death as an intimation of Jesus' martyrdom and his resurrection. What sets it apart from Old Testament teaching is the redemptive theme, Jesus' laying down of his life for the sake of his flock, and his willingness to do so. If the mason had not made a mistake in carving Richard Grossmann's tombstone, what did this choice of epitaph mean? Had he too laid down his life? Had he committed suicide as well? It was almost too incredible to contemplate. 'Sorry,' said Florence as she took back the Bible.

⚘ ⚘ ⚘

June is the beginning of the low season in Tiberias, the lowest town on earth. The temperature and humidity will not start to come down until October. On still days the air feels so thick it is hard to breathe. What tourists there are come out at night to stroll along the lake front by the Galilee Experience, browsing in the shops selling seaside tat. Among the buckets and spades, beach balls and novelty sun hats, the restaurants offering fish and chips, one might imagine oneself back in England, except the bar opposite the Chinese take away is called the Big Ben Pub rather than O'Neill's. This is not, however, a place where one would expect to find a Lebanese restaurant, still less one run by a Lebanese, but there it was, next to the telecom bureau. It was irresistible, a carafe of red wine and a bowl of *foul medames* as good, Ramzi assured me, as in his home town of Nabatiye, to which he could never return. He had been an officer in the South Lebanese Army and once the IDF withdrew from their 'Security Zone' he and many of his comrades in arms had sought asylum in Israel. His chef had been his sergeant, and they both had a battle-hardened look about them. It seemed incongruous to find a Lebanese Muslim taking refuge in a Jewish town, but Ramzi pointed out he could not live in the Palestinian areas nor in a predominantly Arab town like Nazareth because he would be shot as a collaborator. As it was he was always looking over his shoulder. There were a few 'Israeli Arabs' that he had come to know in the year he had been in Tiberias, like Hassan from the telecom bureau who was closing up and joined us. Ramzi introduced me: 'He says three generations of his family were born in Palestine.'

'So you are a Palestinian too?' Hassan joked, but his face froze in surprise when I mentioned the Grossmanns of the Hotel Tiberias, and he gave me that look to which I had become accustomed, a weighing up of what I wanted and how much to tell me. His father had worked for my grandfather, he said. It was my turn to be surprised.

His father had been dead for twenty years, and he knew of no one else who had worked at the hotel who was still alive. 'Maybe you could speak to Mrs Jarjoura in Nazareth. She runs a transport company that used to provide all the taxis for the hotel in her father's day. Maybe she could tell you something about your grandfather's death. My father did not say anything about it.' He had an air of someone who was not telling as much as he knew. 'I wish I had listened to his stories because shortly after he died I started working at the Meyouhas Hostel. I do remember him saying that Umm Kalthoum had visited Tiberias once, so maybe she stayed there. You know Umm Kalthoum? The Egyptian singer? He also said George Bernard Shaw stayed once, but one person I know stayed there for sure was the Baha'i leader, the third after the Baha Ullah I think, called Shoghi Effendi Rabbani. He stayed in room 208. Sometimes Baha'is would come to make a pilgrimage and they always wanted to stay in that room.' Hassan's family were originally from Tiberias, but since 1948 they had lived in Nazareth. 'Did you see that sign by the post office? The one that says Tabariyeh was the first mixed town to be "liberated"? What that means is that in 1948 the Jews expelled all the Arabs and took their property. Sure they didn't destroy the Grand Mosque, but they welded the doors shut. At least your family got some compensation for the hotel. I am not even allowed to spend the night in the town. It is illegal. How have I been "liberated"?' He looked around cautiously to check no one was listening. 'You know in the last five years more than one million Russians have arrived in Israel. You saw all the Russian signs in Haifa? The Israelis are worried about the high Arab birthrate, so they let them in without many questions. They have a "right of return" and they are given our land, and I am not even allowed to live in the town of my fathers. Even the Tabaris who used to own the land are not allowed to live on it. They are now in Haifa. And these Russians are not even Jews!' He repeated the genetic 'proof' that the Jews were not a race but followers of a religion, a proof I had first heard from the doctor in Amman. To change the subject I mentioned the photographs of the hotel that were now in the municipal archives. 'Yes, I have heard of those pictures, and of the photographs of the Jewish farming settlements. Every time they show those pictures, every time they publish them in books, they say, "Look, there was nothing here when we came. Nobody was using the land. Nobody was living there, so how can you say it was your land?" But you should find the book of old photographs that was published by Professor Khalidi from Bir Zeit University. It is a collection that shows the Palestinians were here and long before these European Zionists came. Or there is another book called *Palestine, Our Country* by Shukri Araf. And another by Elias Shakhur. You should read those books. We Palestinians should read them too. You know what the most popular book in the West Bank is at the moment? *Mein Kampf.*' So much for changing the subject, but there are no other subjects in Israel apart from land and freedom.

There was one more place I had to see before I left Tiberias, a place some Christians consider to be the Mount of Beatitudes where Jesus delivered the Sermon on the Mount, but that was not the reason I wanted to visit. It is the site of an event whose memory still inspires pride throughout the Arab world. Needless to say, it is not signposted and no one I spoke to in Tiberias knew where it was, even though it lies just a few miles west of the town. It is the mountain known as *Qarne Hattin*, the Horns of Hattin, where in 1187 Salah al-Din defeated the Crusader army so completely that the fall of the Kingdom of Jerusalem was inevitable.

Salah al-Din's ploy worked. The siege of Tiberias drew the Crusaders out of their stronghold at Sepphoris and on the morning of 3 July they marched east with the intention of relieving the Lady Eschiva's citadel. They marched into a trap. 'Experience had shown,' wrote Hackett in his thesis, 'that unity among the Arab states was an ephemeral and personal affair. It was not to be expected that Saladin's empire would outlast Saladin. The Latin settlement had only to tide over the comparatively short period before Saladin's empire should break up ... to be secure from threat of an organized, large-scale attack for a long time to come.' This was the view put forward by Raymond of Tripoli, even though it was his wife under siege. King Guy of Jerusalem, however, was more inclined to listen to Reynald of Châtillon and the Master of the Templars, who counselled action. They called Raymond a coward, and to save his honour he consented to join the expedition, despite realising, as did Hackett, that 'with no reserves it was folly to risk everything in one battle'. Leaving the spring at Turan at noon the Christian army was harried by Salah al-Din's lightly-armed skirmishers and shepherded up onto the plateau near the village of Lubiya. Here they were forced to make camp, far from any source of water.

The Arab village of Lubiya, 'runner beans', was abandoned during the war of independence. Members of a British Zionist group took over the site as a kibbutz, transliterating the Arabic name to Lavi, Hebrew for 'lioness', turning plough-shares into swords. One of the kibbutzim, a man in his forties with a beard and a briefcase, gave me a lift from the bus stop on the main road and set me down by the cattle sheds on the far side of the settlement. He seemed used to Christian visitors to this Mount of Beatitudes (the other more widely accepted one being above the site of ancient Capernaum on the lake's northern shore). His only enquiry was whether I had enough water with me as I limped off, looking like jackal-food. From the west one can appreciate why the hill is called the Horns of Hattin. It has a double summit joined by a saddle that might suggest horns to the fanciful, though they are so weathered they look more like buds on the crown of a heifer than the head gear of the steers in the kibbutz fields. The ground slopes gently up towards the Horns and it was in these fields that the battle took place.

A line of pylons now marks the route that King Guy intended to take, passing across the southern flank of the hill and descending to Tiberias and fresh water, but as his army set out on the morning of 4 July Salah al-Din threw his main force across the line of his march, pushing the Crusaders towards the summit. It had been almost twenty-four hours since the army had last watered. A hot dry wind blew from the west, like the one that parched my throat within moments of setting out from the kibbutz. Salah al-Din used it to good effect. He set fire to the scrub and the flames pushed the Crusaders further up the hill. They were trapped between the Horns, tantalized by the waters of the Sea of Galilee in plain view below and facing annihilation at the hands of the Muslim mujahideen. It was, wrote Hackett, 'a crowning disaster for the Franks in the East'.

After the battle, Salah al-Din wrote to the Caliph that the Franj had 'remained firm with the firmness of those rushing on death'. The figures given for the numbers of Franks killed and captured that day are not reliable. The most conservative Muslim estimate states that thirty thousand were killed and three thousand captured, while two hundred, including Raymond of Tripoli, escaped. Whatever the truth, the Kingdom of Jerusalem lost so many men it could no longer defend itself, and the number of prisoners on sale in Damascus caused such a glut in the slave market that prices fell to less than a tenth of the usual rate. It is told that a prisoner was bartered for a pair of shoes. One eye-witness reported seeing a single Muslim soldier leading thirty captive Franks roped together across the Hauran.

Among those captured were King Guy, the Master of the Temple and Reynald of Châtillon. Guy and Reynald were brought before Salah al-Din, who gave the King water to drink with his own hands, signalling that he would not be harmed by his captor. He did not give water to Reynald, and sending the King out of the tent, he offered Reynald the chance to convert to Islam. When the treacherous knight refused, Salah al-Din ran him through with his sword and commanded his head be cut off. The rest of the captured leaders were sent to Damascus, together with that holiest of Christian relics, the True Cross, found by St Helena during the construction of the Church of the Holy Sepulchre, and torn from the hands of the Bishop of Acre, lying dead on the battlefield.

Salah al-Din's famed generosity was in evidence when he accepted the surrender of the citadel in Tiberias. He allowed the Lady Eschiva to depart with her family and followers and to take her possessions and money with her. It is on such episodes that his chivalrous reputation rests, but little is heard of his treatment of the Templars and Hospitallers captured at Hattin. Knowing it was not the policy of the military orders to ransom their knights, he ordered them all to be killed. The prisoners were offered conversion to Islam, but most chose death instead. They were handed over to amateur executioners and slaughtered while Salah al-Din looked on 'with a glad face'.

More than eight hundred years after his death Salah al-Din is still a living hero in the Arab world. I had heard his name invoked during Friday prayers in the Old City of Cairo, a pious wish that a new Salah al-Din would rise up to drive the new invaders from Europe, the Jews, into the sea. By the citadel in Damascus there is an equestrian statue of him, as idealised as that of Richard Coeur de Lion outside the Houses of Parliament in London. Yet here at the site of his greatest triumph there is no memorial. It is a lonely place. The wind shook the sear brown grasses, the dry soil scattered with chips of red-brown volcanic stone like petrified gouts of blood. Dust devils danced over it and grasshoppers popped from under my feet as I crossed the bowl of ground between the Horns. I sat in the shade of the holm-oaks growing on its eastern rim and peered down into the great rent in the earth's crust. Immediately below on a triangular plateau, tilted up towards the east and ending in a cliff to the north, stands the village of Arbel, its fields blocks of golden stubble, ploughed chocolate earth and dark green orchards. In the afternoon haze the lake showed blue-grey beyond, its northern shore barely visible, the hills to the east, rising to the Golan Heights, brown shapes that seemed to exhale dust. These hills on the western side, the lands of Naphtali and Zebulon, the wildernesses into which Jesus would retire to fast and pray, my mother remembers covered with wild hyacinths and anemones in the spring, echoing with the barks of jackals on winter nights. These were the hills over which Shan Hackett ranged at the head of a troop of cavalry in a noble attempt, ultimately futile, to keep the peace, the pitiless hills in whose shadow Fritz found rest at last by the shore of the Sea of Galilee. Away to the north the cone of Mount Hermon, snow-capped in winter, bulwark at the head of the Great Rift Valley, looked down implacably on the warring tribes.

In the spring of 1944 Bridget and Elizabeth Hackett, aged eight and seven, left their home in the German Colony in Jerusalem and their grandmother Frieda, and joined their mother on a boat sailing for England. Lizzie (formerly known as Liesl) remembers that Frieda, to whom she was very close, was to travel with them, but she had fallen off a table while changing a light bulb a few days before they were to leave, injuring her leg. She could not make the journey, she said. Bridget, who had been Gita, recalls joining a convoy at Port Said and zigzagging across the Mediterranean to avoid U-boats. The convoy passed to the west of Ireland and docked in Liverpool. None of them had ever been to England before. Margaret and the children went to stay with friends in Wiltshire. At boarding school in north Devon, Bridget and Lizzie did not let on that they were German; once when Lizzie had told a friend she had had to endure taunts in the playground. They already spoke unaccented English, having attended the British Community School in Jerusalem. That made the transition easier, and so the process of forgetting began.

The process of remembering that I had set in train sixty years after Fritz had died is still in motion, stirring up happy as well as sad memories. After my return from Israel it was wonderful to be able to show the three women photographs of the Meyouhas Hostel and the Lido, to hear Margaret laugh in pleasant surprise that the hotel had changed so little, to see her smile as she remembered swimming and playing tennis at the Lido, the parties they had in the restaurant. My mother pointed out the steps she had been climbing when she had pulled the tail of the family's Alsatian; it turned around and bit her face. She has a scar on the bridge of her nose. That was why she had to have a course of anti-rabies shots at the Scottish Hospital. The dog was put down and she still blames herself for that. Lizzie's recall constantly surprised me. Although she was only two and a half when they left Tiberias she remembered the chemist opposite the hotel where the milk-and-honey supermarket now stood, the loud music from the electrical goods shop, the lemonade vendor. Of the three she had kept in closest contact with the German side of the family, driving around Germany visiting relatives in the A35 van that had been bought with her share of the compensation for the hotel. She saw Frieda three or four times more before her death in 1972. Whatever feelings of loss and sadness they felt on seeing pictures of the tombstones in the garden of the Scottish Mission they left unspoken. They were glad to see that the graves were well tended. To the questions whether or not the Grossmanns of Tiberias had been members or supporters of the Nazi Party and whether Frieda had kept a diary the answer both times was no. There were two other surviving members of the family I could ask, Dore and Rix, and as luck would have it their annual reunion at a spa south of Munich was less than two months away. I was cordially invited.

In the meantime I had a number of leads to follow. Fred Hibbert had told me that a considerable archive of Torrance family material had been bequeathed to the University of Dundee library. My initial enquiry suggested that there was enough material relating to the Grossmanns to make a visit worthwhile, but my highest expectations were disappointed. There were files and folders and boxes of photographs to go through, ranging from pictures of the staff and patients of the Scottish Hospital to snapshots of family holidays in India and Europe, all meticulously catalogued and preserved, regardless of historical or artistic worth. There was an intriguing album illustrating the diseases that the Doctors Torrance, father and son, had to treat including anthrax and hydatid cysts, even a picture of a 'woman with breast weighing 5lbs' and one of a 'woman with supernumerary nipples' that had been printed on a postcard blank. Among the snapshots, however, were a handful that included Grossmann family members, providing my first indistinct glimpses of Frieda and Rix on excursions with the Torrances to al-Salt and Irbid on the eastern side of the Jordan and Mount Tabor near Nazareth. There was one full-length portrait of the two of them together dating from May 1926 when Rix was twelve and nearly as tall as Frieda, a good-looking boy in shorts and a matelot jacket, his arm around his mother's shoulders. Frieda's dark hair is parted in the centre and tied back, her warm smile creases her plain kindly face. There were also a large number of professionally taken photographs, mostly by G. Eric Matson of the American Colony Photographic Department, a photographer of considerable talent. His pictures of flying boats on the Sea of Galilee and the Lido were of especial interest to me (one of the Lido, a postcard, asked the Torrances to pass on the sender's best regards to Greta, Brigitte and Fritz), as was a series taken on a journey to Jerash and the Jebel Druze he made around 1934 in the company of Herbert Torrance and Rix Grossmann. Here is Rix by a classical column in a suit with plus-four trousers, square-shouldered and handsome, grown into the sporting frame noted in Karl Ruff's letter. Among the professional pictures there was also evidence of the Grossmanns' involvement in that business. A series of pictures showing the flood of 1938 were stamped on the back 'Hotel Tiberias. Fritz Grossmann', and one bore his handwriting: 'To Dr Torrance from Fritz.' It seemed Fritz had dabbled in photography like his father, but he had not taken these, Margaret said. She remembers being on a visit in the Lebanon when the flood struck. The greatest treasure to emerge from the scrupulously archived dross was a photograph taken by Richard Grossmann senior of the lake shore by the old town wall. It was a beautiful albumen print from a glass-plate negative and must have been taken around the turn of the century. It shows the townswomen going about their daily chores, drawing water, washing clothes and cooking utensils, and a fishing boat, oars stowed and nets piled in the stern, the fishermen landing their catch. On the back is a stamp reading 'R. Grossmann and Co., Photographers, Tiberias (Palestine)' in English and Arabic and Herbert Torrance's handwritten notes: 'No wonder there were outbreaks of cholera and enteric diseases! Father took the "boilers" from the hospital wash-house, took them into the town, so that the people could obtain "boiled water". Yet they used this hot water for washing clothes – & filled their jars for drinking water from the lake.'

I had been hoping to find written material or printed matter referring to the Grossmanns. I thought there might be a register of the graves in the mission garden or some reference to the tragedy that had overtaken their neighbours, but there was none. Such notebooks as there were dealt with medical matters and natural history, and the cuttings included such deathless prose as an article on snakes from the *TV Times* of 27 April 1970. Archivists are not obliged to make value-judgements. It was a long way to go for very little and the greatest boon was the reading time the train journey afforded.

There was more to find in the Thomas Cook archive, a company that also seems, in its early days at least, hardly ever to have thrown away a piece of paper. Large leather-bound ledgers appeared from the vaults containing agreements made between the firm and various hotels, guides and transport operators, all copied out in a beautiful copperplate hand. There were four that concerned 'R. Grossmann [sic], Hotel Keeper, Tiberias', the earliest dating from November 1900 relating to boat tours of the lake. It schedules the charges that Grossmann could make for the various destinations – Tabgha, Magdal, the mouth and outlet of the Jordan, the Baths – and stipulates there should be no more than six persons in each boat, 'the best boats that are in his possession'. Payment is to be made in the firm's 'vouchers', the forerunner of travellers cheques. For its part, the firm undertakes 'to employ the said Grossmann at all times for the conveyance of travellers', and in return 'the said Grossmann agrees & binds himself not to have any arrangements or dealings or anything at all to do with H. Gaze & Son, Rolla Floyd, F. Clark, Perowne & Lunn or any other imitators of the said firms'. (Rolla Floyd was a survivor of the American settlement in Jaffa, staying on to become a dragoman for Thomas Cook's tours before branching out on his own.) The agreement was to run concurrently with the one made some months earlier between the parties concerning accommodation at the hotel, but no record of that contract exists. Exactly when Thomas Cook became first involved in the hotel cannot be discovered from this agreement, but by the time of the next agreement in July 1904 Grossmann is referred to as 'lessee of the building known as the Tiberias Hotel owned by the said Firm' and speaks of an outstanding debt to the company of 14,000 francs. The document goes on to outline the conditions for a further loan of 12,500 francs 'to build a third storey & to furnish it'. Grossmann was to repay the money at

5 per cent over a period of twelve years, when 'the Firm will transfer the property back to his name', so it would seem the capital needed to build the hotel had originally come from somewhere else. Thomas Cook's association with the Hotel Tiberias therefore began between 1894 and 1900.

Over the following seven years business must have been good, as the next agreement concerning board and lodging rates notes that Grossmann had already repaid 10,000 francs of the loan. (In 1911 one franc was worth 9 pence ha'penny, and one American dollar bought four shillings.) He is even referred to as the 'proprietor', though the hotel is still in the name of Thomas Cook, and the firm is willing to lend him a further 50,000 francs on the same terms, but with no time limit. The purpose of this new loan, it is stated, is to enable Grossmann to build and furnish an extension. On each occasion, a set of photographs of the finished work was sent to Head Office in Ludgate Circus. These too were kept. Though the two showing the third storey in 1905 were very faded and had been folded, I had seen neither before and they showed an angle from the roadway that included the town wall and old arch. The ones of the 1911–12 extension on the side of the hill were the same as those in the Tiberias municipal archive, the mortar bright and new, and included several of the rear courtyard and front terrace. Jill Lomer, the archivist, said the figures were unidentified and I was able to tell her who they were, Richard Grossmann senior in his *sola topi* and his two children Dore and Fritz.

The last document was a curious one. Rather than being entered into a ledger, it was a carbon copy of the actual contract and signed by R. Grossmann on 29 January 1912 in the presence of the German Consul in Haifa, Dr Julius Loytved-Hardegg. It was a bill of sale for the entire contents of the hotel for the sum of 50,000 francs. Now it seemed that

Thomas Cook owned the hotel lock, stock and bed linen. As the sum corresponded to the previous year's loan the intention must have been to discharge that debt, and a note on the back of the last page reads 're loan to Grossmann Tiberias'. What was most interesting about the document was that it provided a schedule of the contents of the hotel: 101 iron bedsteads, 110 mattresses, 87 mosquito nets ... 235 chairs ... 1 harmonium ... various crockery decorated 'Hotel Tiberias'. There were 206 wine glasses, 253 water glasses, but only 9 for champagne. Tea pots, coffee pots, milk pots, chocolate pots, cream pots and custard stands. Salt holders, sugar basins, wine coolers, tea filters, nut crackers, menu holders and epergnes – all the accoutrements of genteel Edwardian dining. Whether the contents of the hotel were actually worth 50,000 francs or were merely being put up as security is impossible to determine.

After 1912 there are no further records relating to the Hotel Tiberias, and so no indication of whether the outstanding sum mentioned in the 1911 agreement and due in 1916 was repaid on time. One has to imagine it was not as a result of the world war and Richard Grossmann's death. The silver lining in this case was that the hotel being in Thomas Cook's name at the end of the war probably saved Frieda and her three children from deportation to Egypt with the rest of Palestine's German residents. What the hotel's financial position was after the First World War is also unclear.

When I mentioned the Kaiser's visit to the Holy Land, Jill Lomer produced a folder containing every last receipt and an album of Krikorian's photographs. I knew the Kaiser had not visited Galilee, but I had some time left so I flicked through the bills from the Hotels du Parc and Jerusalem, and was rewarded with something completely unexpected. It seemed that the Kaiser's agents had looked into the possibility of an excursion to the Sea of Galilee and had stayed at the Hotel Tiberias. There was a receipt on headed notepaper for Graf Wedel and his party on 19 October 1898 and for 'Marschall Lejivail Pascha' on 31 October amounting to some 217 francs and signed 'Krafft & Grossmann'. Of greatest interest was the letterhead itself. Engraved in Stuttgart by A. Kunz, it bears the legend '*Gruss aus Tiberias*', 'Greetings from Tiberias', and incorporates a general view of the town, probably taken from a Frith photograph, with a very fanciful representation of the 'Tiberias-Hotel' framed by orange blossom and date palms. It depicts a three-storey building with a flat roof from which flies the Reich flag. The headed paper was probably ordered soon after the building of the hotel in 1894 and in 1898 it still only had two storeys. When the third was finally built in 1904–5 it had a pitched roof. The letterhead indicates the ambitious plans Krafft and Grossmann had for the future expansion of their business.

Always innovative, Thomas Cook was one of the first firms to publish its own in-house magazine, the *Traveller's Gazette*, which carried feature articles on destinations as well as advertisements for the firm's tours and partner companies. It was renamed the *Excursionist* after the First World War. The entries about the Hotel Tiberias in the company's guidebooks were without exception bland, referring to 'modern sanitary arrangements' and no more, so I turned to the magazine in the hope of finding a first-hand account of the hotel. The only reference I came across, however, was in the same vein, adding that it had 'an excellent situation on the slope behind the town' and 'there is probably no more comfortable hotel in the Holy Land' (*Traveller's Gazette*, February 1914).

It occurred to me that there might be other references in the Imperial Airways magazine, if such a thing had existed, which prompted me to approach the British Airways Archive and Museum Collection at Heathrow. This in turn led to a series of communications with their Imperial Airways expert, Dermot Doran, which veered from the pedantic to the bizarre; one of his telephone calls came through while my wife was in labour and was answered by the midwife, to whom he tried to dictate a long and complex message. His first letter had included his correspondence with the editor of a quarterly magazine called the *Wartime Newsletter*, containing 'personal reminiscences of the events of WWII', in which he had sought to correct factual inaccuracies that had appeared in readers' correspondence about a picture of a flying boat, 'Canopus on Lake Tiberias'. His original letter set out 'to generally collate and slightly correct' the published responses, but when the editor questioned his sources there was a certain sniffiness in his reply that his information came from 'the original documents and records on which both contemporary journals and subsequent books have been based (though not always with 100 per cent accuracy)'. I had been warned, and was warned again by his second letter in which he found it necessary to tell me that 'we had to write recently to an Australian journalist proposing a film on flying boats in Australia: "British Airways would not wish to see any confusion . . . arising from historical and technical accuracy being sacrificed for entertainment/journalistic value."' He enclosed a brief history of Imperial Airways and their use of flying boats on the 'Empire Air Routes' which eventually reached Sydney and Cape Town. This letter also contained a helpful five-step plan of action for me to follow, step number three being: 'You weave the information . . . into your draft text re the Tiberias Hotel etc. – and send us a copy – which we will check – and then perhaps a further draft.' Not wishing to take up any more of Mr Doran's time I leave that loom-work to others.

I did, however, follow step five and visited the archive at

Heathrow to read through the *Imperial Airways Gazette*, published between 1928 and 1939. Dermot Doran and the other volunteers, all ex-BA staff, were without exception most friendly and helpful, and Mr Doran was not nearly so pernickety in person as he was on paper. He fetched the bound copies of the *Gazette* and then bustled around at the very peripheries of my vision, blowing unconsciously between pursed lips in a way that was neither quite a whistle nor quite a tune. The magazine exuded the confidence in Modernity and Progress of the interwar years, the bold designs and luxurious decor copiously illustrated under headings like 'The Shape of Things to Come', which in the case of the flying boat proved to be the shape of things past shortly thereafter. The first flying boat to land on Lake Tiberias, of the 'Scipio' class, was here described by one poetic soul as 'a mightily powerful water-witch'. Pictures of the interior of a 'C' class Empire flying boat, the successor to the 'Scipio', showed its promenade saloon, smoking cabin and sleeping berths – 'Look at the comfortable chairing!' For a time flying boats did indeed seem to be the future of commercial aviation. There was even an outrageous piggy-back design, one flying boat on top of another, developed to fly non-stop across the Atlantic. The Second World War put an end to those heady days and prompted the development not only of land aircraft with higher pay-loads and longer ranges (i.e., bombers), but also of the jet engine.

The pioneering spirit of Imperial Airways, their vision to make accessible the furthest corners of the Empire, was not always shared by their passengers. One of the few accounts I found touching on the hotel, by a Mr W.D.H. McCullough, described the inhabitants of Tiberias as being 'like the crowd in a musical comedy'. He goes on: 'After a remarkably good dinner [presumably at the Hotel Tiberias] I strolled down to the sea front and wandered about, gathering my first impressions of the East. I very quickly came to the conclusion that there is a lot to be said for the West.' Another correspondent, the Reverend P.B. Clayton, somewhat flown with Parnassian liquor and on his way to Persia, described his first sight of the empyreal craft at Brindisi: 'In the wine-darkness of the Adriatic an hour before dawn, *Scipio* swam like a fretful whale, ordered to wait around for Jonah. Scarce were we swallowed up, six passengers decanted from a coracle, when Brindisi became a row of yellow stars beneath and then behind us. We now rose high, described a cut between a demivolt and a semiquaver, and made for Byron's holyland. Now the day broke in shreddings of cloth of gold, spattered with flames of fire. Airmen are up betimes. The early worm they covet is the still tranquil air, in which the thievish sun has no time to pick the deeper pockets . . .' And so on in a mix of metaphor, simile and allusion to Palestine where a man of the cloth might have been expected to drench the land with Tyrian purple, but: 'somehow, the air view quite expels the pilgirm spirit during the time of transit'. He recovers his powers of description in time for the landing: 'By now, the Lake of Galilee began to unfold its perfections to our gaze. Clouds encompassed it about through which the sunshine stole like a shy worshipper, constant but never habituated to his high privilege . . . So, with a sigh, and a soft splashing of foam, we found ourselves at rest on Lake Tiberias.' His overseas posting was literature's loss and Persia's gain.

In the meantime Mr Doran had located a report from a less excitable pen, that of Imperial Airways' Traffic Superintendent, Near East Area, concerning the survey flight of the *Ceres* on 6 September 1937. Of more concern to him than the soft splashing of foam were the moorings, pontoons, launches and refuelling arrangements on the lake. He met, among others,

'Mr Grossmann, the owner of the Tiberias Hotel'. 'The arrangements made at the Tiberias Hotel were very satisfactory, Mr Grossmann himself taking a personal interest in all these matters . . . For the departure the following morning Mr Grossmann and all the servants . . . were on the top line, so much so that it is satisfactory to note that the departure was made according to the schedule laid down.' At the height of the service in 1939, shortly before Imperial Airways merged with the original British Airways to form the British Overseas Airways Corporation (BOAC), there were two flights every weekday, except Wednesday, scheduled to land on the lake, one in each direction, and at the weekend there was one inbound on Saturday and one outbound on Sunday. The Sea of Galilee became for a while an international airport.

I did find some references to the hotel in other libraries. The old Baedeker guides helped identify when the hotel became the sole possession of Richard Grossmann – some time before 1906 – so it might be reasonable to assume the first loan he obtained from Thomas Cook in 1900 was used to buy out his partner Krafft. When writing about Tiberias most of the pre-1939 travellers repeat the story about the King of the Fleas holding court there. The adjectives 'shabby', 'squalid', 'miserable', 'filthy' invariably feature in their descriptions. They say very little about the hotel, although they would certainly have visited if not stayed. One climbs to the hotel's flat roof to look down on the town. Another expresses his relief upon leaving Tiberias: 'The quiet and shade of Tabgha was very welcome after the heat and the bustle, the shouting Arabs, and the incessant tourist clatter and clamour of the Hotel Tiberias.' Gertrude Bell calls it a 'nice little hotel' in her diary entry for 26 April 1902, when it was still little.

What irked me most was that I had not found anything to counter Helga Dudman's claims about the Grossmanns, made in her history of Tiberias. It remained the most complete treatment in English, and I was curious to track down one of its sources, Sven Hedin's *Jerusalem*. Hedin had made his name as an explorer and writer in the 1890s, publishing copious amounts of material on Persia, the Caucasus and Central Asia. The Swede had studied geography at the University of Berlin where he was taught by Ferdinand von Richthofen, the man who coined the term 'The Silk Road' for the trade routes across Asia, and his strong pro-German political sentiments stem from this period. In his opinion, a powerful German state was desirable not only as a counterbalance to British imperial expansion, but also to check Russian ambitions in Scandinavia. When the First World War broke out his political support found practical expression. He visited the western and eastern fronts and wrote books about both experiences; while *Jerusalem* is for the most part a travelogue it includes an account of the '*Suësfront*' where Turks and Germans were fighting the British imperial forces in the Sinai. The German edition was published in Leipzig in 1918. Between the wars Hedin continued his explorations of Inner Asia and his voluminous writings. As well as the popular accounts of the expeditions he undertook between 1926 and 1935, he set about publishing their scientific findings; this work ran to 54 volumes. His pro-German sympathies were reawakened, as was Germany's national pride, by Hitler's rise to power. He accepted an invitation to speak at the opening of the Berlin Olympics in 1936, and later toured Germany as a guest of the National Socialists. In 1937 his book *Germany and World Peace* represented a propaganda coup for the Nazis and shows how badly the 72-year-old had been misled. By the end of the war even Hedin had to admit in a letter to a German friend: 'Everything has gone wrong in the Third Reich. Hitler is completely mad.'

In his day Hedin had been the most famous explorer in the

world and author of numerous bestsellers about his journeys in Asia, yet when I telephoned a London bookshop specialising in travel in an attempt to discover if there had ever been an English edition of *Jerusalem*, the assistant had never heard of him. I tracked down a copy of the German edition in a Hamburg bookshop via the internet. It was printed in old Gothic type and well illustrated with photographs and Hedin's pencil sketches. The relevant passage about Richard Grossmann describes him as an 'industrious' man who used his free time to collect natural history specimens for foreign museums. The local wild life must have been their chief topic of conversation as Hedin provides a long list of all the species to be found thereabouts, including leopards and cheetahs. Grossmann's wife is '*prächtig*', 'splendid', his children '*liebenswürdig*', 'friendly', and he is credited with having earned, before the war, '*ein kleines Vermögen*', better translated a 'modest' rather than a 'small fortune', since there is no sense in the German phrase that a 'small fortune' is actually a large amount of money. Hedin then accompanies Grossmann to a reception given by the Turkish authorities in celebration of the anniversary of the adoption of their new constitution. All the town's dignitaries are present, the Mufti, the Chief Rabbi, and after a display of Turkish folk-dancing from the soldiers, a young Jewish girl from Damascus danced 'like Salome', though in a manner that was both 'noble and chaste'. Hedin may have become pro-Nazi in later life, but there is certainly no evidence of anti-Semitism here.

Whether it was a 'modest' or a 'small' fortune may seem like a point of little consequence, but the language of the conflict in the Middle East is mined with nuances and slight changes of emphasis of this sort which when taken together add up to a concerted propaganda campaign. Helga Dudman's use of the word 'disappeared' in writing about the Grossmanns' departure from Tiberias is another example. While it is true they had to leave quickly taking very little with them, that fact does not, as Dudman implies, prove that they were Nazis, only that they were German citizens. (In other territories of the British Empire, Jews of German origin were detained as well; were they also Nazis?) Yet the whole thrust of Dudman's characterization of the Grossmanns is to leave us in no doubt that Nazis they were, who, having wrested a small fortune from a country not theirs, having played host to German officers and the latterly pro-Nazi Hedin, slipped away like the thieves they were at the moment when something righteous was going to be done about their widely suspected and decidedly criminal political sympathies. If it turned out that Dudman's allegations had no basis in fact, I wondered momentarily if I could sue her for libel. What those allegations chiefly rested on, according to Elisheva Ballhorn, was Frieda's diary, and without that I could refute nothing; denials from surviving members of my family could easily be dismissed with: 'they would say that, wouldn't they?' I needed the diary, but in the meantime I hoped Paul Sauer's book about the Templers would shed light on the political affiliations of Germans in the Holy Land immediately before the Second World War.

The only problem was I could not find a copy and searching the internet proved unsuccessful in this case. What I did discover was that the *Tempelgemeinde* in Germany and the Temple Society of Australia (TSA) both have websites where one can read the latest edition of the Templer newsletter, the *Warte*, or an English translation of part of Christoph Hoffmann's magnum opus, *Occident and Orient* (1875), which lays out the founder's religious beliefs and reasons for settling in the Holy Land. The TSA had its own publication, the *Templer Record*, which reads much like a parish magazine, detailing Tea Mornings, Ladies' Afternoons, Working Bees, Services, Retreats, Confirmations. The names are the same, Hoffmann and Herrmann and Lange and Klink and Beilharz and Ruff, and the addresses by the Elders highlight the problems faced by every reforming religious movement once the founders and their heirs have passed on: a dwindling, ageing membership and a re-evaluation of the original millenniarist message in the cold light of the fact that the world has not ended, yet. 'Now, did [Christoph Hoffmann] or did he not seriously believe in the second coming of Christ? . . . To me the question is academic.' I posted a message on the 'Reader Response and Suggestions' page and followed links to other sites where I found a complete text of the reparations agreement between the Australian, German and Israeli governments, and, on the Australian War Memorial site, group photographs of the German internees taken at the Tatura Internment Camp. Some cannot help smiling at the camera, but most are stern-faced, sitting and standing in front of corrugated iron huts with neat little gardens, each group numbered for identification purposes. Here are Fasts and Ruffs and Blaichs, here is Hermann Tietz who attended Fritz's funeral, and this was where Frieda and Margaret, Gita and Liesl might have ended up, if Shan Hackett had not intervened. They might have become Australian rather than English.

I received several e-mails as a result of my posting, a couple from Israelis living in the old German settlements who seemed to be pumping me for information, and one from an Englishman, Martin Higgins, whose mother had been born to a Templer family and had married a Palestine policeman. Martin and his sister had grown up in wartime Palestine, leaving when the British mandate ended in 1948. He wrote to tell me his sister remembered Frieda Grossmann from those postwar days, living on her own in the German Colony in Jerusalem, giving lessons in needlecraft. His sister still had an example of her work, a crocheted egg-cosy in the form of a girl in a bonnet whose dirndl fitted over the egg. Martin had been an intelligence officer, specialising in Eastern Europe, at GCHQ in Cheltenham, and since his retirement he had been researching Templer genealogies, making several trips to the archive in Stuttgart. He also had a copy of Sauer's book, *The Holy Land Called*, and was kind enough to lend it to me.

Professor Dr Paul Sauer's distinguished career has been based on his works on the history of Baden-Württemberg, becoming deputy director of the state archive, and director of the Stuttgart city archives in 1986. He has also undertaken private commissions, notably a history of the Beilharz family which was privately published in Australia by Ludwig Beilharz, who then proposed Sauer should write a complete history of the Temple Society. The result was *Uns Rief Das Helige Land* and Sauer notes in his preface that the Temple Society 'provided funds and promised their total support'. The book found an independent publisher in Germany, but the English translation was published privately by the Temple Society of Australia. As a result of the support and close involvement of the Temple Society, the work cannot be considered to be totally impartial, and Sauer acknowledges this problem in his preface: 'My aim was to present an objective and balanced account . . . Certainly, the assessment of certain periods and historical events, such as . . . an objective description of the National Socialist era, was not easy.' With this in mind I turned to the chapter covering the years 1933–9.

During the political turbulence of the 1850s, when the Friends of Jerusalem was founded, its leaders Hoffmann and Hardegg were ardent supporters of German nationalism. They saw the unification of all German-speaking peoples in evangelical terms, as a step on the road to widespread recognition of the truth of their message, which in turn would lead to a national drive to build the 'spiritual Temple'. In advocating that all German-speaking peoples should unite they were opposed, as was the Württemberg government, to the Prussian plan to exclude Austria from a unified German state. They had left Württemberg shortly after the war between Prussia and Austria that decided the issue in Prussia's favour. Once settled in Palestine they realized their need for financial and political support from the new German Reich, of which their home state was now a part, and the welcome they extended to the Kaiser and their loyalty during the First World War were practical expressions of their patriotism. With Germany's defeat the precariousness of their position in Palestine without imperial protection was painfully apparent. The British deported them.

After another period of political turbulence and financial hardship in Germany, Hitler's rise to power seemed to restore not only national unity but also international prestige. As citizens of a strong German Reich they felt more secure in their position as a national minority in a British-administered territory. Living outside Germany the Templers had no experience of how the National Socialists had set about achieving the 'miracle'. The rebirth of the German *Volk* also coincided with the coming of age of a generation of Templers who had never known the founders of their society, and its spiritual precepts were of less importance to them as a result. As in Germany, the German youth of Palestine was to prove a rich source of recruits. Nevertheless, when Hitler became Chancellor in 1933, there were in Palestine only five members of the National Socialist German Workers' Party (NSDAP). One of these, the 55-year-old Cornelius Schwartz, was a well-respected Templer who would occasionally be chosen to give the sermon at their services. He was appointed the State Party

Group Leader and was soon emboldened to be openly critical of the Templer elders' opposition to the NSDAP, and of their blindness to the great 'national reawakening' in Germany. This he attributed to their 'lack of moral fibre'.

If the Temple elders were not enthusiastic about the NSDAP's vision of a 'national community', Germany's Jews were left in no doubt that they were not going to be included. A boycott of Jewish businesses was announced to begin on 1 April 1933, and Germans in Palestine rightly feared that such an action would lead to a corresponding Jewish boycott. Some Templers also foresaw the antagonism that would be aroused by the displaying of the new German swastika flag and petitioned the consulates in Palestine not to fly it. The NSDAP policy of 'Gleichschaltung', 'coordination', was soon felt in Palestine. All areas of German life were to be brought into line with National Socialist ideology. New teachers arrived in the Templer schools who taught the children the Horst-Wessel Song. National holidays became National Socialist events and non-participation was characterized as a betrayal of one's Volk. Sports clubs flew the swastika at their pre-match parades and cultivated the idea of German physical superiority. Branches of the Hitler Youth and the Band of German Girls were established in every settlement. Gleichschaltung even went as far as to preach a new kind of Christianity, that of the 'Deutsche Glaubensbewegung', the German Religious Movement, which claimed the National Socialists 'conceive the essence of Christianity more purely and nobly' than dogma-bound churches. To the pro-NSDAP editor of the Warte this sounded like a reformulation of Hoffmann's earliest objections to the institutionalized denominations of the church in Württemberg, one of the tenets of the Temple Society itself, and from the May edition of 1933 the newsletter became an organ of Nazi ideology, even promulgating the anti-Semitic theories of

Houston Stewart Chamberlain and Alfred Rosenberg. During 1934 there was an intensive campaign of lectures and compulsory gatherings at which speakers like Schwarz sought to inculcate Nazi ideology in the settlers. By the end of 1935, when the Templers in Palestine numbered some 1300, there were 250 members of the National Socialist Workers' Party. Even those rare voices that spoke with caution about the Nazis' racial and religious policies, like Dr Richard Hoffmann, Georg Wagner and Philipp Wurst, were broadly in support of their quest for national unity. Wagner hoped the NSDAP would bring 'the realization of a perfect community'.

What the Jewish reaction was to these developments is easily imagined. While there were small-scale demonstrations outside the various consulates to protest the flying of the swastika flag, the boycott of German goods was more widespread, especially after the passing in Germany of the 1935 Nuremberg Race Laws. Sauer quotes a newspaper report from the more moderate end of the spectrum: 'For fifty years the Germans and the Jews have been living side by side . . . and the mutual relations were more than good, they were excellent. It was customary to visit each other in the settlements, it seemed as though it was our mutual duty to develop shoulder to shoulder this part of Asia.' That had all changed with Hitler's rise to power; although, says Sauer, 'the German settlers continued their efforts to entertain good relations with the Jewish population . . . [but] they were powerless against the growing suspicion and the increasing animosity of a considerable portion of the Jews.' He is also remarkably coy about whether the espousal of the NSDAP and the inculcation of Nazi ideology led to anti-Semitic feelings and actions among the German settlers. He notes that the Office of Germans Abroad prohibited German subjects from meddling in the politics of their host countries and from encouraging the formation of local

'National Socialist' organizations. The public display of Nazi uniforms and insignia was also discouraged, though Sauer reports one occasion, an athletics match between the British Palestine Police and the German Sports Club at Sarona, when the swastika and the Union Jack flew side by side. Almost the only mention of anti-Semitic indoctrination in Sauer's chapter is this: 'From a Hitler Youth diary, preserved from Jaffa, it is alarmingly evident how high, initially, anti-Semitism ranked in the political training programme. The Hitler Youth leader explained to the boys the ominous paper . . . [the] *Protocols of the Wise Men of Zion*.'

At the approach of war the German consulates advised all men of an age to qualify for military service to return to Germany. Some 247 men heeded the call, most travelling on a Greek boat chartered for this purpose. Those who remained were interned in the Mazra's camp near Acre, where they celebrated with enthusiasm Hitler's fifty-first birthday on 20 April 1940. The rest of the Germans in Palestine – the women, children and elderly – were confined in their settlements around which were placed barbed-wire perimeter fences fifteen feet high. Their guards were mostly Jewish. Sauer reports that news of the German advance through the Low Countries and France caused 'an enthusiastic, euphoric atmosphere in the perimeter settlements'. The British confiscated all radios in May. In July 1941, after twenty-two months behind barbed wire, it was decided that the German internees should be transported to Australia. In all 665 people, of whom 536 were Templers, were loaded onto a train (though not into cattle wagons) and taken to Suez where they boarded the *Queen Elizabeth* for the three-week voyage to Australia. In Sydney they were met by 'heavily armed soldiers with fixed bayonets', and after another long train journey they arrived at Tatura, Camp 3, some hundred miles north of Melbourne. The camp was divided into four compounds, one of which was already occupied by German Australians among whom were a number of Jews who had fled Nazi Germany only to be confined with their tormentors. Sauer writes: 'In the camp, the various N[ational] S[ocialist] organizations, especially the Hitler Youth [HJ] and the BdM [Band of German Girls], now developed bustling activity.' It was not long before the tensions caused by this proximity broke out into unrest. The Hitler Youth in one compound took to singing Nazi songs by the fence dividing it from the compound where the German Jews were quartered, who tried to drown them out with shouts of 'Nazi pigs'. When one of the singers tried to climb the wire the guards fired warning shots. Thereafter the German Jews had their compound to themselves.

The Australian authorities did little to restrain the activities of the pro-Nazi internees. In December 1941 they even returned to them the portraits of Hitler and NS literature that had been confiscated earlier. The Hitler Youth organized a Midsummer Festival during that month. Hitler's fifty-third birthday was celebrated in April. The drama group put on *The Merchant of Venice*. It was not until December 1942 that the camp commandant demanded that all National Socialist activities cease, but portraits of Hitler continued to be displayed, insignia worn and the Nazi salute given. News of Hitler's death prompted a service of memorial, the address given 'in memory of our Führer Adolf Hitler and his friend Benito Mussolini'. A week after Victory in Europe Day, the camp authorities finally banned all National Socialist announcements and the Nazi salute. All symbols, flags, badges, banners and NS literature were to be surrendered as well as all portraits of Hitler. The internees disobeyed this order, preferring to burn the offending articles themselves rather than give them up. Sauer concludes this part of his history thus: 'On 10 July 1945, the internees were forced to watch a film of German atrocities in the concentration camp of Bergen-Belsen. Most of the men and women considered the crimes shown so monstrous that they regarded them as infamous enemy propaganda.'

However uncritical Sauer's account of the Templers' support for Hitler and National Socialism, the facts he reports add up to an unanswerable indictment. Nevertheless, he is keen, as were the leaders of the society immediately after the war, to refute untruthful allegations made about the German settlers in Palestine. The most frequent of these were that the Templers had constituted a Nazi Fifth Column against the British and that they had materially supported the Arabs in their conflict with the Jews. One of the more bizarre claims, and one repeated as fact during his celebrated 1961 trial, was that Adolf Eichmann, the Nazi Head of Jewish Affairs, had been born in Palestine to a Templer family. (He was in fact born in Soligen, a town between Düsseldorf and Köln.) In the face of such accusations the Temple Society felt constrained to issue a public statement: 'We are Germans and we have held a patriotic view. We do not deny for a moment that a considerable number of our members in Palestine believed in the so frequently proclaimed honest intentions of the Hitler Government. However, we would like to meet a Jew who has suffered wrong at the hands of a Templer. If the majority of decent Jews in Palestine were not under such pressure from their own extremists, they would probably be honest enough to admit these facts.' Such a statement did not win them many friends in Palestine, though they still hoped they would be allowed to return to their properties, as they had been after the First World War. Those who had not been transported to Australia remained internees in Palestine, but now the guards who had originally been there to prevent escape could not protect them from attack. Wilhelma was subjected to drive-by shootings. The mayor of Sarona was assassinated. Four young German men were killed in two separate incidents in November 1946. The Mandatory authorities announced that the remaining Germans would be deported, but still the Templers clung to the hope that somehow they would be able to carry on their eighty years of settlement work in the Holy Land.

As the end of the British Mandate approached matters came to a head. One night in April 1948 the Haganah raided Waldheim. Two Germans were killed, a woman and a man in their sixties and a 42-year-old woman was wounded. The leader of the raid claimed to have found soap in one of the houses marked 'made from Jewish fat'. By the end of the month, the last of British rule, almost all the remaining Germans were taken to camps on Cyprus, leaving the Jewish press to declare that Israel was now 'free of Germans', just as the Nazis had declared Germany 'free of Jews'. But still some lingered in Jerusalem, hoping that the city would become an international enclave and they would be able to stay on in the German Colony. Some, like the acting president of the society in Palestine, Nikolai Schmidt, had returned to their homes there at the end of April, but the fighting for Jerusalem's suburbs intensified and soon the Israeli forces were in control of Emeq Refa'im. The Germans took refuge with the Sisters of St Borromaeus and when the shooting had died down returned to their homes to gather up their personal possessions. They found them looted and occupied by Jewish refugees. But still they persisted and some returned to the German Colony in the spring of 1949, living in such of their houses as were still empty, and they even tried to collect rent from the people occupying the others. In April of that year the last Templers left Cyprus on a boat bound for Melbourne, and in November the new Israeli government requested those remaining in Jerusalem to leave. Nikolai Schmidt was in the last group to depart on 13 April 1950.

◈ ◈ ◈

The train from Munich's international airport runs alongside an autobahn that has signposts to Dachau, a town of 35,000 people whose industries include the production of paper, cardboard, electrical equipment, textiles, and ceramics. Rix sat opposite me. He had come out to the airport to meet me, aged eighty-seven and still recognisable from the pictures I had seen of the 20-year-old at Jerash, tall and straight, square-chinned, dressed in a sandy-coloured corduroy jacket and a checked shirt. We went directly to the city centre where Rix arranged for me to leave my bag with a friendly barman in a bierkeller while we did a little sightseeing and had lunch.

I do not remember when I first became aware that I had a great-uncle. Probably it was when I discovered that Fritz was my grandfather. Yet that part of our family history was so little talked about that when I started asking questions about the Grossmanns I was surprised all over again to discover that Fritz had had a brother and a sister, and astounded that they were both still alive. Dore, his sister, had visited England once, but I had been abroad at the time and though I was told about it when I got back it did not register exactly who she was. It was not important to me then. They were not quite long-lost relatives, but that I should never have met them now seemed extraordinary.

Any nervousness I had felt about meeting Rix disappeared almost immediately. Conversation came easily, as due to his excellent English as his humorous manner. He had grown up speaking more Arabic than German, and he still had some typically Middle Eastern traits, such as a sharp upward flick of the chin accompanied by a long blink for 'no', and the hand gesture that looks like brushing imaginary flour off one's palms for 'kaput' or 'nix'. Born in 1914 he had grown up in the Palestine of the British Mandate, so naturally he had learned English at Miss Wagner's small school in Nazareth, but his real English education, he said, had come while he was a prisoner of war in Tennessee.

In 1939 he had avoided internment in Palestine quite by chance, he said. From the middle of August Dore and her family were on holiday in Italy and she wrote that he should join them there. He flew to Rome and travelled on to Cattolica, but no sooner had he arrived than they received word that they should get back to Germany as quickly as possible. The car had been full on the drive south but now with an extra passenger and Rix's luggage it was overflowing. They made it as far as Lake Como on the first day, reaching St Moritz the following morning. The Swiss threw stones at them. That evening they crossed Lake Constance and the German border just in time; next day it was closed for the duration of the war. Rix was twenty-five and required to report for military service. Some years earlier, before his chef's apprenticeship, he had undergone the compulsory military training instituted by the National Socialist regime. As a reservist he had to report to his unit, but he was soon transferred to a special division, later known as the Brandenburgers, made up by and large of Germans from abroad. Most of the Palestine Germans who had escaped internment served in this division, alongside Germans from the old colonies in Africa and the Pacific. They were trained up as a commando unit and Rix saw action on the Russian front where they were used as paratroopers. Rix had had a lucky war. He even got married in the thick of it and had a son. He was one of those who came through without so much as a scratch, and gave the impression that he had known all along it would be so. On the eastern front the first company of the Brandenburgers went into action; no one came back. From the second company three or four returned. He was in the third company and when it was their turn to be deployed there was not a single casualty. He also escaped the murderous winter retreat of 1942–3 having been posted to North Africa by then. As an Arabic speaker he joined the Brandenburger unit of the Afrika Korps, in which Count Lazlo Almasy, 'the English patient', also served, engaged in desert reconnaissance and intelligence-gathering operations. (I realized with a start that it had not occurred to me to visit the German cemetery when I had been at el-Alamein.) In May 1943 he was captured; he was among 250,000 prisoners taken by the Allies at Tunis and he was shipped to America soon after. The last two years of the war he spent in the comfort of the Crossville camp about a hundred miles east of Nashville. The regime was not so harsh, the huts were warm and dry, the food was not bad, the guards were friendly. Only after the war did he experience the hard-ships the conflict had brought to Europe. He was shipped to France and held in a transit camp near Paris. It was the hardest winter of his life, and the coldest for years. The prisoners slept in tents in a muddy compound and were fed food that gave them diarrhoea. The latrine was a ditch with a pole over it on which to sit. He was ill and weak when he was released in the spring of 1946 and made his way to his sister's house in Göppingen, near Stuttgart. There he was reunited with his wife, Thea, and their son Rainer after three years a prisoner; Thea, a Sudeten German, had managed to get away from Bohemia before the Russians arrived. They settled in Munich, but, said Rix, if he had been allowed to return to Palestine, they would have gone straightaway. 'It was my home,' he said in his wistful voice.

We reached his present home by bus, a ground-floor flat in a 1950s block on Torquato-Tasso Street where he had lived since he was widowed. Neither of us had read Tasso's epic poem about the First Crusade, *Gerusalemme Liberata*, in fact there was not much space for books in the flat – a larder and a kitchen, sitting room, bedroom, bathroom. Above the table in the small hallway hung an Arabic motto. Rix had never learned to write Arabic and he wanted to test my claim that I could read the Arabic alphabet. '*Ahlan wa sahlan*', it read. '*Fantastisch!*' said Rix, and '*ahlan wa sahlan*, welcome,' spreading his arms wide. '*Ahlan beek*,' I gave the customary reply. There were other mementoes of his life in Palestine in the sitting room, pictures of the hotel and his mother on the wall, an Israeli tourist office poster, and a collection of miniature head-dresses, turbans and tarbushes, cheap souvenirs from the 1930s. 'You could tell the race, religion and even the sect of everyone in Jerusalem just by what they wore on their head. This one is Druze, you see, this a Sunni mufti, this a Shi'a cleric.' We settled down to coffee and Dixieland jazz. Rix's love of jazz had started in Palestine. 'There were some first-class bands in Haifa in those days and when we had a party at the Lido we always had a band and dancing.' We got out his photograph albums, and there on the first page were the hotel and Lido in their heyday, no date, but probably from 1937. The pictures were captioned 'our hotel in Tiberias' and 'our Galilee Lido', and that of the hotel, taken from the roof of the chemist's opposite, was also a group photograph, the figures on the balconies, at the windows and on the steps identified as '*Mutterle und Onkel Konrad*' and '*mein Bruder Fritz*', '*der blinde Mustafa*' and other employees, Sliman and Karam and Ibrahim, Salibi and Hanna. As important to Rix, I felt, were the two cars pictured '*Fritzens Ford, mein Chevrolet*'. It was Rix's first car and he had been very proud of it. Of Sliman, Rix said that he had not shaved for a week after Fritz's death as a mark of respect.

'I was in Haifa when it happened. I got a telephone call very early in the morning and went home immediately. They had already taken the body away but they had not cleaned the bathroom yet. Nobody knew why he did it.' He dismissed Elisheva's story about a love affair and in a manner that I believed. He mentioned the financial problems caused by the borrowing for building the Lido and the fall-off in business as a result of the civil unrest, but pointed out that the hotel had continued to function after Fritz's death and throughout the war without the bank foreclosing on the loan. 'He was a very serious man, very *schwermütig*.' Rix's dictionary translated that as 'melancholy'. 'He was six years older than me, so while I was a little boy in Tiberias he was at school in Nazareth, and then he and Dore went to study in Germany. I don't remember so much about him from those days, not until I came back to work in the hotel.' Rix had found the work there rather dull. 'You know, people did not stay very long, they were on a group tour or passengers from the Imperial Airways flying boat, so we always had the same menu in the hotel, chicken or fish everyday. I got a little bored.' Working in the Lido restaurant was more interesting, once they had stopped the stove from smoking out the place; Rix pointed out the tall chimney that he had built with his own hands. Sometimes the air passengers stayed overnight, and then the kitchen staff would have to get up very early to make them a breakfast to eat on board, all packed in thermos flasks to keep warm. 'But we had to be careful with the hot water. We could not put it boiling in the flasks. In Tiberias water boils at one hundred and five *grad* and if they opened the flask flying at three thousand metres it would explode.'

There were a few long-term guests as well and Rix

remembered a pair of elderly American widows who had come to the Holy Land, they said, to die. Another permanent resident was Mr Wade, Imperial Airways' superintendent in Tiberias and Rix's bridge partner. There were a few other people in the town he saw as friends – the Torrances, Mrs Feingold, Albrecht the German engineer – but mostly he would go to Haifa to have fun. 'When I was growing up Tiberias was very isolated. My friends were the young Arab boys of the town. We used to go fishing every day, you know, just with hand-lines. One time I was with them fishing off the town jetty. We were lying on our stomachs looking down into the water. It was so clear you could see the fish, and they could see you. There was a big catfish coming to my hook, and the other boys gathered around me to watch. It bit the hook and I pulled up hard. As I pulled I did a little fart and each time I pulled I did another. Everyone was laughing and for a long time after that whenever they saw me they would make with the finger so [forefinger hooked and jerked upwards] and the noise – *pwut pwut pwut*. Even the boys who were not there at the time knew about this. On my first day of school in Nazareth there was a little boy in the street who did *pwut pwut pwut* so I threw a stone at him. It cut him just above the eye. Of course I denied it, but no one made that noise again.'

Although Fritz was identified as one of the figures in the picture of the hotel it was taken from far enough away as to make him indistinguishable from the others. I had but a dim recollection of the only picture I had seen of him as an adult and would not have recognized him if he had walked into the room. But then, turning a page, there he was, on a skiing expedition to Mount Hermon with Margaret (whom Rix called Gretl) and Rix and a certain Dr Bigger. He is not in the picture of Dr Bigger's car stuck in the snow on the way up, the doctor digging out snow from under the wheel to find some traction and Margaret in a big fur coat and a woollen hat beaming at the camera, looking like my aunt Susan when she was young, but here are Dr Bigger, Gretl and Fritz posing in their skis, the doctor in jodhpurs and a roll-neck jumper, Margaret still beaming, and Fritz, slim in a V-neck sweater and white shirt, unsmiling, with an enigmatic look on his face, straight narrow nose, thin lips, high forehead with his slightly wavy hair pushed back. Maybe I find his expression enigmatic because I know what he will do just a few months later – the pictures were taken in the spring of 1938 – and maybe it is his black-framed round glasses that make him look serious and prevent one seeing what is in his eyes. The last picture of the day out shows Gretl, Fritz and Rix standing one behind the other, their long heavy skis interlocking, and again Margaret smiles broadly, though neither brother does. They do not look much alike from the eyebrows down. 'That was a wonderful day,' said Rix. 'The whole mountain was ours.' There were no facilities on Hermon at that time and no marked pistes. Occasionally they would go to Lebanon, to The Cedars, where the skiing was more organized.

On another page were pictures of Rix during the war, a studio portrait of him looking very smart in his Wehrmacht uniform and a snapshot of him and another officer in their barracks at Tunis. Rix had grown a moustache by then and had had one ever since. He is sitting on a chair in the bright North African sunlight, wearing dark glasses and reading a copy of *Esquire* magazine. The next two were group pictures of the prisoners of war in the Crossville camp. Of course I had to ask the question I had not wanted to put to him while we were in public: had he or any other member of the family been a Nazi? 'No, I was not a member of the party, and Gretl and Fritz certainly weren't. Dore and Reinhard were in

Germany, but I don't think they were members either. I think their two eldest children, a boy and a girl, were in the HJ and the BdM, but at school you had to join. My mother never had a political thought in her life. She did not have the time, just like she did not have time to keep a diary. After the trouble started in 1936 we had to let many of the staff go and we did their work. She just did not have time.' I showed Rix the letter about him Karl Ruff had sent to Berlin. '*Fantastisch!*' he muttered to himself over and again as he read through the document. Alex Carmel had contacted him shortly after it had been found, 'and now here it is! You know everything!' He had had no knowledge of the document at the time and no idea what had prompted the correspondence. In fact he had had little to do with his cousin Karl, his mother's brother's son, because he was 'a fanatical Nazi, 150 per cent. He came to Fritz's funeral and he made the Hitler salute over the grave. It caused a real scandal. The family was furious. I had nothing more to do with him after that.' As I showed him the other material I had found – the photographs from Yad Shitreet, the Torrance Archive and Thomas Cook as well as those I had taken on my journey – he kept repeating, 'But you know everything!' and I half suspected this was his way of deflecting further questions. As for the rest of the Grossmann family history and the early days of the hotel he said I should ask Dore, she was the archivist. He was only two when his father had died and he remembered nothing about him. Rix had been born on his father's forty-first birthday and had been given his father's name, Richard Julius Grossmann.

Rix's happy-go-lucky attitude, a life charmed and charming, was no better illustrated than by the fortunate circumstances of the heart attack he had suffered in his early eighties. After he was widowed he became friendly with an American lady who had spent many years in Munich. Occasionally he would go to America to visit her and on one trans-Atlantic flight with an American carrier he had bought, he could not say why, a one-dollar insurance policy. A few days after arriving he had a heart attack and received the best cardiovascular care money could buy, for the price of a dollar. It was, he said, *fantastisch*. His health regimen included a spoonful of whole linseed in his breakfast tea, though he allowed himself a boiled egg as well, and these emerged from underneath a pair of his mother's crocheted cosies. He preferred to take his exercise on a bicycle and having a second in his garage we set off together on a two-hour ride through the beautiful English Gardens. More picturesque than any British urban park I felt vaguely flattered they called these gardens English.

🔥 🔥 🔥

You expect German trains to leave on time, and we pulled out of Munich Hauptbahnhof on the button. You expect the Bavarian Alps to look like a *Sound of Music* theme park, and they did, all onion-domed churches, chalets with wooden balconies, haystacks and grazing cows, ripening maize. I did not know what to expect of my great-aunt Dore. Until I had looked at Rix's albums I had only seen pictures of her as a small girl with dark serious eyes and a tomboy haircut, and suddenly there she was as an old woman, short and somewhat dumpy, her grey hair brushed back from a wrinkled brow, her eyes smiling now as she visited relatives in Australia with Rix. She was waiting for us on the platform at Bad Tölz station in a flowery summer dress and a string of pearls, smiling from ear to ear as she held her arms wide to embrace me. I felt an immediate flesh-and-blood intimacy with this spirited 94-year-old as she linked her arm through mine and led me to her daughter Ursel's car. We sat in the back together and she held my hand all the way to Bad Heilbrunn.

Dore and her extending family had been visiting the '*Jod-bad*', the iodine spa, annually for over thirty years. She and her husband Reinhard had even bought a plot of land on which to build a house for their retirement, but he had died before they could realize their plans. They always stayed with the same family who let out self-catering apartments, but Rix and I were accommodated in the large *Kurpension* next door, built in the traditional Bavarian style, from whose balconies cascaded brick-red pelargoniums. It was a short walk across the courtyard to take a light supper in their apartment, cold meats, cheese and breads, gherkins and home-made pickles, Ursel and her husband Ortwin playing host. Ursel was a hand-some woman, with bright blue eyes and an open generous face. Her hair had been blonde, but was now turning white. She reminded me of my own mother. Her husband, a retired professor of anatomy, looked more like a badger. The longer of his eyebrow hairs reached far up his forehead, and the bristles protruding from his ears and nostrils could have been made into a small shaving brush. The man with the hairiest nose in the world, according to his wife, it took me a while to become accustomed to his Swabian accent, but luckily he afforded me ample opportunity. I caught up with him as he told the story of his elder brother's escape from what would become East Germany in the last days of the war; he had stowed away in the back of a US Army lorry heading west and when he investigated what was in the boxes it was carrying he found they contained Hershey bars.

Dore's husband Reinhard had had a lucky escape as well, but in the First World War. He had joined up in 1917 aged fifteen and served in the trenches. He and another lad were sent forward to reconnoitre and when they returned they found their entire company had been wiped out. He came home from the war with a scar down one cheek and a desire to follow his father into the medical profession. Not having finished his schooling before joining the army, it was a long road to travel and made all the harder by his falling in love. Dore and Fritz had been sent to Germany in 1922 to complete their education and had lodgings with Reinhard's widowed mother in Korntal. Dore was only fifteen, but they were soon secretly engaged, secretly because a medical student could not even be engaged, let alone married. They had to wait five years before Reinhard qualified as a doctor and they could wed, and still they had to keep it secret for another year, because Reinhard's boss would not tolerate married assistants. They lived in Leipzig in a fourth floor apartment and stood in the gods to hear the city's Gewandhaus Orchestra. Dore remembered fondly those first days of their marriage when they had been poor and happy; times were coming when they would be poor and miserable. Their first child, a boy, was born in 1931 and their fifth and last, called Reinhard, was born in 1943. Dore breastfed him for ten months as there was no milk and little food. The arrival of Rix and his family after the war further stretched their resources, having lost all their savings in the monetary reforms, to the point where Dore could do nothing for her mother when she was forced to leave the newly created state of Israel in 1948. Frieda, she said, had been heard speaking Arabic near one of the Haganah checkpoints; a friend had come to warn her that she was thought to be an Arab spy and might meet with an accident unless she left. Frieda had taken refuge with her old friends the Faris family in Beirut where she had managed a hotel on the Corniche not far from the St Georges. Frieda finally came to live with them in 1950, or was it 1951? Ursel noticed Dore was beginning to flag and sent us all to bed, Dore promising more stories the next day, when she would show me her photograph albums.

The new day brought a cloudless late August sky, weather that in New York would hold for another couple of weeks. Ortwin and Ursel and I walked down the hill through beech woods to a small peaty lake where we swam. We had lunch all together in the garden of a rustic Bavarian restaurant, beside a sparkling stream. We ate trout in a chanterelle sauce. There was a group of young hikers wearing lederhosen and drinking *weissbier* from steins. I half expected them to break into a chorus of 'Tomorrow Belongs to Me'. At the end of the meal Rix and Dore used their secret language, Arabic, to sort out the bill before anyone else could pay it. Back at the *Kurpension* the three of us settled down to look through the two albums.

Inside the cover of the first, stuck to the marbled end-paper, was a photograph of the hotel, the one with Rix's Chevrolet in the foreground that I had seen in his album. Next to it was the hotel's luggage label, the colours as fresh as the day it was printed. It showed a view over the town and lake looking south from the hotel, a date palm and the mosque of Daher al-Amr and a fragment of one of his towers in the foreground, the blue lake with a couple of white sails and purple hills beyond. The lettering and the palette evoked the 1930s. The artist had been a little creative with the geography of Tiberias – Mount Hermon's snowy slopes appeared on the horizon at the opposite end of the lake to where it actually stands – but he could be forgiven that licence in creating a label that would have stood out on any trunk. Turning the page took us back thirty years to 1900 and Dore started to tell the story of her parents' early life.

Frieda's father, Paul Ruff, a Templer, had emigrated from the Black Forest with his two brothers in the 1870s and had settled in the German Colony in Haifa where they set up a joinery workshop. (I had photographed one of the brother's graves in the Haifa cemetery without realising it.) Paul married the daughter of another Templer family, Christine Heselsch-werdt, whose brother had founded the Hotel Germania in Nazareth. They had a daughter, Frieda, born in 1884 and a son Alfred three years later. Paul was a giant of a man, full of humour and life, but he died of stomach cancer at the age of forty-three, leaving his widow and their two children to be cared for by her brother. Christine worked in the hotel leaving Frieda to look after Alfred. When Frieda was fourteen she was sent to work as a maid for a doctor's wife in Jerusalem. At eighteen she went to work in the Hotel Tiberias and married the proprietor, Richard Grossmann, two years later.

The Grossmanns were from Stuttgart. They were not Templers, but members of the Evangelical congregation. Richard's brother Konrad was a missionary and colporteur in India. When Richard contracted tuberculosis as a teenager his parents decided to send him to the German Colony in Jaffa where he found work in the Hardegg's Hotel Jerusalem as a pastry chef. (The change of air seemed to do him the world of good – Martin Higgins had sent me a group photograph of the Jaffa Sports Club of which he was a member.) His cheerful disposition made him popular with everyone. 'He was also quite a joker,' said Dore and among the formal pictures of the newly married couple (Frieda wearing black) was one of Richard fooling around, sitting up on the back of her chair so it looks as though he is on her shoulders, with a cap at a rakish angle and making a face that resembles a tongue-out grimace from the Maori hakka. Frieda is laughing uncontrollably. The following year their first child was born, Pauline, but she was a sickly baby and died aged six months of what Dore described as 'Zahnfieber', 'tooth fever', exacerbated by the heat of the Tiberias summer.

When Richard Grossmann first arrived in Tiberias it was neither safe nor sanitary. Bandits preyed upon travellers on the road to Nazareth and on one occasion he was shot at, the bullet grazing his ear. After one outbreak of cholera, he decided to dig the well in the hotel yard, an event I had seen pictured in the Yad Shitreet archive, but not this photograph of him standing by the pump and holding an upturned purse to show the work had cleaned him out. Dore said Frieda had doused in the courtyard to pinpoint the spring. When the next outbreak of cholera put the town in quarantine, the pump was the only source of clean water. Nevertheless, Dore had had dysentery as an infant, though not too seriously, but when Fritz was born he too caught it and could not shake it off. He was still suffering when Frieda caught smallpox. She lay delirious for four weeks and lost all her hair. Her whole body was covered in pustules and her eyes needed to be bathed constantly so that she would not go blind. Once the fever had passed, Dr Torrance recommended a trip to Germany to recuperate and to give Fritz a chance to rid himself of dysentery and become stronger. Frieda had never been to Germany before and in 1909 they arrived at the Grossmann family home in a sorry state, made sorrier by the cruel tongue of her mother-in-law. Frieda's hair had not yet grown back, her face was covered in pockmarks, her youngest child was sickly and her eldest spoke Arabic almost exclusively – Richard's mother's comment, made so Frieda could hear, was 'So this was why we sent you abroad, to marry such a woman!' Frieda travelled on to the Black Forest to stay with her relatives, and there, finally, Fritz got over his dysentery on a diet of blueberries.

In the eyes of the six-year-old Dore there is an impish quality as she sits on a step next to Fritz in a pretty embroidered dress that would not stay clean long. He has his arm on her shoulder, but there is no doubt who is in charge. 'Of course he had to do what I said. We used to steal eggs from under the chickens and because I only liked the yolk he would have to drink the white first. When we did something bad we would climb up the exhaust pipe from the water pump and sit on top of the old town wall until our parents promised we would not be punished. They were worried not only about the height of the wall but also because of all the snakes and spiders and scorpions that lived in it. We were not scared of the animals though. Father always had such animals by him. He had a pet snake which lived in his knapsack and came out when he whistled. As well as cats and dogs, we also had a monkey and a gazelle and a weasel as pets. Once we even had a young hyena in the yard, and another time he kept a vulture that used to sit on his shoulder. He was always collecting specimens which he sent to German museums. When we went to school in Germany, after he was dead, we were very proud to see his name still on the cabinets of insects and animals. He even sent a pair of wild boar to the Berlin zoo.' There was a picture of Richard dressed to go hunting, mounted on a fine pony and wearing a keffiyeh. He acted as a guide to hunting parties, and on one excursion when he was accompanied by Frieda's brother, Alfred was bitten on the thumb by a viper. Richard quickly cut across the bite to draw the venom and cauterized the wound with a brand from the fire.

Before the First World War Richard had maintained good relations with the Turkish authorities. Dore remembered one Persian landlord who visited occasionally and took great pleasure, despite his extensive retinue, in having the two children serve him his meals, for which they earned a gold coin. She had less fond recollections of the local Turkish governor who would come every day to the hotel to eat a vast breakfast of eight fried eggs and two litres of hot milk into which he emptied a whole bowl of sugar. In the evenings he would send a servant to order his dinner, always asking for a chicken with four breasts. He took a liking to the four-year-old Dore and would say to her father that as soon as she was old enough he was going to marry her. He would try to kiss her, until she slapped him hard on the ear. Richard kept them apart thereafter.

Richard junior, Rix, was born just before the start of the First World War. It was a great surprise to Dore as she had not noticed anything different about her mother. The telegram from Haifa read 'Prince born, Mother well.' Richard rushed off to see his new son and Dore did not recognize him when he stepped off the steamer from Samakh as he had shaved off his beard. The war did not effect them much at first, but after the Turkish attack on the Suez Canal food became scarce and expensive. Richard's tuberculosis returned. In the end he could not leave his bed. The pain was still fresh on Dore's face as she recalled the last time she saw him. 'Fritz and I were called in one morning to say goodbye to him. I will never forget his deathly sad face [*todtraurig*]. We were not allowed to kiss him because he was so infectious. That afternoon he had his second serious haemorrhage. He shot himself to save the family.' This explained the biblical reference on his gravestone to the shepherd who lays down his life for his sheep. It was obvious from Dore's demeanour just how great an effect his suicide had had on the children, and it surely must have been a contributory factor in Fritz's subsequent actions. His father had set him an example of self-sacrifice for the good of the family and maybe, in the face of his debts, he thought that what he was doing was noble.

Before the First World War the children had had a private tutor, an Arab woman from Jerusalem, who had taught them French and English, but after their father's death they were sent to relatives in Nazareth, the Wagners, whose daughter ran a small school. The war was coming ever closer and Dore remembered being friendly with a detachment of Austrian infantry stationed in the town. On one occasion the German commander Kress von Kressenstein visited the troops and gave her a bar of chocolate. When the final British push came in 1918 the children were in Tiberias. The first they knew of it was the arrival of the Austrians retreating from Nazareth where they had been surprised early one morning. Many were still in their pyjamas. Their retreat over the Golan Heights had already been blocked and they gathered in the hotel to await their inevitable capture. Fighting at the southern end of the lake was also fierce. Dore watched in horror as the steamer that plied between Tiberias and Samakh approached the town, full of wounded German soldiers and strafed by a British biplane. It burned, she said, '*wie eine Fackel*', 'like a torch'. In the afternoon a troop of Australian soldiers rode into town. Dore remembered them as savages, riding bareback with bloody daggers clenched between their teeth. They took prisoner all the soldiers in the hotel and would have taken the Grossmanns too, but Frieda was able to show them that the hotel belonged to Thomas Cook and they were left alone as a result.

Dore remembered the years after the war as happy ones. The privations ended and the hotel became popular once more. Business thrived and Frieda's brother, Alfred Ruff, came to Tiberias to help her manage the hotel. Frieda even got married again, to a Heselschwerdt cousin called Fritz. He turned out to be a wastrel and was happiest spending her money. Frieda kicked him out, reverted to using her first husband's name, and never spoke of him again. Rix liked him because he had a fast car. There were outings on the lake by boat and picnics on Mount Tabor and the Horns of Hattin. I asked if Fritz had been a happy child. 'Yes, I think so. We had a wonderful life in *Palästina*. He was certainly a serious boy. When we were at school in Nazareth, for instance, he started copying out the Bible. I wouldn't say he was melancholic [*schwermütig*]. That's not the right word. He was *schwerfällig*, he took things hard. As for his suicide, I was not in Palestine when it happened, so I cannot tell you why he did it, only what I heard afterwards. Fritz had borrowed money to build the Lido and because of the situation in Palestine he could not pay it back on time, so his creditors suggested other ways that he could discharge the debt. They asked him to do something he would not do – he was much too *geradlinig*, "straight". So rather than do it he shot himself.' But what did they ask him to do? 'Some say they wanted him to spy on the British officers in the hotel. Others that they would force him to kill his cousin Karl Ruff.' This was a twist in the conspiracy theory I had not heard before, and seemed to make it all the more incredible. Moreover the two actions, either spying on the British or murdering a person whom Dore also called a 150 per cent Nazi, seemed mutually exclusive. It prompted the question, to whom did Fritz owe money? If to the Tempelbank, the German settlers' own financial institution, one would have to determine the political position of those in charge. If they were pro-Nazi, then spying on the British might make sense; if anti-Nazi then the murder of Ruff, though unlikely, was just inside the bounds of credibility. However, I had thought that the debt was due to the Anglo-Palestine Bank, an Anglo-Jewish institution, in which case the spying theory was a non-starter, but the idea its officers might try to coerce one German to kill another was intriguing. Rix then put another kink in the story, suggesting it was the Nazis themselves who wanted Karl Ruff dead; not only was his fanaticism embarrassing, but also if the murder could be made to look like the work of the Jews then the opinion of the

German settlers would harden against them and the result would be a consolidation of Nazi influence among the Templers. To me this was more revealing of the atmosphere of suspicion and intrigue prevalent in pre-war Palestine than of the truth about Fritz's suicide. Dore was more certain on the questions of whether any family member had been a Nazi and whether Frieda had kept a diary, answering 'no' to both.

Turning the pages of the albums a curious feeling crept over me. The loneliness I had felt while growing up, which stemmed from the fact that my father was the only son of an only son and my mother's sisters had no children, the envy I had felt towards friends who had large families, whose Christmases and holidays were spent with cousins and uncles and aunts, the feelings of rootlessness exacerbated by the army life, having lived in five different places by the time I was seven and then being sent away to boarding school, the sense of dislocation I had experienced on discovering that the person I had thought of as my grandfather was biologically unrelated to me – all these factors had combined to produce a feeling of not knowing where I belonged, an inability to answer the simple question, 'where are you from?' with any certainty – and now here were pages of pictures of relatives I never knew I had, people I would probably never even meet, but still family. I felt my sense of self broadened, deepened, reaffirmed by their mere existence, my identity anchored in a wider family history. Yet for all I had discovered about that history there were still surprises in store. There was a loose photograph between two pages and turning it over I found myself looking at a picture of the most hated man of the twentieth century. It showed Adolf Hitler, the national saviour, sitting in an open-topped car on a country road surrounded by a small crowd of admirers. His driver has stopped to let them see the Führer while three SS officers in shiny leather coats with

fur-trimmed collars, their caps showing the skull and cross-
bones insignia, scan the crowd for danger. A fifth member of
his entourage wears a white leather coat and a strange leather
skullcap that makes him look like a court jester. The crowd
is made up mostly of women and two beautiful blonde girls
are being held up for the Führer to admire, his gaze locked
together with that of the smallest. Two right arms raised in
the 'Hitler greeting' jut into the bottom of the frame. While
the rest of the composition is a jumble of faces and bodies,
there is an empty space between Hitler and the little girl, a
stillness at the centre of the picture traversed by the look each
gives the other, the curious stare of the innocent and the
crocodilian smile of the mass murderer. It is this direct and
mutually pleasing connection between the two that makes this
photograph disturbing, like watching footage of a child playing
near a leaking drum of radioactive waste. How could this girl
have come so close to evil and remain unaffected? What was
this picture doing in my great-aunt's family album? 'The little
girls,' said Dore, 'are my husband's brother's daughters. Their
family used to take their holidays near Berchtesgaden where
Hitler had his mountain lodge. The girls were out walking
one day with their nanny when Hitler saw them and ordered
the car to stop so he could say hello. Their parents were furious
when this picture was published in the newspapers.' They did
not want to keep a copy of the photograph, but Dore had
seen the historical value of the image and had saved it.

One of the most poignant pictures in the albums was of
Frieda on the journey she made with Dore to Israel in 1969.
She stands alone on the terrace of the old hotel with the
mosque of Daher al-Amr in the background looking out over
the town that was her home for nearly forty years. She is
eighty-five years old, bent and leaning on an umbrella, her
white hair tied up in a braid, and written on her face are the

memories conjured up by standing in that spot once more, where the happy, newly married girl was photographed with her madcap husband. Her expression betrays more sorrow than joy as she remembers the hardships and disease of her first years in Tiberias, the loss of her infant daughter, her husband, her eldest son, two world wars, the loss of her business and her home and her eventual expulsion from the land of her birth. She stands there on the unswept terrace before the old hotel, at that time empty and boarded up, a lonely pathetic figure, and it occurred to me that if the story of the Grossmanns in Palestine had a hero, it was she. She had kept the business running and provided for the family through it all, only to be interned, deprived of her property and her livelihood, and turned out of her homeland. Even that she had survived, even that, and here she was, returned to visit the scene of past joy and past sorrow, a town she still considered her home though it was now part of a different country to the two she had known, the place where her husband and daughter and son were buried. They visited the garden of the Scottish Mission and Dore wrote: 'we were much comforted to find [the graves] so well kept'. Frieda died peacefully on 22 January 1972. Dore, herself a widow by then, spent the night watching over her, but fell asleep near dawn and dreamed she heard her mother's last breath.

As a leaving present, Dore gave me her copy of the picture I had glimpsed as a teenager, the one of Fritz at the Lido with his two daughters, Gita and Liesl, one on either side, holding his hand. It was, said Dore, the last photograph taken of him.

▲ ▲ ▲

For all the assurances I had been given by my family that the Grossmanns had been neither members nor supporters of the

National Socialist German Workers Party I could not shake the suspicion that what Helga Dudman had written about them in her book *Tiberias* might actually be true. That suspicion arose for two reasons: first, because they would deny it, wouldn't they? And secondly because I desperately wanted to believe them. I did not want to 'find' my real grandfather only to discover he had been a Nazi. Despite what my relatives had said, and despite the information Alex Carmel had given me, I still had no concrete evidence with which to refute the charge that 'they too were Nazis'. And on what evidence did that rest? On Frieda's diary, according to Elisheva Ballhorn. Without the diary I could not challenge the book's statement. Even if I managed to retrieve the diary I would still be faced with the problem of trying to prove a negative, hard enough even when innocence is presumed, but when it comes to matters concerning the Nazi Party that presumption does not seem to apply, especially in the Israeli version of events. Anyone who sets out to challenge the basic assumption that in 1939 all Germans were Nazis lays themselves open to charges of seeking to revise history and Holocaust denial, just as anyone who criticizes the policies of the Israeli government is an anti-Semite. The Holocaust itself is so institutionally fetishized that it has become the universal justifier for both the existence of the Israeli state and for all that it does. As such it is jealously guarded, to the point where the state of Israel cannot allow itself to recognize that any other peoples in the twentieth century were subjected to similar genocidal persecution, as though that admission might somehow diminish the magnitude of Jewish suffering. The Israeli position was made abundantly clear by their reaction to the proposed World Genocide Day and their refusal to tolerate the inclusion in the remembrance of the Armenian genocide, though cynics and real-politikers might suggest this had more to do with maintaining friendly relations with the Turks, perpetrators of that massacre, whose country is one of the few Muslim states to recognize Israel and with whom a huge deal for tanker shipment of fresh water was being negotiated.

When I had met Elisheva I had said I was prepared to accept the consequences of my investigation, no matter what it turned up; my chief concern was to establish the truth. As a result I was not prepared to take what my relatives said on trust, and by the same token I could not accept what she had said without question, especially her most damning claim about the Grossmanns – that they were Nazis. I felt she had been largely responsible for the appearance of this statement in Helga Dudman's book, and, now that she was unable to produce the evidence she claimed proved its truth, I felt angry. The elaborate preamble to her remarks, the parading of her rigorous concern for historical truth, I had come to regard as a smoke screen to cover her own unsupported claims, a ruse to make me believe what she had to say without reservation. I drafted several progressively less petulant versions of a letter to her, none of which, I am glad to say, I sent. When I did write to thank her for all the help she had given me while I had been in Tiberias, and to ask if there was any way I might be able to obtain a copy of the diary, I was at once encouraged by her offer to contact the Lady of Jerusalem, as she became known in our letters, who was in possession of the document, and disappointed that she persisted in the same cloak-and-dagger charade of not telling me who the Lady was or enabling me to get in touch with her directly. Her declared reason for this secrecy was the promise she had made to the Lady, yet I suspected she feared that if she lost control of this piece of information she would be left out of the loop. Despite this frustrating aspect our correspondence became increasingly friendly, but I had no difficulty imagining how her repeated enquiries of the Lady of Jerusalem might become annoying. As time wore on it did occur to me that my relatives were right, that the diary might not exist at all, until Elisheva found among her papers three photocopied pages that the Lady had given her when she had visited the Tiberias archive. There was no mistaking Frieda's handwriting – I was able to make comparisons with the photograph captions – and the names Grete (her name for my grandmother Margaret), Rix and Dore confirmed its authenticity. True to her conspiratorial mindset Elisheva swore me to secrecy about having sent the pages. It was tantalising to have a fragment of the diary, and to wait helplessly while she made a hash of what she presented as extremely delicate negotiations with the obdurate Lady of Jerusalem. My greatest fear was that Elisheva would so antagonize the Lady that she would be unwilling to part with even a copy.

September began bright and clear. My wife and I were looking forward to the birth of our first child, Fritz's great-grandson, towards the end of the month. On the eleventh I went to see my grandmother and aunt to talk to them some more about their life in Palestine and show them the pictures of the German internees in Tatura Camp that I had found. My wife called after lunch to tell us to turn on the television. The Twin Towers collapsed, while Palestinians danced in the streets of East Jerusalem. I remembered the man I had met in Syria, a migrant to the United States home to visit his family, who was so proud his wife worked in the World Trade Centre. A pall of smoke that could be seen from space spread over the future.

In the early hours of the following morning my wife went into labour ten days early, the result, it seemed, of some primal physiological response to danger, and we were transported to a different world of sleepless nights, huddling together in our whelping den for comfort. The boy, Barnaby, 'son of the prophet', had a stomach ache that lasted three and a half months. The bassinet in which Barny 'slept' once stood in a house my mother-in-law had rented to an Arab and his European wife. They had had a daughter while they lived in London. The man was one of Osama bin Laden's older brothers.

When we emerged into the daylight once more it was to discover that a country whose population had been reduced to living in caves by twenty years of war had had its caves blown up, that there existed an Axis of Evil which the mis-elected United States government, dominated by ultra-conservative arms dealers and oil merchants, was preparing to smash with evangelical zeal. It seemed George W. Bush's comment about embarking on a 'crusade' had not been a slip of a slip-prone tongue, but a statement of intent; he was indeed planning the first Christian offensive against radical Islam for seven hundred years.

Despite appearances, other things had been happening in the interim. The Temple Society of Australia had commemorated on Armistice Day the passing of sixty years since their internment in Palestine, the beginning of the end of their founder's eschatological settlement project in the Holy Land. Martin Higgins attended and returned with news that he had heard a new twist to the story of Fritz's suicide. He recommended I write to the person from whom he had heard it, Felix Haar, who greeted me in reply as his father's cousin's great-grandson. 'This makes me your grandfather's second cousin and you a fourth cousin to our seven grandchildren here in Melbourne, if my thinking is right.' Martin, who had done extensive research on Templer family trees, was not joking when he said all the families were related somehow. Another roster of relatives I never knew I had was revealed. Felix went on:

In Tiberias, there was only one 'Mutterle' for all of us . . .
[Frieda] was the soul and dynamo [of] the hotel . . . The ladies'
afternoon teas were 'Mutterle's speciality. Seated at the head
of the long table, 'Mutterle' directed the movements of the
milk, sugar, cake and the cups of good English tea. My few
words of English [were] enriched with 'could you please pass
the sugar? . . .'

Felix had been only twelve years old at the time of Fritz's
death and the memory of it soon faded. He had been one of
a group of 305 internees who were exchanged for British and
Jewish prisoners from Germany. The group also included my
grandmother's sister, Gisela Auer, who had been trapped in
Palestine by the outbreak of war. It was around this time, he
wrote, that he had first heard the story of Fritz Grossmann's
death. After the war he decided to emigrate in 1950 and
join the Templer communities that had been established in
Australia. There he became friendly with one of the old farmers
from the Templer settlement of Betlehem, Carl Herrmann.

Not long after Carl died in 1991, we were with his widow
driving home from a visit to friends. There the story of Fritz
Grossmann and his dilemma came up and I got a comprehen-
sive report . . . Fritz and Carl were very close friends. Fritz came
to Carl one day and told him about his predicament. He had
drawn the 'black ball . . .' at the [Freemasons'] Lodge. The
order was to kill Karl Ruff . . . Fritz would have been absolutely
safe, no policeman or judge would have got himself involved
in this case, but Fritz was no murderer and saw finally no other
way out but to kill himself as the law of the Lodge demanded.

This was indeed a new take on the conspiracy theory of Fritz's suicide and the first time I had heard the Freemasons mentioned in that connection. I was not too surprised though; where conspiracies are concerned the Masons are never far away. Felix's further theorising as to why they might have wanted Karl Ruff murdered then took off into the realms of international conspiracy, a world where Warburg's bank gave financial support to the NSDAP, reckoning that Nazi persecution of the Jews in Europe would be the surest way to increase Jewish emigration to Palestine. This scenario casts Hitler in the unlikely role of Zionist agent, and indeed in the years before the war, before the Nazis tried out other 'solutions', Jewish emigration was encouraged, the methods of persuasion, culminating in *Kristallnacht* in November 1938, becoming ever more brutal. *Kristallnacht* itself was prompted by the assassination in Paris of a German diplomat by a Polish Jew. Felix's theory was that the murder of Karl Ruff was planned in June 1938 with the intention of provoking a similar anti-Semitic backlash in Germany, which in turn would increase Jewish emigration to Palestine. What the theory did not explain was why the Freemasons might be in favour of the creation of a Jewish state. All in all, it reminded me of another conspiracy theory then doing the rounds. I heard it first from my friend in our local curry shop, a Pakistani Shi'ite with Persian ancestry, and I read later that it had gained widespread currency in the Islamic world. It was that the attack on the World Trade Centre had actually been planned and executed by the Israeli secret service, Mossad. Why else, he said, had all the Jews who worked there received advance warning not to go in on 11 September? The purpose of the attack, according to this theory, was to provoke a US-led campaign against Israel's Muslim enemies and distract world attention from Israel's own campaign against the Palestinians.

The Taleban had been destroyed. Iran and Iraq were in the firing line. Jenin refugee camp was being flattened. For him these events were proof enough. In conspiracy theories the outcome proves the premise.

Just so with the claims in Helga Dudman's book about the Grossmanns – their 'disappearance' from Tiberias proved they were Nazis. Elisheva backed up this claim by citing the number of '*Heil Hitler*'s Frieda's diary contained. Indeed in the three pages she had sent Hitler's name appeared twice, which made me wonder if those pages had been selected for that reason. However, neither mention was accompanied by the word '*heil*', 'hail', nor any expression either of approbation or dissent. In the first instance Frieda is writing about a party she attended for the silver wedding anniversary of '*Herr u. Frau Tim. Wurst*' at which the German ladies of the Haifa colony gave Frau Wurst a trunk with an inscription on the lid, an uneven couplet attributed to one 'A. Hitler': '*Es mögen Männer Welten bauen, / Es steht und fällt ein Volk mit seinen Frauen*', 'It might be that worlds are built by men, / But a people stands and falls with its women.' The author might have been a controversial figure, but the sentiment is hardly more inflammatory (or more original) than James Brown's song 'This is a Man's World'. Frieda does nothing more than record a fact, and it is the same with the second appearance of that dread name: '*Adolf Hitlers Geburtstag wurde in Haifa im Club schön gefeiert*', 'Adolf Hitler's birthday was nicely celebrated in the club in Haifa.' This entry for 20 April 1939 does not even make it explicit that she attended the celebration of this German national holiday.

Eventually Elisheva admitted defeat in her attempt to secure the diary from the Lady of Jerusalem and agreed that I should try my luck with her directly. Irène Lewitt was her name, a Swiss by birth and also in her eighties, who did voluntary work at the Israel Museum. She was perfectly charming on the telephone and declared herself willing to send me at her own expense the original diary once she had made a copy, a task which seemed to take an inordinate amount of time. Finally it arrived, a year after I had first heard of its existence, and I understood why it had taken Irène so long to photocopy. Flakes from its pasteboard covers fell off as I took it out of its envelope and the binding was shot. Not only was it in a delicate condition, but also the pages were as thin as airmail paper and more numerous than I could ever have imagined. Here it was at last sitting on my desk, though not flat, the black covers warped, the red cloth spine loose. The sticker on the front identified it as a *Kopierbuch*, a copy book, which explained why the pages were so thin. On the sticker was written '*von Frieda Grossmann für Dora Vorster*', and printed '*vom . . . 192 . . . bis . . . 192 . . .*' – Frieda's frugality showing through once more, as it did in the accounts ledger photograph album, in her use of inappropriate and outdated stationery. Not that a copy book in itself is inappropriate for use as a diary, but Frieda's writing implement of choice was a dip-pen and often when it was freshly charged with ink the letters would soak into the paper in an illegible blur. Because of the thinness of the paper only the right-hand page was intended to be used – these were numbered 2 to 500 with a few unnumbered pages at the end – and because she was using ink Frieda only wrote on every other numbered page initially, but around page 300, when stationery was becoming scarce, she took to writing on every one. There were approximately 350 pages of writing, and the left-hand pages seldom remained blank, but carried stuck-in newspaper clippings, pictures, prayers and sentimental poems. I had much more sympathy with Irène Levitt when I attempted to photocopy the document.

Frieda's first entry is for 18 March 1939. It starts in the

matter-of-fact way that characterizes most of the entries: 'Today Grete went to Haifa to go skiing in the Lebanon with her friends the Boutagys and Dr Bigger.' The lack of self-consciousness or the sort of 'Dear Diary' apostrophe of the novice suggests that this was not the first time Frieda had kept a diary and that earlier volumes must have existed, including one covering the tragic events of 1938. These were probably still in the hotel when it was ransacked in 1948 and ended up on the street outside with the photograph album. It made me wonder if they had also been saved and might one day resurface. This volume, whose last entry was for New Year's Eve 1942, had been found (so Irène said) in the Fast house in Jerusalem's German Colony by a Haganah fighter who had passed it on to Irène, because she worked at the Israel Museum, decades later. There is no reason to suppose that Frieda stopped writing her diary when she came to the end of the copy book. In all likelihood there was at least one subsequent volume, 1943-?, that either was not recovered in Jerusalem or, if Frieda had found a note book of a similar number of pages, was still current when she left the city for Beirut and went with her.

The first thing that must be said about Frieda's diary is that it provides no evidence whatsoever of either Nazi sympathies or membership of the NSDAP. Contrary to Elisheva's assertion that it was peppered with '*Heil Hitler*'s, the Führer's name appears only three times, in the two contexts already mentioned – the inscription on the trunk and the celebration of his birthday (the celebration of the British monarch's birthday is also recorded) – and for a third time when reporting news she had read in the *Palestine Post* of an unsuccessful assassination attempt in Munich. There is not one anti-Jewish or anti-British comment, nor a single pro-German one; once the war has started she takes no joy in Germany's early victories. Her thoughts are with the soldiers of both sides, a nation's youth, who must fight and die. The coming winter causes her to think how cold the soldiers fighting in Northern Europe must be; the summer makes her wonder how those in the North African desert can bear the heat. Her every comment about the war ends with prayers for a quick end to the hostilities, the madness, the senseless waste. Her constant wishes for worldwide peace and unity are the closest she comes to expressing a political opinion. I sent a complete copy of the diary to Elisheva, partly by way of thanking her for having 'facilitated' its recovery, and partly in the hope that on seeing for herself just how apolitical a document it is she might change her opinion about the Grossmanns being Nazis, or at least question its basis.

As one might expect of any diary Frieda's is filled with the mundane events of daily life, and as she was a religiously minded, family-orientated grandmother with a wide teatime acquaintance, a widow who ran a hotel, most of the entries touch on these subjects. Besides her German friends and relations, the cosmopolitan nature of her circle and her good relations with all sections of Palestine's population is apparent from their names: the Misses Lee, Ferguson, Palmer, Keith, Wryce and Lady Downes; Sitt Zareefy, Mrs Khadder, Faris, Haddad, Boutagy; Mrs Silberstein, Goldstein, Saki, Feingold and David; Miss Vartan, Mrs Markarian and Dr Krikorian. Even during the period of her internment (17 June 1940–15 April 1941) her concerns are unchanged – who is married to whom, what their maiden name was, how many children they have, who needs her help, who is sick and what they have, who has died, who took the service, who came to tea or to the Red Cross sewing afternoon, how the grandchildren are – 'froh u. munter, Gott sei Dank' ('happy and full of beans, thank God'). Her days at the hotel are taken up with washing the linen, camphorating the carpets, whitewashing the rooms, fixing the range in the Lido, buying towels for the kitchen, coping with the staff shortages and worrying about their debt and the lack of business. It is clear that the passengers from the Imperial Airways flying boats and the British civil servants and the soldiers stationed at Nazareth, who came to lunch and tea in the Lido and sometimes stayed overnight in the hotel, were keeping the place going, just. Their main creditor was the Anglo-Palestine Bank whose policy towards the Grossmanns seems to have been remarkably lenient, not foreclosing on the loan even though they could not cover interest let alone repay the principal. There were other creditors too, private investors, the Hardeggs of the Hotel Jerusalem, Andreas Beck, Frau Christian Pflugfelder and the Torrances, and these received their interest, except the Torrances who had made their loan interest-free. It was hard to imagine any of these kind souls involved in blackmailing Fritz either to spy or to assassinate.

Although business picked up during the early years of the war, the hotel's financial situation was complicated by the new regulations concerning Trading with the Enemy. A Custodian of Enemy Property was appointed and it was in negotiations with his office that Margaret came into her own, her connections with the British community proving an advantage. At the start of the diary, March–April 1939, Margaret's position at the hotel and in her mother-in-law's estimation is somewhat hard to determine. There seems to have been some tension in their relations. Frieda remarks that 'Grete does not feel comfortable and at home with us, and instead of sticking together we have been damaged . . .' Margaret moved out of the hotel and took a house in Haifa, at the time that Shan Hackett was attending staff college there, though the two had not yet met. There also seems to be an element of blame for Fritz's suicide attached to Margaret in Frieda's mind, the understandable reaction of a bereaved and bewildered mother, but without any basis in fact. Relations were strained further by a point of contention with Rix, who wanted to buy a new car out of hotel funds, but this was blocked by Margaret as an extravagance the business could not afford – as the hotel's book-keeper she was well placed to know. There was also a stand-up row between Gisela Auer, Margaret's divorced sister who had come out to Palestine to help with the children, and Resi, their nanny. Reading between the lines, Frieda took Resi's side and Gisela left Tiberias in high dudgeon, never to return. When Rix went to join Dore and her family on holiday in Italy and was prevented from returning by the outbreak of war, Frieda was left alone with her worries.

When Margaret returned to Tiberias shortly after the outbreak of the war, Frieda makes no comment, but she is very happy to have the children nearby once more – 'they fill the hotel with laughter and noise' – and appreciative of the hard work that Margaret puts in on the books and the legal and financial negotiations. The first wild hyacinths appear before Christmas and everything carries on as normal. The High Commissioner comes to stay with his wife and goes duck-shooting on Lake Huleh. The girls have new dresses for Easter. The flying boats land, refuel, take off, the passengers having lunched in the Lido. Everyone spends some time in bed with a temperature. Frieda makes apricot leather. And then towards the end of May 1940 comes the news that the Germans of Tiberias are to be interned; 'the die is cast,' Frieda writes. The two Grossmann women and the two children were allowed to stay on for a few extra days to put the hotel's affairs in order. A Christian Arab who had worked for Frieda before, Sam Jureidini, was engaged as manager and the Grossmanns left Tiberias for the Schneller School in Jerusalem. 'Farewell

beloved Tiberias, lovely lake, dear house, and Fritz's grave!
Will we be permitted to see you once more? We are in God's
hands! Now and henceforth.' They stayed in Jerusalem for
three weeks before being interned in the Sarona camp.

Margaret and the children were brought to Sarona a few
days after Frieda's arrival by one '*Major Hakett v. der T.J.F.
Force*'. It is his first appearance in the diary, though he and
Margaret had met in the hotel the previous Christmas. He
becomes a frequent visitor and celebrates Christmas Day 1940
with them in the camp. Frieda assumes that he and Margaret
are engaged – in an aside on 2 January 1941 she states that
'Grete and Frl. Ernst want to marry Englishmen'. The next
time he visits he is referred to as her fiancé, when in fact they
were not officially engaged until the following spring. What
prompts the first aside is the distribution to only a few internees
of forms declaring opposition to the Nazi regime. Frieda tran-
scribes the text in full:

I hereby affirm that

a) I am hostile to the Nazi regime, and that I arrived in
   Palestine comparatively recently. I left . . . under German
   domination because I was subjected to oppression by the
   Nazi regime upon racial, religious, and/or political ground.

b) I am hostile to the Nazi regime and I have lived in Palestine
   for a substantial period and I have formed ties of association
   and sympathy with Great Britain.

Frieda crosses out 'hostile' and underlines 'sympathy', her
comment: 'It might have been better for me to do otherwise,
but I want to remain German.' There is, however, no suggestion here or anywhere else that in crossing out 'hostile' she is
declaring herself to be in sympathy with the Nazi regime,
although when she came before the board considering the

release of those who had received the forms, she was, she says, 'unable to answer all the questions to [their] satisfaction'. At a further interview she was reassured that she would not have to renounce her German nationality and when a list of those to be released was posted on 7 April 1941, her name was on it.

For Frieda her time in Sarona seems to have been something of a holiday, despite the curtailment of freedom of movement, the rationing, the overcrowding and the occasional air raid. She was relieved of the onerous task of keeping the hotel afloat and gathered around her were friends and relations she had seen but rarely in peacetime. At last she had time to relax and time for herself. She started taking piano lessons. She tended a small patch of garden where she grew 'salad' and vegetables. She was visited often by friends from Tiberias, and by Sam Jureidini who was usually the bearer of good news about the hotel, prompting her to anticipate the day when it would be free from debt. Her only cares were that her brother Alfred was not there, having been interned in Waldheim, and that there was so little news from Dore and Rix; neither state of affairs improved on her moving to the Fast house in Jerusalem, nor was she entirely free to move about the country. She wanted more than anything to return to her home, but was prevented from doing so by the authorities because of Tiberias' proximity to the Syrian border. She did, however, manage to obtain on occasions a 24-hour pass to visit Galilee, but failed in her application for a Palestine passport. In this attempt and in all that she wrote she makes it clear that she regarded Palestine as her homeland (*Heimat*). When she was offered the chance with the other internees of 'repatriation' to Germany she refused.

Margaret, stepping out with a British officer, had considerably more freedom, frequently taking the children to the beach at Jaffa. Frieda reports in February 1941 that Shan Hackett had already received permission to marry Margaret, but no date had been set for the wedding and their progress to the altar of the Anglican cathedral would be far from smooth. First came the Allied invasion of Syria and Lebanon, Operation Exporter. Shan was absent from Jerusalem for a month and then limped back in the middle of June with shrapnel in his shoulder and hip and the Military Cross on his chest. He spent time recuperating in Jerusalem's military hospital and Frieda records his rapid recovery. Less than three weeks later 'his wounds have healed well, but his shoulder still hurts when he moves it.' A week after that she writes that 'Major Hakett', whom she now calls Shan, has received new orders. This would have been his appointment as Secretary to the Commission of Control, whose President was Major General Chrystall, Hackett's former commanding officer in the Trans-Jordan Frontier Force. Four days later, on 18 July, he attended its first informal meeting with the Vichy French commanders at the Grand Hotel, Ain Sofar in the Lebanon. General Chrystall in his opening address made reference to King Arthur and his Round Table and there was something chivalrous in the terms of the Convention which ended the hostilities in Syria and guaranteed such of the Vichy troops unwilling to join the Free French safe conduct back to France. Shan managed a few days in Jaffa with Margaret during August, Frieda reports, but he was back at the Grand Hotel in September for the tenth and final meeting of the Commission, accompanied by his assistant secretary Captain Walter Milner-Barry. The meeting concluded, the representatives sat down to lunch, at the end of which General Chrystall rose to propose a toast. 'All of us know and love France. Many of us have served alongside her gallant soldiers. All of us look forward to the day of her restored greatness. I am going to propose the toast of France, and say how much I hope the day is not far distant when she will be reunited, and inhabited once more only by her own peoples.' The minutes conclude: 'The toast "La France" was then drunk with the greatest cordiality on all sides by Free French, British and members of the T[roupe] F[rançaise du] L[evant] alike.'

Shan and Margaret were reunited in Jerusalem in October. It must have been a golden time for them, the beautiful autumn weather making them forget the uncertainties of war, but Shan was somewhat in limbo. The office of the Commission of Control had moved to Jerusalem and there was still work to be done requiring him to visit Syria on occasion. Yet, his secondment to the TJFF over, he was keen to rejoin his regiment, at that moment fighting in the Western Desert. The unforeseen consequence was that his permission to marry was revoked. Margaret was distraught. Shan had been courting her for over two years. Their plans to marry were long-standing.

But Shan had not given up. He had gone over the head of his commanding officer and had managed to obtain permission to marry once again. They were married ten days later on 21 March 1942. Only death could part them thereafter and they had been married for fifty-five years when Shan died. If he had not been so persistent, my mother may never have met my father.

For all Frieda's fortitude in the face of the trials and hardships she recorded in her diary there was, however, one memory that gave her constant pain: that of her son Fritz's suicide. It was always with her, but never more so than on the anniversaries of his death or his birth. On the first anniversary of his death she cannot help but rehearse the events in her mind.

28.6.39. On this day one year ago Fritz and Grete and their dear children came back from Nablus where they had been staying for four days as guests of Dr Bigger. Richard went to Haifa at noon and met Fritz just before he left the town. In the afternoon Fritz, Grete and Dr Bigger took tea with us in the hotel and then went on their own to the Lido.

At six in the evening Fritz drove up in his car to pick up the children, who had stayed with me, and take them home to Resi, who would put them to bed. Fritz hugged his children and I lifted them into the car, saying be careful they don't fall off the seat when you drive away. I felt a strong desire to go up to the house with them; why didn't I? We had so little time to talk, but we understood each other and worked together so well.

29.6.39. A year ago today at 5 in the morning Grete telephoned.

Mother, mother, Fritz has killed himself!

How can a person endure hearing such a thing? How did I come to be dressed?

Dr Bigger was in the house and I woke him and he drove me up there.

And there lay Fritz, o my beloved son!

What was it that you could not bear and could not tell me? What happened in Nablus, or elsewhere, that made your life so unbearable you could leave your sweet children?

There was no recall possible, no making-it-better! Fritz, you good man, you had left this world and gone over to a better one!

Alfred and Richard came from Haifa at 8 a.m. The consternation of the populace was terrible. Many friends and acquaintances came from Haifa, Jerusalem, Nazareth to take part. At 2.30 our dear Fritz was laid in his grave. Pastor Berg gave the address.

So this terrible tragedy fell on us . . . and on his beautiful life's work, the Lido, which he built with so much trouble and care and love, despite the difficult times. And the children, o the poor dear children, must grow up without a father, just like my brother Alfred and I, and my own children, and now Fritz's poor children. It is too sad.

Yesterday I went down to put flowers on the grave and Miss Vartan and Sitt Zareefy came with me.

By the time the second anniversary comes around, the war has started and Frieda, Margaret and the children have been interned in the Sarona camp. 'This day also we have lived through, without the outside world seeing our inner pain . . . May he rest in peace and may we meet again in eternity.' She quotes an anonymous English poem that Miss Keith had given her the previous August:

> Perhaps if we could know
>> The reason why they went
> We'd smile and wipe away
>> The tears that flow – and wait – content.

The third anniversary, a few days after Germany attacked Russia, finds her in Jerusalem:

My heart is heavy with pain. It is the third year . . . since my dear son Fritz went away from us. This night he fought with death. How many hours did he sit and struggle? And I did not know that his soul was so troubled and his heart so broken and lonely. What, you poor good man, caused you so much grief that you preferred to take this course rather than stay with us?

You are with God and released. You have gone over and do not have to experience this terrible war.

Until I too am called, I will care for your children as

well as I can, despite all our hardships. They will not want
for love!

The following year there is no mention of the anniversary in
Frieda's diary. She is too busy looking after the children. Lizzie
fell over while running at the British Community School sports
day and cut her arm. The cut became infected and she was
in bed with a fever.

Frieda's pain is still palpable after all these years. Every time
I read these entries tears well up in my eyes, even though I
never met her or her son. And for Frieda there was no moment
of catharsis, no answer to the question why, no contentment,
despite her faith, in her anticipation of their reunion in the
afterlife. Not knowing why, she too is prey to believing any
explanation that is offered, no matter how far-fetched. She
records a conversation she had in Haifa with her uncle Gottlieb
Ruff on 15 December 1939:

> As I was taking my leave Uncle Gottlieb asked if I knew
> whether Fritz, our dear good Fritz, had belonged to the Free-
> masons. I had to answer no. Uncle wondered whether the
> Freemasons had demanded something of him that he could
> not carry out and for that reason he chose to kill himself. It
> is so terrible not knowing. Fritz never said anything to me
> about it. He is free, the poor man, and how glad would I be
> if I were already with him.

Terrible indeed not to know, not to have an explanation we
can understand for the mysteries of life and death. I had heard
so many stories about Fritz's death that I did not know what
to believe as true. There seemed to be no way to come at the
truth emotionally or any reason to believe one of my inform-
ants over another. Neither did there seem to be a rational

explanation for Fritz's suicide as there had been in his father's case. I toyed with the idea of a statistical analysis, a way of finding the average by discounting the explanation I had heard least – the affair – and that I had heard most – the conspiracy theory – and arriving at a mean: depression. Indeed that was the explanation I favoured most, but only because it was what I wanted to hear? Wasn't believing the cause to have been depression just an easy way out for me? The least messy explanation? Putting the blame on the victim merely a cop-out? Not, I recalled, when depression has been shown to be hereditary.

Finally, my grandmother told me something of Fritz's last depression. It had been deep for a number of months. He had tried to keep it hidden, but Dr Bigger had noticed his black mood and that, said Granny, was why he had asked them to spend a few days with him and his family in Nablus. Fritz's spirits seemed to lift while they were there, but on the morning they were due to return to Tiberias, Rix had telephoned with the news that a little girl of whom Fritz was very fond had drowned at the Lido the day before. Fritz was distraught and Margaret feared the news would start him downhill again, but on the drive back to Tiberias he remarked how much better he felt. Whether he was lying to conceal his despair from his wife or some fresh incident awaited him in Tiberias cannot be known.

One detail, Granny noticed, that Frieda had omitted from her first anniversary entry was the fact that she had given Fritz the gun. It was the revolver she kept in the hotel. As Palestine's internal crisis worsened during 1937, both sides became increasingly desperate to procure any weapons they could. Frieda felt the gun would be safer out of the hotel and hidden. Fritz buried it in his garden. Margaret remembers, after she had discovered his body, looking out of an upstairs window and seeing a hole and a pile of earth where Fritz had dug it up again. It was the same gun his father had used to kill himself.

△ △ △

So much has happened since I started on this investigation. The second phase of America's global Crusade started, and finished with the fall of Salah al-Din's and Saddam Hussein's home town. Al-Qa'ida is alive and well, as perhaps is Osama bin Laden, and still at war with America and her allies. There was a new plan to divide what was once the British Mandated Territory of Palestine between Jews and Arabs. They called it 'The Road Map', but for there to be a map there must first be a road and the roads of 'Palestine' have long since been blocked by Israeli soldiers and bombed busses. They have not been safe since 1947, when the fighting between the two sides broke out again, when Shan Hackett returned to the Galilee to command the TJFF in the last days of its existence and Frieda Grossmann was giving her last crocheting lessons in the Fast house. My 21-year-old father-to-be was also nearing the end of his service in Palestine. He had been shot at by both sides and was lunching a little way down the street when the bomb went off in the King David Hotel. He was on one of the last boats out of Haifa, the *Empress of Australia*, whose funnel was peppered by the *feu de joie* of friendly Arabs on the quayside. He had been born in 1926, three years before the first serious anti-immigration riots in Palestine. The conflict has lasted almost his whole life. Palestinian terrorist attacks are certainly among my earliest memories of world events, and I have become weary of it all, weary of the pro-Palestinian liberal press, weary of the intransigence and sectarian hatred inculcated in the youth of both sides by 'religious' teachers, wearied by America's election-conscious unconditional support of the rogue Israeli state, by Israel's inability to respond to adverse comments with anything other than counter-charges of anti-Semitism, by the ridiculous self-righteous rhetoric of Palestinian extremists. The most sensible thing anyone has said about the conflict in recent years comes from an unlikely source, the orthodox Chief Rabbi of Great Britain, Jonathan Sacks. His book *The Dignity of Difference* brought complaints of betrayal from the hard-line Zionist lobby both in and outside Israel; its central messages are: 'We are not fully free if others are oppressed' and 'No one creed has a monopoly on spiritual truth.' This last assertion was deleted from the paperback edition.

Professor Alex Carmel died in the autumn of 2002. Elisheva Ballhorn suffered a small stroke. Closer to home, Dore Vorster succumbed aged ninety-six after a rapid decline, and Rix had an operation to remove a tumour from which he never fully recovered. He is now in a nursing home. But life has beginnings as well as endings. My wife gave birth to our second son, Fritz's second great-grandson, shortly before Dore's death. I look at him sometimes and think how like Fritz he looks when he was a baby – maybe I am imagining the likeness. There was another picture in Dore's album of Fritz as a youth that I think bears a strong resemblance to my brother. Now I find myself studying my own face in the mirror as I shave and wondering if I can see Fritz there and wishing that I could.

INDEX